No Ordinary Man

WILLIAM FRANCIS QUINN
HIS ROLE IN HAWAII'S HISTORY

～ *No Ordinary Man*

WILLIAM FRANCIS QUINN
HIS ROLE IN HAWAII'S HISTORY

By Mary C. Kahulumana Richards

HAWAII EDUCATION ASSOCIATION
Honolulu, Hawaii

Hawaii Education Association

1998 by Hawaii Education Association
All rights reserved. Published 1998
Printed in the United States of America

Library of Congress Cataloging in Publication Data

Richards, Mary C. Kahulumana.
    No Ordinary Man: William Francis Quinn, His Role in Hawaii's
    History.

    Includes index.
    1. Quinn, William Francis, 1919. 2. History—Hawaii. 3. Politics—
Hawaii.

Contents

Part IV

Part V

⁓Author's Preface⁓

William Francis Quinn, last appointed governor of the 50th State, enjoys a special role in the nation's history as the only last-and-first governor of all the United States.

Quinn and his family arrived in Honolulu in 1947. He was 28 years old and came to join the law firm of Robertson, Castle & Anthony. His rapid, meteoric rise to prominence in civic and community affairs climaxed with his appointment as Governor of the Territory of Hawaii by President Dwight D. Eisenhower in September 1957. With the advent of statehood for Hawaii and his victory in the 1959 special election, Quinn became the first Governor of the State of Hawaii.

This book tells of those momentous years in Hawaii's history and speaks of Quinn's youth and education. He graduated from St. Louis University in 1940 with a B.S. degree (summa cum laude) and earned an L.L.B. (cum laude) from Harvard Law School in 1947. His service in the United States Naval Reserve with duty in the South Pacific from March 1942 to February 1946, during which he advanced from Ensign to Lieutenant Commander, is highlighted. During these early years and beyond, William F. Quinn is revealed as a family man, devoted to his wife Nancy and their seven children.

Chronological chapters closely follow the critical and exciting five years that spanned William Quinn's administrations. It was a period of transition, of dramatic and rapid change. These were the glamorous, patriotic early years of Statehood when flag-waving, marching bands, and military salutes were "in." These were the days when government revolved around Iolani Palace, when the governor and lieutenant governor offices were upstairs in the royal bedrooms, and the legislature held court in the formal dining room and the throne room.

During those years, nature with all of her violent fury went on a rampage. On four occasions it was necessary for Governor Quinn to declare major disaster emergencies to alleviate suffering and to deal with the damage cause by hurricane, volcanic eruption, tsunami, and severe drought. Despite the setbacks of natural disasters and crippling strikes, Hawaii enjoyed a growing prosperity. Quinn developed and initiated a 20-year general plan with a capital improvements program geared to emphasize construction of water projects, roads, airports, harbors, parks, and the like. His limitless energy and dynamic, impelling oratory made him Hawaii's best salesman to mainland investors and many other groups.

The Governor did not, however, lack opponents. More than a few of them were in his own Republican party. Unfortunately for Quinn, this was especially true in the State Senate, causing him bitter confirmation defeat with many of his appointments. The opposition he suffered and the attendant widely publicized disputes are discussed with quotes from the local press.

Of special interest to Quinn was the establishment of the East-West Center as a meeting place for international concerns. With the Center as the core, Hawaii would be better able to fulfill one of his dreams. He emphasized the important role of Hawaii as the "hub of the Pacific," a phrase he used repeatedly. He believed that Hawaii should be the economic, cultural, social, and political hub of the Asian and Pacific rim.

At the Governor's Mansion, Washington Place, the Governor and his First Lady received and entertained a seemingly endless stream of presidents, kings, queens, prime ministers, world leaders, and stars of stage and screen.

I wish to express my gratitude to Bill and Nancy Quinn for recalling so many public and personal experiences. They willingly shared not only their family mementoes, but also personal letters, photographs, and hundreds of newspaper clippings. Most of the latter were collected and recorded in ten large volumes by the governor's office during the Quinn years (1957 through 1962).

The book is filled with anecdotes told by people who were there, former staff members and lifelong friends and acquaintances. I am grateful to them for their contributions.

A big mahalo goes to George Chaplin, Editor-in-Chief (Retired), *The Honolulu Advertiser*, for contributing his excellent preface to *No Ordinary Man*.

My special thanks also go to my daughter Melainie Fitzsimmons for her detailed index and to friend and mentor Ted Berkman, author and professor of non-fiction at the Santa Barbara Writers Conference.

I also owe many thanks to the following interviewees for the generous amount of time and thought they gave to the questions I asked:

Anderson, Marty	August 28, 1992
Cabot, Nancy	February 1993
Cades, Russell	November 1991
Chaplin, George	October 20, 1993
Chaplin, George	August 1996
Cornuelle, Herbert	October 27, 1993
Durant Marian	June 1992
Everly, Hu	February 27, 1994
Felix, John Henry	September 1990
Hubbard, Lucille	April 1990
Hughes, Robert	November 3, 1993
Mason, George	September 1990
Mason, Dot	April 1995

MacNaughton, Malcolm	July 1992
Midkiff, Robert	October 28, 1993
Sahney, Lila	September 7, 1993
Smyser, "Bud"	October 1990
Tuttle, Dan	October 29, 1993
Twigg-Smith, Thurston	August 26, 1993
Walker, Henry, Jr.	July 1992
Walters, Jess	August 10, 1990
Wiley, Iris	September 15, 1993
Woolaway, Art	November 17, 1993

All interviews and conversations were conducted by me in Honolulu.

Resources and publications consulted in the writing of *No Ordinary Man* include: *Hawaii Pono* (1961, Harcourt, Brace & World), by Lawrence Fuchs; *The Honolulu Advertiser*; *Honolulu Star-Bulletin*; Hawaii State Archives; Hawaii State Library (Hawaiian Film and Catalogue Library); "Selected Addresses and Messages of William Francis Quinn," compiled by Jess Walters and published by the State of Hawaii; and "The Watamull Foundation Oral History Project 1987: William Francis Quinn," produced by the Watamull Foundation.

Signed,
Mary C. Kahulumana Richards
Honolulu
1997

≈ Publisher's Note ≈

It is an honor and a pleasure for the Hawaii Education Association to present this biography of William F. Quinn, the last territorial and the first state governor of Hawaii. The author is well-known as an observer and a writer concerning the Hawaii scene. She is a long-time family friend of the Quinns. As a result, Mrs. Richards provides an intimate and home-like view of the Governor's unique role in the history of Hawaii.

The story of Quinn's role in the formation of the Fiftieth State is thought-provoking and even exciting. His administration spanned a period of rapid change in the history of Hawaii and of the Nation. As a Republican, Quinn was able, in the face of growing negative odds, to preserve a brief foothold in Hawaii government for the developers of modern Hawaii against the rapidly developing Democratic Party. He worked tirelessly to structure a new state government even as Democratic efforts concentrated on the dynamics of constructing a new and different political picture, replete with a growing reservoir of new citizens. He won election as the first state governor by defying most estimates that the rapidly expanding Democratic Party would be accorded this honor.

Since public education was the major issue of both Democrats and Republicans in 1959-62, Governor Quinn was hard-pressed to keep up with the Democrats in this arena. Years of neglect did not ease this burden borne by Governor Quinn who, almost by happenstance, was running as a Republican.

The Hawaii Education Association continues to encourage studies about the development and future of public education in Hawaii. Presentations such as this will hopefully provide understanding and new insights into the never-ending process of preparing for the future of democracy in America. In the years since Governor Quinn's last administration (1962), Democrats have controlled all three branches of Hawaii government. Yet, public education continues to be a prime arena of public concern. The problems of achieving truly effective public education appear to perplex and continue to plague both political parties. Thus, as Hawaii relentlessly continues to seek ever-better public education, history and the role of political leaders in such history should both instruct and encourage our people to find the "magic key of success" for Education that is so basic and vital to the future of our Nation.

The Hawaii Education Association
By its President,
Dr. Hubert V. Everly

☙ Foreword ☙

William Francis Quinn played an unmatched role in modern Hawaii history. As the last territorial and first state governor, he had the privilege and challenge of overseeing an exciting and fundamental transition.

On an island chain farther from a continent than any other, Hawaii was the only major U.S. jurisdiction where a majority of people had their cultural and ethnic roots in Asia/Pacific rather than Europe. It was a vibrant society eager for dynamic change.

It was a time of high drama, when mainlanders were beginning to recognize that the Pacific was supplanting the Atlantic as our country's top trading partner and that Hawaii offered opportunities for investment. It was just before the jet age, but there were already visions of what could lie ahead for the Islands in tourism, general business development and cross-cultural exchange.

Bill Quinn, in many ways, was a natural for the times and the tasks that would face him. He was a man of integrity and intellect, handsome, articulate, with a ready smile, keen wit, an actor's talents and a rich Irish tenor's voice.

A young Harvard lawyer and World War II Navy veteran, Quinn had been invited to the Islands in 1947 to join a prestigious law firm. He became highly active in the community-in theatricals, in speech-making, in enlivening countless gatherings with his rendition of the "Hawaiian Wedding Song."

If politics was even remotely on his mind, it wasn't evident. Were it not for an invitation, he would not have become a Republican precinct worker in 1952, nor four years later yielded to urging to enter the race for a territorial Senate seat against Herbert Lee. He lost, but he was in good company with Peppi Cooke, Joe Itagaki and Mary K. Robinson.

When discussions initiated in Washington led President Eisenhower in 1957 to appoint him as territorial governor, no one was more surprised than Quinn. He had been in the Islands only 10 years. He saw his future in the law. But he was gutsy, rarely lacking in confidence and, already in love with Hawaii, he welcomed the chance to take the helm.

It was a yeasty era. After decades of feudal Republican rule, the Democrats had won the state Legislature. Understandably, they were feeling their oats. They, among others, recognized that, although a fiscal conservative, Quinn was a social liberal and, given different circumstances, could as well have been a Democrat. But he wore the GOP label with gubernatorial power, and the Democrats made life pretty rough for him.

Many of his appointments and his frequent travels to "sell" Hawaii were sharply criticized. One of the problems, of course, was that Bill Quinn was not a born politician. He did not think and respond viscerally. The careful lawyer, with respect for details, he examined every aspect of an issue before making a judgement; the time involved frequently negated any possible political hay he could have made with speedier decisions. Short of sacrificing principle, he was not averse to some compromise. But on basic issues, when he felt he was right, he dug in his heels.

What both political parties agreed on was the imperative of Hawaii gaining statehood. There were differences in strategy, but the reality is that Alaska came in first, with Hawaii following in March 1959. When President Eisenhower signed the historic measure, Quinn was at his side.

Quinn's two years as territorial governor impressed Hawaii voters and in the first state election in 1959 a population that had voted Democratic since 1954 surprisingly chose him. He brought boundless energy and enthusiasm to the vital job of restructuring Hawaii's government. *TIME* magazine saw Quinn and Hawaii facing a "whole new bright future."

But Bill Quinn faced obstacles not only from Democratic opponents, but from mossbacks in his party who refused to accept that time had passed them by, and especially from his lieutenant governor, Jimmy Kealoha, who from the outset undercut his boss in his own yearning for the top spot. Although Quinn defeated Kealoha in the Republican primary, the damage done to him was considerable, and Jack Burns won by a substantial margin and went on to prove a productive governor.

At his headquarters on election night, Bill Quinn, with his usual class, coupled his concession with the singing of "Irish Eyes." He went out, head high, to take the presidency of Dole Pineapple and then return to the law.

Mary Richards, in this biography, provides a warm, revealing picture of a highly capable, dedicated man who got Hawaii statehood off to an admirable start. There is a strongly personal flavor to her account, a detailed mosaic of Quinn's recorded remembrances, commentaries by a host of political participants and outside observers, editorials and news stories. Mrs. Quinn—Nancy to so many—proves herself a loving and insightful wife and mother, a gracious First Lady who calmly maneuvered an impossible official and domestic schedule in support of the governor.

Readers who were here at the time will relive an extraordinary slice of Island history. Those who came or grew up since will get an inside view of Hawaii keeping a date with destiny.

George Chaplin
Editor-in-Chief (Retired)
The Honolulu Advertiser

≋Chapter One≋
Young Man in a Hurry

"Student deferment be damned. . ."

BILL QUINN
Harvard law student

In Harvard Square just off the university's campus, noisy confusion burst the rain-darkened winter silence. Attention focused on newsboys, bundled against the cold, lining the sidewalks. "EXTRA! EXTRA!" Incessant voices heralded grim news. Holding papers high above their heads, the newsboys shouted that disaster had hit the United States at Pearl Harbor.

December 7, 1941.

Two young men wrapped in throat scarves and weather jackets emerged from the old movie house arcade in the square. Bill Quinn, the taller of the two, and Hamilton White were second-year law students at Harvard and roommates in a boarding house just off the Cambridge, Massachusetts, campus.

Stunned and outraged by the attack on their country, the two raced back to their residence. Long into the night, huddled close to a burning log in the fireplace, they planned how to join the coming fight.

Monday, December 8, with the temperature at 7 degrees, the morning radio cracked with spits and spurts as broadcasters filled the air waves with rumors. Alarming reports came of sabotage, shell explosions and imminent invasion of the Hawaiian Islands in the Pacific.

Harvard's academic routine shifted abruptly. Students who

had enrolled in the reserves or had attended military schools left immediately for duty. By the time Christmas vacation began 10 days later, Bill Quinn had decided to enlist.

He packed his bag, strapped his tennis racket over his shoulder and took the train home to St. Louis.

He felt good about his decision. He hadn't consulted any superior. He did not notify Harvard that he wouldn't be returning after the holidays. Before leaving, though, in his Midwest twang he announced to his buddies across the hall, "Student deferment be damned! I don't like the special treatment."

Bill expected his father's objections to his quitting Harvard Law. Still, he was not prepared for the ensuing outrage:

"Damn it, you never should have left school! You've thrown out your education like garbage....You're an idiot!...You're no son of mine." Bill would never forget Charlie Quinn's words.

Billy, as his parents called him, stood firm.

"I can't continue school and not fight. Besides, I've already signed up for Naval Intelligence. They'll be calling me soon."

His father stiffened. C. Alvin Quinn, known as Charlie, was a dapper man who dressed in business suits, with a crisp white handkerchief in the pocket; he stood a head shorter than his 6-foot-1-inch son. This day, his usual aplomb was gone. His face reddened and swelled; his voice cracked with anguish.

"Are you crazy? What you've done is senseless. Impulsive! You belong back in school!"

His father clenched his fists. Bill heard the bells in the tinseled Christmas tree jangle, an odd counterpoint to the older man's shouting.

"You have a deferment as long as you are a student. Nobody can change that. Nobody! Get your law degree first, boy, and quit wasting your time around here."

It would be three months before his father spoke another word to him.

Bill James, a Navy recruiting officer in St. Louis, urged his childhood chum to apply for AVS, Aviation Specialist.

"You're officer material," James told Quinn. "You'd be stupid just to enlist."

James set up an interview for Quinn with Air Combat Intelligence. Bill went through the interview, but a part of him had always hoped to become a pilot; he went to the Navy and Army Air Forces for conferences as well. Both commands turned him down—bad eyesight. He had no choice but to wait for orders assigning him to officers' training school. Instead, there were additional interviews; still the orders didn't come.

All his former classmates and buddies were gone, in college, in the service or married. His father forbade his driving the family car; he had no spending money. His presence at home only made a bad situation worse. Charlie Quinn remained angry. Bill's confidence dipped to a depressing low.

His mother knew Billy was determined to stand fast despite his father's wishes. Betty Dorrity Quinn, the epitome of an Irish woman with golden blonde hair and blue eyes, was gentle, full of forgiveness and fun. Charlie Quinn left the spiritual nourishment of the family to Betty; he attended Mass with the family at times. Betty, a good Catholic, made sure the children went every Sunday and on holy days. She comforted Bill but could do nothing to ease the rift between father and son.

January came and went, depressing broadcasts continued from Europe and the Pacific on the state of the war, and still Bill Quinn heard nothing about his enlistment.

While Quinn waited, Drew Pearson, writer of the "Washington Merry-Go-Round" column, exposed the Aviation Specialist program that had been recommended to Bill. Pearson wrote that the unit was started by a leading Wall Street stockbroker connected to the Washington establishment. Pearson gave evidence that the AVS was a special little Navy program for

special people, mainly young stockbrokers who'd become officers and did not have to do much. The story prompted the Navy
Department to redesign the AVS. Applicants were quickly
recalled for more interviews. Bill traveled to Chicago for his
hearing, signed up and returned to St. Louis to await his call to
service. Still nothing happened. It was now well into February.

Bill's father remained silent and unforgiving. Charlie Quinn
could be a difficult and embittered person, but he hadn't always
been so. Charlie had worked as a salaried man all his life. His
father died when he was very young, robbing Charlie of any
chance at a formal education.

At age 10, Charlie, the oldest, left school and worked to help
support his brothers and sisters. When he was 20 and living in
New York City, he worked for Amalgamated Leather Company,
owned by a prominent businessman who took to him. Soon the
fair-haired boy, Charlie was given privileges such as seats in the
boss's box at the Metropolitan and access to his horse and car-
riage. Years later, Charlie would reminisce about going down to
lower Third Avenue in formal attire to show off to the folks in
his old neighborhood.

C. Alvin Quinn had a passion for walking canes and a reputa-
tion as a lady's man. He remained single until his mid-30s, then
married Betty Dorrity. They moved to Rochester, New York, but
by the time Billy, the second son, was 2, the Quinns moved to
St. Louis, Missouri, the Gateway to the West. This exciting river
town had become a major shoe and leather center, and Charlie
went there as part of Amalgamated Leather Company. He was on
track for success. Soon, though, Amalgamated Leather, in which
he had placed all career hope, was sold. There were five brothers
among the new owners, and they sat at the top of the company.
Charlie stayed where he was with no chance of promotion.

He was offered an opportunity to become marketing manager of a competing company a little later but turned the offer

down; he was reluctant to risk his family's security. Ironically, that company grew, and the man who took the position Charlie rejected eventually became the governor of Delaware. These things burdened and embittered Charlie.

His life wasn't all grim. Charlie Quinn had a flare for music and dance. He saw to it that music was an important part of the family's life. Billy's older brother, C. Alvin Quinn Jr. (called "Fat" because he'd been a plump boy), studied piano; Billy first studied the violin, later opting for voice lessons. Sister Betty Lou became an accomplished pianist, and Betty, their mother, had a lovely soprano voice. She joined in singing when Charlie, in an occasional festive mood, would grab one of his canes and burst into song and dance.

Charlie's cane collection was unique, and at one time he was the only man in town who walked Lindell Boulevard strutting to the tap of his cane. Unfortunately for Billy, Charlie also used his cane as a rod, and he broke more than one over his second son's back. He had no patience for Billy's flamboyance. Charlie continually compared Billy to his older brother, "Fat," an upright, responsible young man who received many honors and became president of his high school class.

Nonetheless, Billy was an exceptionally bright student, if not a class officer. He skipped an elementary grade, making him a year younger than most of his classmates when he started high school. He walked into his high school assembly on opening day wearing knickers. Billy heard the guffaws, swallowed his embarrassment and never wore knickers again.

During his teens, Billy preferred girls to studies. Now and then, he'd skip a class to meet a young lady at Messier's Drugstore. Sipping Cokes, flirting and sneaking kisses were more captivating than math or history.

The principal called young Bill in. Quinn recalled the dressdown.

"'Your I.Q. tests here show a high potential, and look what you're doing! We've expected good academic achievements....I insist that you do better, and I'm going to make it difficult until you do.'"

Billy paid little attention until his third year, when he made new friends from a Jesuit boys school. He realized he needed the discipline of the Jesuits. He asked his mother to be transferred to St. Louis University High School, where his friend Bill James went.

There was one hitch. St. Louis University High would accept young Quinn only if he repeated his third year; he was short of language credits. He needed four years of Latin and two of Greek to get his diploma.

He made the transfer, repeated his junior year and was recognized for superior academic achievements. He sang solo with the glee club and won a contest in his first attempt at extemporaneous speaking.

Disciplinary problems arose again. When he was still a junior in his new Jesuit school, he decided to enjoy the senior privilege of the smoking room. He was caught by a "scholastic," a teacher not yet a priest but wearing a Roman collar.

"You're not supposed to be in here," the scholastic had said.

"Well, my friends are in here and I thought I'd join them for a morning smoke."

Bad Boy Bill Quinn had done it again. This time his penance was to memorize all five stanzas of *Abou Ben Adhem*. The scholastic ordered Bill to recite it when he was ready. That morning Bill attended his classes, but he was busy memorizing. By noon he sought out the scholastic and rattled the poem off as fast as he could. The scholastic steamed with frustration over the arrogance of this young student, but there was nothing he could do.

Another incident, more serious, brought the wrath of the

dean. Students were required to attend benediction on Friday afternoons in the chapel. Bill decided one Friday to join a couple of friends for a sociable afternoon about town.

The first thing Monday morning, Dean Roach walked into Bill's chemistry class and boomed, "Is Billy Quinn in this class? I'd liked to see him."

Quinn stepped outside the room. The huge, commanding dean with curly black hair coming up over his Roman collar demanded, "Did you leave school early on Friday?"

"Yes, Father, but I..."

"Get your books and go home."

Just like that, Billy was suspended.

His mother did a lot of talking to get him back in school. For penance, however, Billy had to walk the far fence every day at noon for two weeks. Despite his attempt at military parade bearing, his long, skinny legs gave him the look of a colt ready to bolt.

His disobedience aside, he managed well and was awarded first honors at the end of the school year. He returned in September as a senior; by then all of his friends were graduated. Bill Quinn, the young man in a hurry, wasted no time. He went to St. Louis University and asked to be admitted into the School of Arts and Sciences.

"I've had four years of high school; can I get in?"

Of course, they said no. Bill had no high school diploma. Undaunted, he applied at the School of Commerce and Finance, and he was accepted, providing he had fourth-year English. His mother arranged for a tutor; his father looked the other way and Bill began one of the great experiences of his student life. His tutor, a Jesuit, talked every afternoon with Bill about books, poetry and writing.

In his first year of accounting, Bill did well with red lines and ledgers but he was bored. "It's god-awful," he felt. Ever pragmatic and determined, he returned to the School of Arts and Sciences and pleaded with the dean, Father Mallon.

"I've got to get in here. I'll go to summer school....I'll do whatever you say, but I've got to be where I feel I'm getting some education."

He was accepted; again he needed additional credits to meet the requirements. So for two years he attended summer school. At the university, he got into theater and glee club and chose philosophy as a major. Pride in his poetry soared when Marshall McLuhan gave him an A. He loved academic life and went after it vigorously.

At the end of Bill's junior year, the dean announced a special honors program for the next seniors. The special course was patterned after the Great Books Program at St. John's and Chicago Universities. Bill was sure that the program was designed for him.

"That's what I want to do," Bill said to Father Mallon.

But Mallon disagreed, Quinn recalled. "This program is for people who have been doing this all along. This is for the all-A student. You have one year in business."

He named the irrelevant subjects that were on Bill's record. Bill argued that he had gotten all A's in philosophy, he loved it and knew that philosophy was for him.

Bill wouldn't give up. He talked and talked. Finally, a special arrangement was made for him. He agreed to read assigned material during the summer plus take an examination on return to school. Bill went with his family for their usual six weeks at Lake Michigan, then went to the university library to pick up his assigned books. Not one of them was translated; they were all in medieval Latin! He borrowed a Latin-English dictionary and began, one word at a time. Murderous at first, the words got easier; at least he only had to look up every other word. Pretty soon he didn't need the dictionary and he was on his way. He passed the exam, becoming one of an elite group of six.

If ever there was one concentrated year of education, this was it. Starting with the Bible, the scholars—two English majors, a math major, a geology major, a history major and Bill, a philosophy major—read a book a week. The works were considered the greatest of all time. Once a week, they'd meet with the university's experts on each particular book. They were not required to attend other regular classes.

At the end of the year, the six faced tough finals. First was an oral exam held by the department head of each major. Bill Quinn stood before 10 philosophy professors who threw questions at him for two hours. A six-hour written exam in philosophy followed.

The two days of testing culminated in an open assembly for everyone in the university. Questions were fired at the six scholars on the great books and on any subject pertaining to them. At St. Louis University 1940 graduation, Bill received his bachelor of science degree summa cum laude.

Bill invited about 50 fellow graduates to the Quinn house for a celebration. As the party warmed up, Charlie Quinn joined in, getting the others to sing and dance. A little while later, Bill's dad led a parade of celebrants down three flights of stairs, along Lindell Boulevard, in and out of the Chase Hotel, and back up the boulevard to home. Charlie Quinn was quite a showman that night. Though Bill could only surmise that his father was proud of him, he had never heard Charlie say it.

Bill Quinn had a flare and a taste for the theater, but he took the advice of a mentor, Father Dan Lord, who told him to use his singing and acting talents for his own enjoyment, but to pursue law as a career. Bill Quinn went on to Harvard University Law School.

~

It was the end of March 1942, and he was fed up with waiting in St. Louis for orders that would take him into the war. Bill returned to Cambridge and law school. He arrived just as spring vacation started, borrowed a friend's lecture and case notes, and studied for the two weeks. He figured he could catch up on what he'd missed from January through March and get through the rest of the semester successfully. Classes resumed, but after only a few days, he received a call from his father late one afternoon.

"There's a telegram here for you," Charlie Quinn said. "It's addressed to Ensign William Quinn."

"What does it...would you open it?"

"'Proceed without delay to Commandant Ninth Naval District to serve as assistant aviation aide to COMM 9.'"

Bill left Harvard that very evening for St. Louis, went directly to the Naval Office, held up his right hand and was sworn in as Ensign William Quinn.

≈ Chapter Two ≈
Nancy

"She was wearing a plaid skirt, knee socks and had freckles on her pug nose. My friend nudged me and said, 'There's a girl you should know; that's Nancy Witbeck.'"

BILL QUINN

"Ensign Quinn, sir." The yeoman, in starched blue denim with a soft cap pulled to a point over his forehead, saluted the man before him in a gray plaid suit, his name bar pinned to the lapel. "Welcome to Great Lakes Naval Training Base, sir."

Bill Quinn briskly returned the salute of the sailor who met him at the main gate, about a mile from the center. Quinn pointed to two bags that he had carried from the station.

"I'm sorry, sir, but we aren't allowed to carry bags," the yeoman answered.

Bill believed him; so, for the mile trek the enlisted man, with short, snappy steps, led the way while the officer, carrying the luggage, sweated behind.

Only two days had passed since Quinn had been sworn in. He had no training, no indoctrination, no past connection with the Navy, hadn't ever been aboard a Navy vessel. Yet he was reporting for duty as aide to the commandant of the Ninth Naval

11

District, COMM 9. He wasn't even a "90-day wonder." He was as green as the weeds that sprouted through the concrete walkway. He had arrived in a new world.

For three weeks, Bill couldn't get a uniform, and his civvies emphasized his amateur status. Commander Richard Whitehead, aviation aide to COMM 9, the man who was to be his boss, was in Canada, trying to bring back to the United States Navy American fliers who had joined the Royal Canadian Air Force. Before Whitehead returned to the Great Lakes Center, other orders came for Bill. Ensign Quinn was sent to the farm fields of Peru (pronounced Pea-roo), Indiana, where a national program of aviation training was being initiated.

The government was condemning lands for the duration of the war. The properties would revert to the owners at the end. They planned takeoff-and-landing fields in other towns, like Kokomo and Anderson, with headquarters in Peru. Hundreds of farms in Indiana and Illinois were involved in this large naval training program.

With his year and a half of Harvard Law School, Ensign Quinn found himself useful despite his junior naval status. As the government proceeded with the land acquisition, legal questions on appraisals and leases arose that had to be answered before the training program could begin. A delegation of angry landowners protested the appraisal price of their lands. They raised such a fracas, it appeared that the project might sink before it was launched.

Bill watched naval officials handle the sticky situation with great diplomacy. He wrote in his diary:

> *It's a shame but nothing can be done for them. The land that has been watered for years with their sweat will be watered one last time with their tears...but the War must be won.*

Because of his work on the land negotiations, Quinn got to know many people in town. Single, good-looking, personable, and dressed in khaki instead of the usual Navy man's blue or white, he was included in every kind of social function and was made an honorary member of the Elks.

During his time in Indiana, Bill was given a short leave. He returned to St. Louis and to Nancy, his childhood sweetheart whom he planned to marry. During those months he had awaited his call to duty, he and Nancy had fallen in love all over again.

A half century later, Bill could remember the day he first met her. "She was wearing a plaid skirt, knee socks and had freckles on her pug nose. My friend nudged me and said, 'There's a girl you should know; that's Nancy Witbeck.'"

She was as pretty as any movie queen, with dark-brown wavy hair touching her shoulders. Her face, round like a cherub's, was soft and glowed with love. She usually wore either a gold cross at her throat or a strand of pearls atop her cashmere sweater. In warm, mellow spring, St. Louis turned yellow, pink and green; Nancy dressed in pastels to match, sometimes with a wide straw hat.

Nancy Witbeck Quinn's memory of the young Bill Quinn is equally vivid:

"Whenever Bill sang on the radio, Mother and I, just the two of us, would sit and listen. Of course, I had a crush on him from our very first date."

During junior and senior high school, Billy Quinn sang a lot, on the radio, at school dances and in church concerts. He wasn't bashful about his clear tenor voice, and while Frank Sinatra may have been the nation's favorite, many young ladies of St. Louis never missed the radio hour featuring their classmate. He was their star; he made them proud and set them to dreaming.

From their early years, Nancy and Bill kept track of each

other. Billy and his brother Fat went to summer camp in northern Wisconsin on Catfish Lake every year. From camp at age 16, Bill wrote his first love letters to Nancy:

> *Well, here I am up here again and it is swell to be away from St. Louis, except that I'm away from you....*

Popular Nancy dated other beaus, and Bill continued to play the field. Invariably, they would get back together and meet for late dates. When Bill was at Harvard in 1940 and 1941, their correspondence increased, and like many others, they wrote to each other about the possibility of war. Hitler was storming across Europe. Up and down the East Coast from Maine to Florida, entire cities staged blackout drills. Sirens shrieked, basements were converted to underground shelters, helmets and gas masks were issued.

In answer to Nancy's questions, Bill wrote:

> *I don't really see that a blackout in St. Louis would do enough good to outweigh the confusion that results. The experts seem to think that in the current picture of the War, any bombing of America will be a token bombing of the coast in order to persuade us to keep our forces at home. For St. Louis, I should recommend bombing defense drills in all the 24-hour-a-day plants, the ones that would be the objects of a desperate inland attack.*

They also shared family thoughts.

> *It does make Dad happy now that I'm up here, doesn't it? We've had many misunderstandings, Dad and I, because we think entirely differently and we are both proud to a fault. That*

is one thing which I constantly pray for...a true Christian humility.

Their courtship bloomed during the few months Bill was waiting to be called up. At the time, Nancy had long and tiring days. She held a responsible secretarial position at Curtiss-Wright, one of the country's largest airplane manufacturers. Her airport office was an hour's drive from home. Almost every evening after dinner, Bill arrived to see Nancy. They listened for hours to the RCA radio mounted atop a dark-brown record cabinet in the Witbeck parlor. When her parents were out, they'd dance a bit, Bill would sing, talk philosophy or quote poetry.

One evening, Bill regaled Nancy about the summer before he entered Harvard when he was a cast member of a repertory company in northern Michigan. They were learning one play while rehearsing a second and performing a third, he said. He loved the theater, he effused, and told her how he had really wanted to pursue an acting career. Nancy listened with great interest. Then Bill, a peacock fanning his feathers, related his grand romance with a leading lady:

"She was in the Erie, Pennsylvania, Theater when I entered Harvard. With Cambridge only 17 hours away by rail, I spent several long weekends with her and didn't return to law school until Tuesday. That didn't do much for my keeping up with the best students in the country and my grades showed it," Quinn laughed years later.

This revelation, added to his long list of girlfriends, was too much. Nancy had had it.

"Fish or cut bait," she said flatly. "I'm tired of being second fiddle. If you're going to get serious, then get those other women out of your system or tell me goodbye."

They named their wedding date in short order.

The party announcing Nancy's engagement was at the Witbeck home. Bill, unable to take leave, was on duty in Kokomo. He wrote her his concerns:

> *Hope you got the flowers all right in time for your party and I hope that it was a success. Just wish I had had a ring there when you did the announcing.... I don't want you embarrassed because of my lack of funds. From now until July, I'll spend about $1.50 a day, excluding rent. We ought to have about $30.00 in the bank on July 15, when the next pay day rolls around.*

Bill and Nancy were wed on July 11, 1942, during a nuptial Mass in the majestic College Church of St. Francis Xavier at the University of St. Louis. Dean Mallon, Bill's advisor and friend through his student years at the University, performed the ceremony; Betty, Nancy's sister, and Charlie Quinn, Jr., Bill's brother, were the attendants. The wedding party knelt at the foot of the three-towered altar and were framed in the kaleidoscopic lights of the stained-glass windows. Nancy and Bill perched like doves in the brilliant sun shining into the English Gothic edifice, she in a long white tulle gown with a short white veil, and Bill, handsome and splendid in his dress whites.

Some weeks before, Nancy converted from the Episcopal Church to Catholicism. Her switch caused deep feelings within her family. To abide by the rules of her new church, Nancy had to get special permission to have her non-Catholic sister be her maid of honor; she could sense her mother's resentment.

On top of that, the church forbade performance of the Wagnerian wedding march, contending that the United States was at war with Germany and besides, the music was about pagans. Mother Witbeck finally voiced her opinion:

"It's bad enough that my daughter is being married in the Catholic Church, but now they can't even have the wedding march played."

Bill came to the rescue. He took Nancy to pay a call on the archbishop of the Catholic Diocese in St. Louis.

Bill introduced his fiancee as Miss Nancy Witbeck. The archbishop asked, as though he hadn't heard, "What is your name, my dear?"

"Nancy Witbeck."

"I mean, what is your real name, my dear?"

"My name is Nancy," she repeated.

"That's not a saint's name. Is your name Ann?"

"My name is Nancy."

The archbishop discoursed on everything from saints' names to the why-nots of the wedding march. His Excellency finally gave permission to have the traditional music played, then he blessed and sent them happily off with their wedding plans.

On the eve of their marriage, Bill received a telegram from Captain Whitehead: *Return to Chicago immediately.*

Following a small reception at the Witbeck home on Stanley Avenue, the bride and groom took the train. Instead of returning to Peru, Indiana, and the white, $50-a-month honeymoon cottage that the good folk of the town had arranged for them, they headed for Chicago. The newlyweds stayed at the Edgewater Beach Hotel and went apartment hunting. They ended up in a basement apartment on the border of Evanston and Chicago. It could have been the set for "My Sister Eileen."

"When we looked up through the street window, we only saw feet walking by," Nancy recalled.

Ensign Quinn was now the aide to Captain Whitehead which was to have been his first assignment, and their offices were at the Board of Trade building in downtown Chicago. They were to organize another training program. Whitehead had the idea of converting the legendary sidewheelers, which had toured the Great Lakes and the Mississippi, to airplane carrier decks. The sidewheeler's superstructure was simply stripped down to a base deck; it looked much like a carrier deck.

"Once the fliers had sufficient field training, they could practice and takeoff just like it's done at sea," explained Quinn, "The end result was that about 15,000 fliers were trained on Lake Michigan in full view of Chicago."

Serving as personnel officer for this nationwide command, Quinn saw the staff grow from three—Admiral Putty Reed, Captain Whitehead and Quinn— to 53. The ensign's job was to write orders and handle organization of the headquarters itself. Eventually a lieutenant commander was assigned to take Quinn's position.

Bill, restless and tired of shuffling papers, wanted more action. He drafted orders for himself to the Air Combat Intelligence and sent them to Admiral Reed. The reply was swift and sharp. The paper came back with a slash, some acid comment and "NO" written on it.

Quinn countered, "Sir, I've done my job here and you've got this big staff now, and I really want to go to ACI school," and with another breath, "and I think there's a class opening in a week or so."

Eventually he was ordered to take an additional course in antisubmarine warfare at the Naval Air Intelligence Center at Quonset Point, Rhode Island. This was exactly what Quinn wanted — special training that would prepare him for action at sea.

On the personal front, however, it would be a difficult wrenching. Billy Jr. had already been born, and Nancy was pregnant again. Shipping out meant that he was to be separated from his growing family. The Quinns both knew Bill might be gone a long time.

Nancy moved back to St. Louis, where she and Billy Jr. would live during Bill's absence. She traveled by train to Rhode Island so she and Bill could be together for Christmas 1943 prior to Bill's shipping out.

"I was supposed to meet him around 5 p.m. Christmas Eve, but the train froze on the tracks in Albany. I didn't arrive in Providence until midnight, and there was no Bill in sight," she recalled.

"Everything was arranged for her arrival," Quinn said, "including lovely little quarters at the Spinning Wheel, a bottle of sparkling burgundy and her presents. There were no cabs to be had, not in that weather, so I borrowed a trench coat, donned my hat and gloves and started a 20-mile walk to the train station."

Bill ran, walked, slipped and slid through the slush and snow. Finally he hitched a ride and arrived at the station just as the train pulled in.

"There were hundreds of people pouring out of that train. I ran up one side and down the other, back and forth again and again until I realized that I was the last person on that platform."

Bill went into the stuffy station; its stark wooden benches were empty, and not even the ticket taker was to be seen. Finally he spotted her at the second platform; she was seated atop her suitcase, right in the middle of the entrance hall, looking like a Norman Rockwell painting—pregnant, her hat askew.

They got to the inn at 5 a.m. as the Christmas Day dawn cast thin shadows across the deep snow. Nancy objected, but Bill set up the two thick-rimmed bathroom tumblers and tried to pull the cork on the chilled wine.

"No, Nancy, we've got to have a Christmas toast right now.

Here, open this beautiful gift."

He worked and worked on the cork until his thumbs were sore. WHAP! Suddenly the bubbly splattered on the wall and ceiling. A few drops were left to pour. The laughter that morning would become a pleasurable memory during the separation ahead.

Their holiday was brief. The day after Christmas, Nancy returned to little Billy and her parents in St. Louis. Bill's orders sent him to San Francisco to await transportation overseas.

≈ Chapter Three ≈
Overseas 1944-45

'My bed is an Army cot, at least six inches shorter than my frame...I can truly be called hung-over."
BILL QUINN
Correspondence to Nancy Quinn

Ensign Quinn boarded a small Jeep aircraft carrier and sailed from San Francisco to embattled Guadalcanal. They traveled far into the broad Pacific during the long, nonstop, no-action cruise. The men slept, ate, played cards, read and wrote long letters home. Bill wrote many letters to Nancy, signing them "Billy."

In one he said:

> *I have started to read Tolstoy's War and Peace...one of the greatest novels ever written. Coming in three lengthy volumes, it is fit material for a cruise such as this.*

His voracious reading didn't keep him from observing his shipmates or the ship's structure.

> *My bed is an Army cot, at least six inches shorter than my frame. Since the mattress is six inches shorter than the cot, things become somewhat difficult. I can truly be called hung-over.*
>
> *There is an amazing thing about naval vessels, particularly combatant ones. Every inch of space is used and used econom-*

ically. Large numbers of men live aboard, and are provided with all the living facilities found in any well-equipped hotel. The ship carries all the gear necessary to accomplish her mission as well as power plants and fuel, to see her through.

He wrote, too, about the beauty of the night.

> *Darling, what a thrilling experience I just had. It is now 9:30 and I went out on the deck to get some air. One has to feel his way around since we darken the ship and proceed without lights at sundown. The sky is literally covered with stars, of all colors and of varying degrees of brilliance...never have I seen such a sky.*
>
> *I'm starting on my third volume of War and Peace...1,000 pages down, 500 to go. The night is hot, too. As hot as some of the still, sultry July nights in St. Louis, when one has to do nothing more than just sit in order to work up a sweat.*

His mood changed as they sailed deeper into the Pacific; the skies grew darker, the clouds heavier and the horizon menacing.

> *I left you a month ago tomorrow. For a week I've been on the water, constantly going further from you. I love you darling.*
> —*Billy*

At last the carrier reached Guadalcanal. From there Quinn was flown to Munda in the Solomon Islands, where he reported for duty as air combat intelligence officer with Fleet Air Wing One. Air Wing One was made up of search squadrons, including a squadron and a half from New Zealand and five U.S. Navy squads. Quinn briefed and debriefed pilots about their flights. These were mainly antisubmarine squadrons: two-engine planes in search of fleet-endangering enemy squads.

The Allied squadrons flew along the various shores, looked for submarines, reported their locations, and used depth charges and bombs to destroy them. Each time they returned, they reported all sightings to Ensign Quinn. This information was routed to the Commander in Chief of the Pacific—CINCPAC—in Hawaii. From there the information would be disseminated to the Pacific fleet.

Munda was not like the romantic, coconut-fringed, moon-lit lagoon islands of Polynesia. Some war correspondents called Munda the "most remote place on earth." Impenetrable mud flats and dense forests surrounded the shoreline. Mangrove trees with long branches snaked out into murky river banks. Munda's swamps were crammed with a brown network of roots like a city jammed with overpasses, crisscross streets and dark alleys. Air Wing One's camp, set deep in the mesquite (*kiawe*) wilderness, was a series of tents and tent cabins close to the newly laid airstrip, a recreation area complete with volleyball court and a large tent for the officers' club.

Bill was punctual with his letters home. He hoped they were received in the same daily order as they were sent. Nancy's mail to him usually arrived in batches; a week or two of waiting for her news always left him longing.

> *Tomorrow is Ash Wednesday and the beginning of Lent. I can remember so well last year's Ash Wednesday when we said "Does it seem possible that Lent is beginning and when it is over we shall probably have a child." Remember? Now we have our wonderful Skooter and are awaiting McCooch's entrance.*

Once settled in his quarters, Quinn's ambitious nature simmered and his creative juices started to flow. With more and more Japanese operating in the area, Ensign Quinn, anxious to share his special training in antisubmarine warfare, decided to put out a daily information sheet. He gathered various intelligence reports and his study notes, used those as reference and typed his articles. He gave it a masthead, wrote instructions on what to do in a certain situation, what tack to take, how to approach, etc. He added bits of humor. The men enjoyed what they read and wanted more.

All of a sudden, Quinn was called up by his commanding officer. The Joint Intelligence of the Pacific, JICPOA, was not pleased. Quinn recalled the dispatch:

WE UNDERSTAND THAT SOMEBODY OUT THERE IS PUTTING SOME SORT OF INTELLIGENCE MATERIAL OUT AND WE DON'T DO THAT. THERE IS ONE PLACE THAT ANYTHING INITIATES FROM AND IT'S RIGHT BACK HERE.

Quinn was directed to stop publishing his paper, immediately.

Bill was chagrined; the men were outraged to lose a bright spot in their dreary days, but this was war, and that was that.

At the start, life moved on Munda like the weather, slow and humid. There were light moments, as when the New Zealand chaps shared one of their favorite drinking songs:

Monday I touched her on the ankle
Tuesday I touched her on the knee
Wednesday with success, I lifted up her dress
and Thursday her chemise - Gor' bly me.

And so it went with its catchy tune and a marching beat to a successful conclusion.

There were naps after lunch. At 2 o'clock every afternoon there would be a huge thunderstorm. It would clear by 3 and a

volleyball game followed. The whole camp would come to life.
Quinn, though, was thirsty for news of his family:

> *Stephen is four months old now, isn't he? How about giving*
> *me another description...color of hair, whether he has a nose or*
> *not, eyes, mouth, ears, has he a cauliflower ear like Billy?*
>
> *It is blowing outside now, and smells as though we are in for*
> *a pretty good-sized storm. This is the damnedest country out*
> *here, with its earthquakes, typhoons, furiously hot weather and*
> *disease. It seems like the Almighty recognizes that it is a part of*
> *HIS world to be destroyed and HE is warming up to do just*
> *that.*

All at once, the Wing got busy. Seven Japanese subs lurked
just north of Bougainville, waiting in ambush. The enemy
thought the American fleet would sail from MacArthur's area in
New Guinea. CINCPAC learned this top-secret information
from an ultra-secret Japanese code CINCPAC had cracked.
Quinn, the only antisubmarine man in the vicinity, briefed the
pilots. The Wing squadrons preceded the surface vessels, spotted
the enemy subs, and the combined forces destroyed all seven
submarines.

Shortly after this, the South Pacific forces were split between
four-star General Douglas MacArthur and Admiral William F.
Halsey, the daring "Bull." Halsey didn't want to lose Fleet Air
Wing One; he ordered the squadron to Espiritu Santo in the
New Hebrides. Now there was only half of one squadron, yet
there was still the complete command in place that had administered seven. For six weeks, there was nothing to do all day, every
day. These were drab days. Worse than the creeping fungus of
heat rash itching in a man's crotch was the silent, dread disease
of boredom. Bill collected one quote after another from the men
as they sputtered the hours away.

Life in the Rear Area

Hundreds of men with nothing to do but drink
And curse and talk of sex but never think
"Break out the bottle, let's get drunk tonight"
"Christ—one craps after another; he's in a bite"
"Did you get a squint at Bob's buxom date?"
"Where in the hell did he find that sucker bait?"
"What's the show tonight?"
"Another two point five."
"Did John ever pay you that dough he owes?"
"Why that deadbeat. I'd give it to him right in the nose."

There was more, then the final lines:

These men are safe, no danger do they face
But separated from love and gentleness,
they can only seek to dissipate
the apathy of irresponsibility
By turning to crudeness, drink or dice
To all forms of masculine vice.
Society's problems with battleworn men
Will be great but what of all of these
Acute in their knowledge
of their ill-earned ease and uselessness
Derelicts are being made.
To them also a debt must be paid.

Finally. Orders. "Proceed forthwith" to Saipan where the invasion was about to begin. Air Wing One could only reach its post by flying to Hawaii, then back. Truk, a strong Japanese naval base, had to be skirted. They had only one night in Hawaii, then they flew to their destination. Bill wrote Nancy of his frustration:

*And did I tell you that we went through Honolulu—liter-
ally on the fly? We got there at 10 p.m. and left at noon the following day. As a result we got into the city for about an hour
during the morning and saw absolutely nothing, except crowds.
It was heartbreaking to be as near to the USA and then turn
around and go the other way. Also, had we been there a while, I
could have made a reservation to call you up. But no soap!*

The ships and squadrons of Fleet Air Wing One were already
at Saipan when Quinn and the rest of the staff joined them.
Saipan was so stormy that seaplane tenders and supporting ships,
unable to make the hazardous entrance to the inner harbor,
anchored in heavy seas in the outer harbor. The Air Wing One
staff landed on the rough waters. It was three days before the
actual attack on Saipan.

Admiral Hoover, Commander of Naval Air Forces Pacific—
ComAirPac—had vital intelligence information for Air Wing
One that could not be entrusted to radio transmission. None of
the Wing's ships had small boats stable enough to handle the
rough seas leading to the inner harbor. Admiral Hoover sent a
lieutenant out in a heavy craft to deliver the information to the
Wing. Great ocean swells pounded the side of the command ship
as a rope ladder was dropped for boarding. Bill Quinn, a lieutenant junior grade by this time, was on deck with some of the
crew peering into the foaming water watching for their visitor.
The rain squalls were fierce and salt spray stung their eyes. Finally
the boat arrived and the lieutenant made a leap for the ladder.
One step, then a slip; the lanky officer missed his footing and
plunged into the dark surge between lifeboat and ladder. But for
the fast rescue work of the ship's men, his skull might have been
crushed. The officer, his cap still on his head and the message
envelope locked in his fist, stepped aboard. Henry Fonda,

Broadway and film star, stood dripping and smiling before them. Lieutenant Fonda was an air combat intelligence officer on Admiral Hoover's staff. Quinn took him to his quarters while Fonda's uniform was dried and pressed. Bill poured him a drink of light rum, illegal as it was, but the information got through and Fonda was saved from death at sea.

Fonda was "certainly an unassuming, regular kind of a guy, modest and full of humor. We were really sorry when he had to get back to his ship," Quinn remembered.

The Air Wing units remained at Saipan for a few weeks after the Allied invasion. Tents were raised along the shore and most of the island was in Allied hands, although some Japanese hid in the hills and sparse fighting continued.

When action on Palau started, Fleet Air Wing One was ordered there. A battle raged at Peleliu, and the squadrons were ordered to a large bay off the island of Babelthuap, more than 500 miles from the Philippines. The Wing was to support the pending Allied invasion of the Philippines.

During this period, Quinn found himself in serious trouble. The squadrons were flying searches when a disastrous typhoon hit; four U.S. destroyers were lost. The Air Wing One pilots must have observed the building storm and reported it, CINC-PAC concluded. The command reasoned that the failure to warn the fleet was the fault of Wing One intelligence. CINCPAC accused Quinn, Wing One's air intelligence officer. The command figured Quinn, who had interrogated returning pilots, had failed to forward the weather information to Honolulu. If he had, CINCPAC would have been alerted to the typhoon. The commander of Air Wing One demanded an accounting from Quinn.

"I was facing a court-martial unless I could prove without any question that I had interrogated every pilot on conditions, got the reports of the bad weather together and sent it all back to

CINCPAC," Quinn remembered.

For at least 48 hours, Quinn was in hell. Headquarters wanted somebody's head, and Quinn's was going to be the one severed. Of course, it was a false accusation; Quinn and his Wing One were able to prove it. The fault rested back at CINCPAC in Honolulu, where someone irresponsibly filed the weather information without notifying the command.

There was yet another problem in store for Quinn, a more personal one. When the squadron was recalled from Palau and sent back up to Saipan, it first flew into Ulithi, in Yap. Here compadres got Bill plastered and took all his money in a craps game. It remains a bitter memory.

"I got up the next morning and I was so sick, I couldn't stand it. I was sending about 90 percent of my money back to Nancy, but there was still some money accumulated. I picked up that cash when we left Palau. It was a substantial sum and I planned to buy Nancy a special Christmas present—the diamond ring that she never got. But boom! Every single cent was gone. My so-called dear friends! And of course, the person I was maddest at was the dope in the mirror."

When they arrived in Saipan, the squadrons and ships of Wing-One joined a U.S. task force sailing out to attack Okinawa. They reached Okinawa before the landings; excitement aboard grew. This was the big one. This was what the men had been trained for and hoped for—a chance to pay back the enemy.

"Every night we were covered by a cloud of smoke. While protecting us from the enemy's sight, the vapors filled the decks with stench and haze similar to exploded gunpowder."

The mornings, however, burst with sun-filled contrast. Each day, the Wing's seaplanes searched the China and Korea coasts for the enemy.

Meanwhile, kamikaze pilots by the dozens attacked the ships in the harbor. High in the sky, individual planes would circle targets, then dive into destruction. For the sacrifice of their lives and the elimination of the enemy, they were promised eternal imperial glory.

"We have learned since," said Quinn, "that those kamikaze pilots were partially drugged before takeoff."

Okinawa's harbor was loaded with U.S. ships: large and small aircraft carriers, destroyers, destroyer escorts, cruisers and the seaplane tenders of Air Wing One. The staff of Wing One, including Quinn, was aboard the St. George. There was a huge crane aft, used to pick up the large planes and lift them back onto the deck. Enormous holds below stored tens of thousands of gallons of aviation fuel.

In early May 1945, "Condition One Easy" was ordered, meaning, be at general quarters but continue ship's work. Below in his cabin, Quinn suddenly heard the five-inch guns: "Boom! Boom!" Then the 40-millimeter, the 20-millimeter and the 50-caliber guns roared. He put on his life jacket, grabbed his gun and ran up on deck. There he watched, petrified, as a kamikaze pierced the low-hanging clouds.

This was no amateur. This was an experienced pilot in the latest Japanese fighter plane. The aircraft ripped through the bursting flak and headed for the open hold. It crashed at the base of the crane, the strongest part of the deck. The plane and its pilot smashed into the crane. Its engine went through the deck, killing four people and injuring 24. But had the pilot hit the fuel storage only 30 feet away, none would have survived. Fortunately, too, the heavily strengthened deck section caused the plane's bombs to break open with a low-order detonation. If they had exploded, the whole ship would have gone up. The men of the St. George were lucky indeed.

By July 4, 1945, the landings on Okinawa were over and a major steppingstone to Japan was secured. Lieutenant Quinn received his orders to go home. He had been overseas for 18 months; he had two sons, Billy, age 2, and little Stevie, whom he had yet to meet. He was flown to Pearl Harbor. For a second time, Quinn was in Honolulu, but for the second time, he had no opportunity for sightseeing. He wanted to get home.

Chances of getting out of there in a hurry were grim, he'd heard. The place was mobbed with men trying to get back to the States. Quinn, eager to see Nancy, found an influential friend who helped him fly out the same day to San Francisco. But that city was choked, too. Quinn couldn't find room on an eastbound train. He and a couple of other officers registered in a penthouse suite at the Sir Francis Drake Hotel and lived the next six days in style while they awaited transport. They ate, drank, talked and talked some more, caught up on sleep but mostly partied.

In her first phone conversation with Bill since his departure, Nancy, always practical, said, "I don't really think you can handle meeting your two children and me and all the family all at once. Why don't I meet you in Chicago and then we can return home together?"

Their reunion was all they had dreamed of, full of love, laughs and joyful tears. They headed back to St. Louis, where the whole family had gathered to greet Bill. For the first time in Billy's life, his father, Charlie, embraced his son. It was August 4, 1945.

The next day (August 6 in Japan), the United States dropped the atom bomb on Hiroshima.

≈Chapter Four≈
The Road Back

"Hawaii? Where is Hawaii?"

NANCY QUINN,
laughing.

When his R&R leave was over in August 1945, Bill drove from St. Louis to Florida's Banana River Air Station and his last military assignment. By instructing at the air station, he would earn enough points for his release from the Navy. His family could be with him during his duty at Banana River.

Nancy and the two boys followed by train a couple of weeks later. For Nancy, it was an arduous overnight trip. There was no way to rest in a skinny berth with two wiggling children. All she could think of was sleep; she planned to hand the boys over to their dad while she caught some shut-eye. But things weren't going to work out that way.

Bill met them at the Banana River train depot, nothing but a platform in the middle of a muddy field. He was alarmed, distracted.

"We can't go to our own house...I was there last night...that whole area has been evacuated.... There's a hurricane coming! It's started building..."

The air swirled and the sky darkened. Bill grabbed their bags, stacked them in the car and drove to the Cocoa Beach Hotel. The hotel was dark, the power off. Bill had packed some cereal, bananas and milk; that was dinner. There were two cribs and a double bed. Sleep, however, was impossible. The wind roared and the rain lashed relentlessly at the old structure. About midnight patches of plaster began to drop from the ceiling. Through the rest of the night, Nancy and Bill moved the cribs from side to side to keep the babies dry and out of the pelting debris.

By dawn the violence had subsided; the rapping of broken blinds and a faint whistle from the dying wind were limp remains of the preceding night. The Quinns moved quickly, packed their car and headed for the beach house where they were to live. It was like driving through a city dump; heaps of trash scattered by the violent winds blotted and dotted the scene. When they got closer to the shoreline, the roadway was awash with rocks and sand, toppled trees and telephone poles. It looked as if a series of land mines had exploded.

"Some kind of a welcome, Billy Quinn," Nancy said laughing. Bill laughed too.

By now they expected the unexpected, but what they faced at their new home was not to be imagined. When they stepped out of the car in the lean-to carport, all four Quinns were swarmed by mosquitoes—big, fast, biting devils. The pests virtually covered their heads, mouths, arms and ears. The babies cried. Bill rushed to unlock the door but dropped the key. Finally, they plunged into the front room, slamming the door behind them. The planes that sprayed the beaches with DDT every day to kill the mosquitoes were not able to fly during the storm. In 24 hours the insect population had exploded.

Their five-month stay at Banana River, rough at the start, was a happy reunion for Bill and Nancy and the two little boys. The commanding officer of the station offered Bill the permanent rank of lieutenant commander if he would stay on with the Navy. Bill was tempted; he had a family to support and he had no funds. He still wanted to be a lawyer, though, not a career Navy man.

He started planning. What could he do while attending law

school that would bring in a hundred extra dollars a month? He made a list:

1. *"Teach a history of or introduction to philosophy."*

2. *"Team up with a pianist and sing from 5-7 p.m. at the hotel near law school."*

3. *"Wild idea. Write to Bendix Corp., purchase a washing machine and rent it out to various couples in need."*

Bill wrote to the acting dean of the Harvard Law School, Edmond Morgan. He remembered Morgan as a fine professor, an authority on the law of evidence and an amicable man with his students. He wrote that his discharge from the Navy was imminent; he expected to be a civilian by Christmas. He said he intended to return to law school in January 1946; he needed a part-time job to defray living expenses. The GI Bill benefit of $85 a month would not be enough to support his wife and two children. He needed additional income. He asked Morgan if there were any way to get a law-related job, such as a researcher or a library assistant.

Dean Morgan answered, "Of course I remember you." He reminded Bill that coming back to school after four years would be hard enough without working, too.

"My recommendation to you is that you come back and spend full time at school," the dean wrote. "I took the liberty of looking up your academic record...and I find that it was good enough to warrant your getting a scholarship. Since the GI Bill is paying your tuition, the school will give you the cash equivalent." And it did.

"God bless Dean Edmond Morgan," Quinn said later. "My big break was all due to his initiative."

Bill accumulated enough points to be released from the Navy and shortly before Christmas, the four Quinns started the drive back to St. Louis for the holidays before moving on to Cambridge, where Bill would return to Harvard in January.

The car was loaded with two cribs, two mattresses, bags of bedding and clothing and pieces of luggage. They drove along Sandspur Road for their last glimpse of the beach.

Birmingham, Alabama, was the first stop. Overnight the temperature dropped so low their old Buick's engine froze. They had to have the car towed around town to warm it up. It was afternoon before the motor first sputtered. The mechanic smiled when the Quinns cheered, packed themselves into car and drove away.

At their second stop, in Jackson, Mississippi, they spent a night in a motel and lost the car key. It was midmorning before they found a locksmith. Finally, though, the civilian Bill Quinn, his wife and two children made it to St. Louis.

After the holidays, Bill traveled ahead of the family to Cambridge in the same troublesome Buick. The farther north he drove, the whiter the expanse grew before him. At times he wasn't quite sure of the road's edge; he had to creep along with both hands frozen to the wheel; there was no heater in the car.

He stopped at a combination gas station and small store with a large pot-bellied oven. Bill backed up against the warm stove and savored its comfort; suddenly something was burning. It was his heavy winter coat, now scorched and barren of fuzz, right at the seat. By the time he got to Cambridge, he felt worn, shabby and in need of a new coat, which, of course, he could not afford. He hoped for an early spring.

At Cambridge, Quinn intended to see if he could go directly into third-year law studies. He wanted to get his degree and get to work. Before he joined the Navy, Quinn had had a year and a half of law, but had not taken any second-year exams. Pragmatic as ever, Bill went to see the assistant dean about going straight into third-year law. The assistant dean thought this a "most unusual request." The law school was already on an accelerated tri-semester program to get people out faster, he explained.

The assistant dean did promise to review Quinn's record after the first semester and, if good, he'd be permitted to move directly into third year without taking the second-year courses again.

Still in need of money, Quinn, with his persuasive skills, got on the board of student advisors and was paid an honorarium of $125 a month. Without any requests home for money, Nancy and Bill managed well.

"We were still appreciating the fact that we were together after three years of separation. This was my new life," said Nancy, "to settle down with Billy Quinn."

The Quinns moved into a second-floor apartment just off Porter Square, a terrible neighborhood, according to Nancy.

"I was totally shocked when I heard the street kids saying the word s-h-i-t. I don't think I had ever heard anyone use that word before." She didn't want her boys to hear that kind of talk, so she took them to play in Harvard Square.

"Our apartment was a large room on the second floor and had its own long, narrow stairway entrance," Nancy recalled. "There were two crib-size niches in the attic where the boys slept. Adjoining the linoleum-floored living room was the kitchen, complete with a gas water heater and a wood stove. Our heat came from down in the basement; we had to stoke our own small furnace every morning.

"We were some distance away from the campus...there was no place to park our trusty Buick. Bill had to illegally park in a filling station after it closed and then get over there by 6 o'clock in the morning to get the car out."

Nancy and Bill worked hard to make their family life comfortable and secure. His routine was intense, filled with work and endless hours of classes and studies. There was no time for Bill's passionate interest in theater, nor was there time for him to join a choir or sing in a musical play. He settled for a movie a week, or a song or two while sipping beer with his study mates.

Winter thawed to spring, then summer arrived. Nancy hoped to surprise Bill with a July 13 birthday party. Two days before, however, she had to tell him.

"I really meant to surprise you but the party may have gotten a little out of hand." She'd invited the dean and several professors and was worried that maybe she'd missed someone that should be included.

"She had gotten half the law faculty and many of my friends all coming to this party in this tiny apartment," said Quinn, "Well, we got two students to come and serve. Nancy asked a couple of friends to come and help peel shrimp and that's what they did most of that day."

The party was planned for 5 to 7 o'clock, acceptable hours for Cambridge at the time. At 4 p.m. the bell rang. Still in his T-shirt, Bill hurried down the long flight of stairs to open the front door. There stood Dean and Mrs. Morgan.

"Oh, did we come on the wrong day?"

After learning of their early arrival, the Morgans went off; promptly at 5 p.m., they returned.

The Morgans were the first and the only guests for the first 10 minutes. They were gentlefolk. The dean, a distinguished scholar, had a pleasant, benevolent manner. Mrs. Morgan, close at his side, quietly smiled. She spoke only once: "No, thank you."

They did not drink. They, in fact, had come for tea.

Bill, beholden to Morgan for his scholarship arrangement, found himself stumped for conversation.

Finally, a few more people came. The Morgans left.

In July, Cambridge is hot and sticky, yet in that small room neither the professors, the students, nor their wives appeared uncomfortable; they were having too good a time. The two white-coated waiters circled, serving pitchers of straight-up martinis and manhattans, the fashion of the day. The party didn't thin out until 9:30 when one of the professors almost fell from the balcony. He had to be carried down the long stairway and driven home.

Outside, neighbors sat at their doorway listening to the din and wondering who these people were. It was a smashing party, one not to be repeated. Ever since her arrival in Cambridge, six months before, Nancy had been storing bottled refreshments with Bill's birthday in mind. They were on such a strict budget she could buy extras only once in a while.

In September, Bill received a letter from the secretary of the law school informing him that his grades were quite good; he could proceed into third-year law and graduate in February. It all appeared within reach, now: his career, a job and security for a growing family. Nancy was pregnant; their third child was due in early December.

The next step for Bill Quinn was to line up work for when he obtained his law degree.

"It was approaching autumn and before I could arrange to interview at any law firm," Quinn recalled, "I received a letter from the secretary of the law school saying that there was a gentleman arriving who wanted to interview the graduates."

Bill went to the interview and heard from another student who had just completed his that the man was from Hawaii.

"Hawaii?" Bill thought about the time he and his mates spent one miserable night there before flying to Saipan. "Well," he mumbled, "I'll go in and see him. It'll be good practice." He met J. Garner Anthony, a lawyer just this side of 50, distinguished and swarthy. He wore a wide-brimmed hat with a brown feather lei around the crown. His hair was dark with silver edges and his suntan reflected his life in the tropics. Anthony was head of Robertson, Castle and Anthony, one of the largest law firms in the Territory of Hawaii.

The two men talked. Because he was not the least bit interested in working for Anthony, Bill was at ease. Garner Anthony was flushed with the great victory that he'd experienced in the Supreme Court that year of 1946. He had succeeded in getting martial law in the territory declared unconstitutional. Bill was impressed by the man and inspired by the discussion of constitutional law.

That night Bill told Nancy about his meeting a man from Hawaii. "Hawaii?" Nancy asked, "Where is Hawaii?" They both laughed and thought no more about it.

A few weeks later, Quinn started a round of interviews. He had appointments with firms in St. Louis, Chicago, Washington and New York. He found out that regardless of class rank, nobody paid more than $250 a month. The nation's law firms were not competitive in salaries.

Bill hoped some firm would consider his family responsibilities and offer him a better salary; he continued with his interviews. While on the road, he got a call from Nancy, at home in Cambridge. She sounded quite excited.

"There's a cablegram here for you. It's from Garner Anthony in Hawaii..."

It was a job offer. Anthony said he'd pay half the moving expenses and offered Bill $333 a month.

"So what else is new, Nancy?"

It was November. Nancy looked out the window; it was snowing and sleeting. The elms and oaks were bare and the wind moaned a bleak song.

"The children go out in their snowsuits and they play and they get wet and they have to tinkle and they come in and I take the wet snowsuits off and I put the dry snowsuits on and that's the way it goes all the time."

"Maybe we ought to go to the South Sea Islands," said Bill. "We can always come back."

"I'd like nothing better."

That settled that. He canceled the rest of his interviews, wired acceptance to Garner Anthony and went back to Cambridge.

When the word got around that the Quinns were going to the Sandwich Islands, it caused a lot of comment.

"Where is it?"

"Do they have any schools there?"

"Are you two missionaries or something?"

Timmy, their third child, was born on December 12 in Mt. Auburn Hospital. The holidays were quiet that year. Nancy was nursing her newborn; Bill was studying for his final exams. There would be a graduation sometime in February but he wasn't going to stay around for it. Again they packed up the kids, the cribs and mattresses into the '36 Buick and drove back to St. Louis. They felt like Okies escaping from a wrathful winter's storm.

The departure for Hawaii was tearful and very difficult. It was particularly hard for Grandfather Witbeck. He had been close to Billy, Jr. and Stevie during those war years when Nancy lived at home. To see them go so far away was almost too much for him.

Lorena, Bill's mother's maid, came to him. "I'd like to go with you, Mr. Bill."

"I can't afford to pay you very much, but I'd be delighted, and if you come you'll be a member of our family, and when I make it, you'll make it, too," answered Bill. Mother Quinn agreed that Nancy needed help with the children. "It's going to be such a long journey," she said.

They would leave St. Louis by train for the three-day trip to Los Angeles, where they'd board the Matson Line's Matsonia to Hawaii. Bill James, Quinn's long-time buddy, arranged a farewell at Union Station. Both families and a few friends gathered to say goodbye. Suddenly, from the other end of the station, came the blare of a trumpet and the boom of drums. A small contingent of boys marched into view. With two of them playing drums and one tooting a horn, they preceded a couple of other youngsters who carried a 30-foot banner. It read: "U.S. DEPORTS QUINN ... FAREWELL, OLD PAL."

Everyone thought it very funny, except Charlie Quinn, who was furious.

That was the way the Quinns left St. Louis in the spring of 1947.

PART TWO

≈Chapter Five≈

Boat Day

*The Matsonia approached port carrying a capacity
load — the passenger list recorded 800, including
five Quinns: Mr. William F., Mrs. William F.,
Mstr. Billy, Mstr. Stevie and Mstr. Timmy.*

Rounding Diamond Head and entering the waters off
Waikiki, the *SS Matsonia* gave a long blast of her whistle. The deep, throaty sound on the morning breeze
signaled an exciting day for Honolulu; Boat Day was a
day of welcome. A day of aloha, with music, dancing
and embraces.

Boat Day in Honolulu meant the arrival of one of Matson's
passenger ships, the *Matsonia*, *Lurline* or *Mariposa*. Every 10
days one crossed the Pacific to Hawaii from San Francisco or Los
Angeles.

On this April day in 1947, Bill Quinn gazed across the waters
to Waikiki and saw peace and tranquillity. It was a far different
scene from the one he had experienced in his brief stops in
Honolulu during the war. Oahu appeared mended, orderly and
clean.

When World War II brought Quinn briefly to Honolulu, the
ships' cruises, which had carried visitors to the Islands and
returned *kamaaina* home for 15 years, had been suspended. The

Islands had been under military rule; there had been no pleasure travel. In those days, the blackout spread a suffocating blanket of darkness. The nights rumbled with sounds of military tanks, the clank and groan and thunder of the heavy machinery.

As the Quinns arrived to start their new life, the cruise liners had been back in business for two years, and Hawaii once again teemed with lighter activity. Gas masks were put away, beaches had been cleared of barbed wire, and what had been victory gardens were once again grassy play yards.

The brilliance of the sun scattered bursts of diamond lights in the white foam behind the ship. Canoes twisted and turned in the blue, whitecapped sea as brown-skinned youths waited for a toss of a silver coin from the decks above. The divers spiraled into the depths, rose to the surface with broad smiles and coins between their white teeth.

At the rail on the promenade deck, the Quinns felt the warm sun and, as promised in the songs of Hawaiian musicians aboard the night before, the breeze caressed them. The family watched the exotic scene, a bit forlorn in the face of the throngs gathered on the pier, everyone dripping with garlands, waving, smiling and talking. The fragrance of the flower lei was everywhere. An overwhelming longing for her home, their family and friends came over Nancy. Back in St. Louis, people had called Hawaii "the end of the world." She realized how far away they now were and that there was no one to greet them. They were the only ones, she thought, just standing, gaping at the overflow of happy embraces.

Musicians performed on the pier, resplendent in white shirts and trousers and red satin sashes. The beautiful duet performed by the band's baritone and soprano captured Bill's and Nancy's attention. The two sang in compelling, passionate tones; although the words were in Hawaiian, the romantic message was clear.

Finally the Quinns disembarked. As they stepped from the gangplank, a tall, lanky, distinguished gentleman with white hair asked, "Are you by any chance Mr. Quinn?"

The stranger eagerly introduced himself. "I'm Alfred Castle." He smiled and shook Bill's hand. "And this is Dorothy Anthony, Garner's wife." He introduced a petite, gray-haired lady who stood quietly at his side.

The couple presented the Quinns and Lorena, their nursemaid, who was carrying baby Timmy, with garlands of ginger, gardenia and carnation. Their fragrance was as welcome as St. Louis flowers in May and twice as captivating. Nothing like this ever happened back home.

Garner Anthony, busy in court, was unable to meet the Quinns, Castle explained. Castle, a partner in Robertson Castle & Anthony, had a princely manner and an air of goodness that reassured the anxious family. Nancy forgot her pangs of homesickness amid this warm reception.

Castle drove them along the waterfront to the Moana Hotel in Waikiki, where they were to spend their first night in paradise. A graceful wood structure, the Moana was five stories high with a grand porte cochere cornered by four stately Grecian columns; a wide stairway led up to a gracious, open-air lanai-lobby entrance. Two steps in, they caught sight of the surf and sandy beach of Waikiki, livelier, prettier than a picture postcard. Of course, Nancy and the children spent the afternoon at the beach. They got terribly sunburned and learned Hawaii's blistery lesson in a hurry. Bill, eager to meet with members of the firm, missed the experience. No sooner had he secured the family in their rooms, then he walked to the bus station and rode into town— to Robertson, Castle & Anthony.

Another partner of the firm, Tommy Waddoups, was about to take off on vacation, Bill learned. Waddoups' friends, Josephine and Analu Ikua, would be house-sitting at his Portlock Road home. The Ikuas were willing to rent their home on Elelupe Road in Kuliouou to the Quinns. It was a nice, modest house in the valley and would do very well for the newly-arrived family.

The Ikuas invited the Quinns for Sunday lunch at the Waddoups' home on the beach. During the conversation about Boat Day, Bill asked, "What was that song that was sung as we were docking?"

Josephine replied, "Oh, you must mean *Ke Kali Nei Au.*"

"That was a lovely duet; Nancy and I really enjoyed it."

"It's known as the Hawaiian wedding song," she said, "I have the music."

Josephine, a professional singer, was a natural soprano. Together with Thelma Akana and Alice Freeland, she was a member of the popular Halekulani Girls Trio, which entertained at social gatherings about town. Josephine carried herself with great dignity. She wore her silver hair pulled back atop her head and always tucked a brilliant flower or two close to her cheek.

Josephine taught Bill the song, carefully, word by word, so he'd get the pronunciation.

That week, Bill and Nancy had another invitation, this time to a baby luau—their first luau and it was a big one, given by a physician in honor of his son's first birthday. Bill and Nancy tasted everything.

"It was the first time that we tasted poi, and I remember choking on it as it stuck to the roof of our mouths," Nancy said.

Josephine, on the stage entertaining with her group, stepped to the microphone and announced, "I have a surprise for all of you. I've got a *malihini haole* boy here and I want you to hear something."

With that, she signaled Bill, and he stepped up and sang *Ke Kale Nei Au* with her. The crowd was delighted and wanted more. With so many people crowded under the tent on a warm afternoon, Nancy wilted amid the crowd under the tent and wished that she could go home, but Bill kept singing.

Next they were guests of the Garner Anthonys for the annual Bar Association dinner at the Pacific Club, successor of the
British Club, whose charter dated back to 1879. The Pacific
Club, the first businessmen's club in the Islands, was a unique
and prestigious place.

The large oval lanai dining room was crowded with black-tie
lawyers and guests who were strangers to Bill and Nancy. There
was, however, a musical trio moving about from table to table—
Josephine with the *Halekulani Girls*. She came up to the
Anthonys' table. "Come on, Bill, sing with me."

The brand-new lawyer in town was being asked to perform
before a rather august gathering. Of course, he did. After the
song, he spoke with an attractive, white-haired lady, Nancy
Corbett, who asked if he'd ever done anything in the theater. She
was the wife of Judge Gerald Corbett and was prominent in art
and theater circles.

"Yes, I have." Bill answered. "As a matter of fact, I was in
summer stock."

She asked if he'd heard of *Mister Roberts*.

"Yes, I read the book and I understand that it just opened on
Broadway within the last few months with Hank Fonda as
Roberts and that it's a great success."

She told him a local theater was going to produce it. She
asked if he'd come and read for a part.

They made a date to meet Elroy Fulmer, director of
Honolulu Community Theatre. Fulmer, the drama teacher at
Punahou, a prestigious private school, was admired by both his
students and faculty. He had a penchant for humor, a vivid imag-
ination and a great respect for the theatrical world.

"He handed me the Roberts part to read," Quinn recalled.
"So I read it and he thanked me and said I'd hear from them in
a few days."

Within a week *Mister Roberts* was cast, and Quinn had the lead. One of the competing hopefuls, Alex Castro, was told he had a good chance. "Except that, there's one outstanding person. His presence on stage is commanding, he has the respect of the men, he's a natural leader. He's got it hands down. His name is Quinn and I think he works for a law firm," Fulmer was quoted as saying.

"Fulmer did a superb job of casting," said Ward Russell, business executive, who at the time was vice president of Honolulu Community Theatre and volunteer production manager. "Quinn was a new face on the scene, but he obviously was a good actor with an excellent voice."

Pete Wimberly, an architect, did the sets and Russell did the lighting. "We were always yelling at each other. It was really a game but the cast thought that we were really mad, particularly Bill. He'd never heard that kind of business going on in the theater before."

Bill was bewildered by more than that:

"Almost all the guys in the cast playing the crew of the supply ship Reluctant were local and had gone to school together. Fulmer didn't try to get them to learn their lines," he said. "They came to rehearsal with a case of beer and I began to think, what in the world have I got into? I'm trying to learn all these lines and these guys are having a party."

In John Mason Brown's Review of the Broadway opening of *Mister Roberts,* he wrote:

> "The Reluctant is an unceremonious and disorderly bucket guaranteed to lay any self-respecting graduate of Annapolis low with thrombosis. She is a war casualty—the casualty of so deadly a weapon as boredom. The members of her crew continue to be as raffish, mutinous and prankish as they ever were. Although the play's dialogue is a little less

dictaphonic than it was in the book, the speech is still auda-
cious... the language is sailor's talk."

For the local production, Fulmer knew how to get the best
from the crew-cast—they learned their lines by osmosis without
ever losing the slightest bit of spontaneity. Several of them,
including Quinn, had served and saw action in World War II.

The Honolulu Advertiser reported:

> There are a number of striking coincidences connected
> with the selection of Mr. Quinn to play the role of Mister
> Roberts. Both were lieutenants in the Navy. In the play
> Mister Roberts had quit medical school to enter the Navy
> when the war broke out. Mr. Quinn had quit law school.
>
> During the early part of the war, Mr. Quinn was holding
> down a safe desk job, all the time trying, as Mister Roberts
> was, to win for himself a transfer to combat duty. Mister
> Roberts won a transfer to active duty in the Pacific. So did
> Mr. Quinn.

The theater's program said, among other sidelights:

> *William F. Quinn* (Mister Roberts) was a natural for the
> title role for tonight's play. With one very important excep-
> tion, everything that happened to Mister Roberts in the play,
> happened to Mr. Quinn in the last war. His four battle stars
> represent action in the Solomons, Saipan, Palau and
> Okinawa.

When Fulmer learned that Quinn knew Hank Fonda and that
he had actually helped to save the actor from drowning during

the war, he asked Bill to write Fonda. The actor responded quickly with a long letter:

"Dear Bill, glad to hear that you've got the opportunity to play this great part. Let me tell you about a few things that have happened."

He went on to talk about how, when they had an opening pre-run in Boston, considerable censorship had been imposed on the play. The worst was the very first line at the opening scene when crew members are sitting topside polishing binoculars:

"One sailor looks, does a double take and shouts, 'My God, she's bare-assed.'

"In Boston they had to say, 'My God, she's naked.'"

Fonda told Quinn that that went over with a big thud.

He also told of how the goat went over the side and relieved himself in the orchestra pit.

They used a sanitized part of Fonda's letter to publicize the local production, Quinn remembered.

Fulmer, worried about some of the rough lines, invited certain arbiters to preview the production. "After all," he explained, "Hawaii is still a missionary town."

Una Walker and Louise Dillingham, both socially prominent, came to a dress rehearsal. When it was over and the lights went up, they were asked what they thought. Quinn recalled Mrs. Dillingham as saying, "Well, you just use the word 'ass' too much."

Quinn promptly told her Fonda's experience in Boston. And they said, "Well, maybe so."

"Some of the other lines that were really bad just went right over their heads, I guess," Quinn recalled. "I think we put on the most unexpurgated version of *Mister Roberts* here that was put on anyplace, including New York," he said.

And it was a hit. By the third night, there was standing room only and hundreds were turned away at the box office.

What the audiences didn't know, as they laughed and cried along with the rackety crew, was that during actual performances that band of reprobates tried to trap Mister Roberts. One evening toward the end of the play, when Roberts is about to depart from the *USS Reluctant* and report for new duty, the crew gathered around him to give him a farewell gift. They had enclosed a card with a few sentimental lines written on it, and they urged him to read it aloud.

"Read it, read it," they shouted in unison. Mister Roberts responded, opened the card and up popped an obscene, air-filled condom. With a hard swallow, a choked voice and tears in his eyes, Quinn managed to stay in character; he bit his lip so hard that it bled.

In another performance, they added something to the scene where Doc, played by Jim Wahl, an NBC correspondent during the war, and Mister Roberts are alone together. It's a serious moment; the two men share a farewell toast.

They clinked glasses, and took the drink in one swallow. With that, the pair were instantly flushed and breathless. Instead of water, it was straight, undiluted gin.

As Henry Fonda wrote in his letter to Bill, "There's nothing I can tell you about Roberts except that you're in for the time of your life."

Indeed, it was exactly that, and it was the best kind of introduction into a community that anyone could ever have.

≈ Chapter Six ≈
Stepping Up to the Bar

"Walk with the home folks instead of the angels..."
WILLIAM F. QUINN
GOP Lincoln Day Address, 1948

U nder territorial law, a lawyer had to be an Island resident for a full year before he or she could be admitted to the Hawaii Bar. Even though Bill Quinn was first in the Island bar exam, he had to wait before he could practice law and represent clients in court. That didn't slow him down. Quinn provided assistance to many clients of Robertson Castle & Anthony. He was their youngest lawyer, and with his irrepressible energy, he was busy.

There was a battle going on between the city bus company and the police. Quinn's firm was called in by the privately owned bus company. When the bus drivers went through the narrow streets of Honolulu (few had been widened since horse-and-buggy days), they'd often have to make a "hula turn"—pull far to the left in order to negotiate a right-hand turn. Each time they'd pull out on the other side of the street, a police officer would give them a ticket. It didn't require being a member of the Hawaii Bar to appear in police court, and Quinn did so every day. He would go in with about 30 bus-driver tickets and he'd fight each one. It was good practice and he learned to understand pidgin fast, though he couldn't speak it.

Another time, Quinn went into court on a federal matter. Presiding was Judge Delbert Metzger, a striking man with white hair, chiseled features and a square jaw. Quinn had not yet passed his required year's residence.

"He swore me in and admitted me to the Federal Bar although I was not yet admitted in State (Territorial) Court," said Quinn.

A couple of months later, still in the first year, a case was coming up and Quinn was to try it. Garner Anthony went with him to make the introductions. Judge Frank MacLaughlin, also a Harvard graduate and 10 years older than Quinn, was presiding. MacLaughlin called both Anthony and Quinn into his chambers and Quinn recalled later what MacLaughlin said: "Garner, Bill can't try this case. I know Bill. But the fact is, he's not yet admitted to the bar."

"But I am, your honor," Quinn interrupted, "I was admitted by Judge Metzger a couple of weeks ago."

"Judge Metzger had no right to do that," Metzger said. "You can't be admitted to the federal bar if you're not admitted to the state (territorial) bar."

Thus the book of registrants admitted William F. Quinn to practice in the Hawaii Federal Court in both 1947 and 1948.

When Quinn's one-year requirement was almost—but not quite—completed, he was sent to the country town of Wailuku, Maui. This was a major case, *Bank of Hawaii and Royal Indemnity Company vs. Y.W. Char and W.H. Crozier*, involving several prominent lawyers from Honolulu.

Contractors Char and Crozier were being sued for failure repay money they borrowed to build the Hana Belt Road.

When Quinn arrived, lawyers informing the court which clients they represented. He sat in the last chair at the back of the crowded room to hear the calendar dates for the start of proceedings, scheduled to begin a few weeks later.

Maui Judge Cable Wirtz called out, "Is anybody here representing John Gomez Duarte?" Quinn recalled.

"I am, your honor," Quinn's voice boomed across the aisle.

Quinn's clients, Mr. & Mrs. John Gomez Duarte, were the indemnitors and had guaranteed the bond.

"I'm not yet admitted to practice, but by the time the matter comes up I will be," he called out.

Quinn, the newest kid on the block, startled several old-timers and the lawyers in the courtroom. Some thought his answer presumptuous. Russell Cades, the attorney for Royal Indemnity, laughed when years later he recalled that day.

"It was a startling statement, all right, but we didn't pay much attention as we had our minds on a lot of other things. I wasn't worried about some novice lawyer...."

The trial began in the late summer of 1948; by that time Quinn was indeed a registered attorney. It turned out to be quite a case and his first triumph. Though relatively inexperienced, Quinn cleverly proved there was a technical flaw in the bond issue. Cades, representing the plaintiff, viewed Quinn's passionate oratory on the motions as "pie-in-the-sky." Nevertheless, Quinn eventually succeeded in getting Mrs. Duarte, who had all the money, out of the case.

The court sessions were intermittent, stretching the trial out into the new year. Each time the court reconvened, Quinn along with the other lawyers would spend their weeknights in the Wailuku Hotel rather than fly back to Honolulu. In those days, Wailuku was a remote, fold-up-the-streets-by-8, nothing kind of town. During those evening hours after dinner, Cades and Quinn struck up a friendship. They found a mutual interest in philosophy, music and theater, and had long discussions on theology.

"Bill and I got to be good friends and I learned a lot from him because he had a different point of view," said Cades. "He learned from a Catholic priest, and my view was from studying comparative religions."

That was in the evening; the next day they'd have to be in

court opposing each other. On weekends, they'd fly home and be with their families.

The Quinns' home then was a modest three-bedroom house on Portlock Road they purchased two months after their arrival in the Islands. It had been a military house that was moved onto a large piece of property at Portlock. There was space for the growing family. Portlock was a small community with friendly neighbors, lots of playmates for the children and a sandy, wide beach with gentle surf. It was far from downtown but "I was so busy raising a family that the distance didn't matter," Nancy said.

The case on Maui continued through the fall of 1948 and into 1949. Harry Truman had been elected president, defeating Thomas Dewey. The Republicans were in the doldrums. In January 1949, O.P. Soares, lawyer for the defendant Willie Crozier, approached Quinn. Soares headed the GOP in Hawaii. "We've got our Lincoln Day dinner coming up in February. Would you make our Lincoln Day talk to the Republicans for me?" Quinn recalled Soares had asked.

Oliver Soares was a *kamaaina*, educated in public schools and trained as a lawyer. He was well known throughout the Islands; in the courts, as a reporter, as a Deputy United States Marshal and a member of the Territorial House of Representatives. He was a round, stocky man with a Sydney Greenstreet look. He sported white linen suits and atop his head, a Panama hat banded with a blue feather lei.

"I wasn't a member of either party and told him so," said Quinn, "but I guess he liked the way I had been addressing the court or something. At any rate, I felt that the Republicans were scratching around for new life. So I said yes."

When Quinn left law school, someone told him he ought to be a politician and had asked what his party affiliation was. Quinn responded he'd never been in a party nor ever voted in a federal election.

He remembered saying at the time, "Well, I could either join the Democrat Party and drag my feet or the Republican Party and push." Now, he had accepted an invitation to speak to the local Republicans.

He went to the library and researched Lincoln. He figured that since the Republicans planned a Lincoln Day dinner, they wanted to hear about the 16th president.

Quinn flew in from Maui for the dinner. Eugene Beebe, a prominent lawyer and a Republican leader, drove him to Kewalo Inn, a popular dining and dancing spot whose owner, Joe Itagaki, was one of the few *nisei* Republicans.

The restaurant stood opposite Kewalo Basin, where fishing boats tied up, and a block away from Hawaiian Tuna Packers. The war had wiped out Hawaiian Tuna Packers, the territory's only fish cannery, which was now slowly rebuilding its boats and gradually increasing its production. Sunsets over the harbor were always beautiful; when the wind shifted and blew from the west, however, the aroma from the cannery could quickly take the romance out of an evening.

Kewalo Inn's second floor had a large dining room with a dance floor, but it wasn't much of a facility for speakers. Quinn looked around for a podium and settled for a music stand to hold his notes. The crowd gathered early; he recognized Art Rutledge, representative of the unions and the chairman of the county committee. O.P. Soares, dressed in his white suit, introduced Quinn to the head of the Republican Club, Mary Noonan. Noonan formally introduced him to the gathering.

Everything about the affair turned out fine. The sunset was glorious, the gentle trade winds kept everyone cool and kept the cannery aroma at bay. Quinn traced Lincoln's career and pointed out how that Republican leader had the flexibility to shift with the political tides of his times.

"We must have the courage to drop 1920 politics. We must

recognize that such things as unemployment insurance, slum clearance and many other reforms are here to stay."

He added, "Dewey's defeat can also be traced to the political fact that a strong issue will defeat a strong man.

"We can recapture the leadership of the country if we try to walk with the home folks instead of the angels," Quinn said.

The 75 party faithful liked what he had to say and they applauded enthusiastically. That evening Bill Quinn joined the Republican party.

The next morning *The Honolulu Advertiser's* headline read: *'Walk With Home Folk Instead of Angels'*, Quinn Tells GOP Party.

"The Lincoln Day address was probably his first public appearance as an orator," Nancy Quinn recalled. "His diction was so good, and he always had a knack of being able to speak appealingly to groups on subjects that he knew nothing about."

The annual affair turned out to be the calm before the storm for Hawaii Republicans.

The Republican Club was to rebuild the local GOP, after the national election disaster in 1948, by launching a strong drive to interest new, young voters. With Soares and Noonan at the helm, they aimed the revitalization toward spreading the base of the party. The club sponsored a regular program on radio, then opened a lounge for teens with dances every Friday night.

A faction in the party, anti-Soares and anti-Noonan, was disturbed by the new approach. The old blood was concerned; these builders of the GOP feared they might be forced out. Despite the Republican slippage nationally, in Hawaii the GOP wielded considerable power. For 50 years, the Republicans had reigned, but there was no cohesive "party." Each one had his own interests, his own appointments and his own career. Commentators would credit this aristocracy as a major factor why, four years later, the Republican stronghold was overthrown by a unified, powerful Democratic Party.

"The old blood members of the Republican Party aligned with some *haole* elite to fight against Soares and Noonan and their program," Quinn said.

"At a meeting at which I was present," said Quinn, "they indicated that they would withdraw their financial support from the Republican Club. As a consequence there was a vote and they dumped O.P. Soares."

That move caused a furor at the very time when continuity, dedication and integrity were critical for survival. By the time the Republicans realized their party was being crushed by financial and structural problems, it was probably too late to cope with the tide of change.

⇒Chapter Seven⇐
Changes and Challenges

"Pro Deo, Pro Patria...For God, For Country"
WILLIAM F. QUINN
to Young Men's Institute, 1950

W orld War II had inexorably altered the very structure of life in the Hawaiian Islands. A revolution, a fight against racism, discrimination and inequality, challenged the tightly controlled territory with its paternalistic one-party (Republican) system. December 7 was the catalyst; from the flames of Pearl Harbor rose an unprecedented era of change.

"Ironically, the people helped most by the Pearl Harbor attack were the Japanese-Americans, who on December 7 seemed the most threatened," wrote U.S. Senator Dan Inouye. The greatest thing that the Japanese-American soldiers of the 442nd Regimental Combat unit had going for them on their return to Hawaii and civilian life, they realized, was the veterans' GI Bill. Immediately following the Japanese attack on the harbor, these men were discharged from the Territorial Guard. At first, because of their race, they were denied enlistment in the U.S. Army. In January 1943, the Army finally accepted them. They received basic training on the Mainland and served in the European zone.

For their brilliant successes in battle, the 442nd Regiment became the most decorated unit in the U.S. Army. Returning home as veterans, they became college-educated lawyers, determined that Hawaii would change.

"Remembering the servitude and the thwarted ambitions of their fathers, who labored in the sugar cane fields under burdensome contracts, they set about to study hard, enter politics and right the wrongs done to the Japanese community of Hawaii," wrote Lawrence Fuchs in his book, *Hawaii Pono*.

"The worst thing that happened when these young, articulate men returned was that none of our major *haole* law firms would hire them," said Quinn. "Here they wanted to join the Republican Party, the only party they had ever known, and they were turned down."

James Morita, corporation counsel for the City & County under Mayor Johnny Wilson, offered them positions in the counsel's office under the condition that they become Democrats. Among these young *nisei* were Spark Matsunaga, Dan Inouye, Ed Honda and others, second-generation Japanese-Americans who represented the largest single voting bloc in Hawaii.

"At that time, the Democrats were the underdogs. Here was an opportunity to build the Democratic Party with all these veterans that the Republicans ignored," said Quinn.

Besides politics, there were other changes. The growing population needed schools, homes and roads. Matson ships now transported visitors on a weekly schedule to and from the West Coast, and United Airlines was soon to open direct one-airline service from Hawaii to 62 Mainland cities. Pan American Airlines named the Islands the "Clipper Crossroads." The newly renovated Royal Hawaiian hotel, which had served as the center of rest and relaxation for the armed forces for five war years, reopened its doors to travelers. A new lunch and dinner spot called the Queen's Surf opened at the edge of Kapiolani Park. It was on the old Chris Holmes Waikiki Beach estate and featured Sterling Mossman in the "Barefoot Bar." Downstairs by the Chinese garden alongside the beach wall, the Beamer family, Mahi and Keola, with cousin Sunbeam, performed at the weekly luau.

Across the street from the Moana Hotel a cottage-type restaurant opened. Its striped green and white canopy stretched above a courtyard entrance marked by flaming gaslight torches. Braced to a tall coconut tree was a sign that spelled BROILER. Peter Canlis, proprietor, host and chef, saw his dinner guests as the audience and his broiler as the stage, with the chef in the lead role. He placed his broiler and its glowing copper hood in the dining room where everyone could watch Canlis broil the steaks and fish.

Don the Beachcomber opened his restaurant in a Waikiki vacant lot that eventually became the International Market Place; Trader Vic reopened his exotic dining hut across the street from the Old Plantation on Ward Avenue. Richard Smart's "49th State Revue" used Roosevelt High School auditorium as its theater and featured the "Flanderettes," the popular USO dancers and singers who had entertained the troops in Hawaii and in the South Pacific. By the fishing boat docks, Kewalo Inn hosted singer Alfred Apaka, and Don Ho moved from his mother's restaurant in Kaneohe to Waikiki; all his Windward buddies followed. The tourists were back and in larger numbers. They wanted to go to a luau, hear the wedding song, *Ke Kali Nei Au*, ride in a canoe and see the view from the top of the Pali.

Portlock Road

During the post-war period as the city grew, so did the suburbs. Ancient landholdings, once the domain of high chiefs, were subdivided into leasehold properties. Hind-Clarke Dairy and the surrounding Hind estate opened vast holdings to residential development and called it Aina Haina (Hind Land). Paved roads, electric lines and water pipes were put in; cattle, pigs and chickens were moved out. Farther along the southeast shore at the foot of the extinct crater of Koko Head, giant saltwater ponds reflected the ebb and flow of the sea. Flower farms climbed dry, red, stony slopes, and only the deep valleys were lush green. There on the southeast point of Oahu was Portlock Road, where the Quinns lived.

Virtually every month brought new young families to the street. By the early '50s there were 93 families with a total of 128 children. The Quinns had helped increase that population by the birth of their fourth son, Christopher, in March 1950, three years after their arrival in Hawaii.

When they first moved to Portlock, the Quinns didn't have a car, so Bill hitched to work. Every morning he'd be out at the highway entrance. Tommy Waddoups, Malcolm MacNaughton or Deal Crooker usually picked him up. Tongues wagged. "Isn't it funny that the Quinns have a black nanny but no car," neighbors remarked. Lorena, who had traveled with them from St. Louis, moved after a few months, ending this gossip.

Chummy and Ward Brown, the Durants, the Wilders, Gibby and Doris Rietow, Lou and Howard Hubbard, Malcolm and Pinks MacNaughton, Jean and Ken Conningham and the Quinns were part of the "original gang" of the area.

Jim and Betty Wilder, with their Albert Ives house design, were among the first *kamaaina* couples to build on the Portlock strip. Betty, then the society editor of the *Honolulu Star-Bulletin*, ran a big spread in a 1953 Saturday edition whose headlines read: "ORGANIZED COMMUNITY, Recreation Program Provides Fun and Safety on Portlock."

Complaints had come in about the children. An old-timer asked, "Whatsa mattah you people on Portlock Road? All got acres and college education and can't keep da keeds off da street!"

In response, the neighbors had formed the Portlock Community Association. Recreational programs helped to cut down the children's off-the-curb playing. A huge concrete slab on a vacant lot became the center of activities. The slab had been the foundation of an Army amphibious tank-repair shop during the war, a reminder of the years when the islanders lived with the fear of invasion.

The 13,000-square-foot slab served as the site for parties and as a sports arena. With a couple of spectator benches, volunteer coaches and appropriate gear, it was the hub for skating, volleyball, tennis and basketball. On special holiday nights, there'd be dancing for parents, with a record player and speaker hooked up to someone's house, gas torches, a bring-your-own spread, and Bill and Nancy Quinn singing *Ke Kali Nei Au.* "The slab was more like everybody's club," Malcolm MacNaughton remembered.

"Our friends there were like part of our family," said Nancy. "Our next-door neighbors were the Durant family, Elbridge and Marian and their two sons, Mike and Bob. After our Christopher was born, Elbridge used to tease me: 'You can't have any more babies unless you ask me first...as soon as they can crawl, they crawl into my yard.'"

Besides children, the street had a large pet population. There was no leash law for animals in those years and there were a few problems. The Quinns' Snuffy, a neutered German short-haired pointer, was an offender. He created his own style of vandalism— he snatched laundry off backyard lines and proudly brought his treasures to Nancy.

"The terrible part was trying to figure out who belonged to the clothes," said Nancy. "Besides, it was very embarrassing, particularly when there were personal things like lingerie." Snuffy was just a day old when Nancy and Bill brought him home. His mom had given birth to too many pups and couldn't take care of all of them. Nancy got out an old bassinet, bought a nursing bottle made especially for puppies, and religiously fed the little pups every three hours. "No wonder that Snuffy follows you around and brings you gifts, Nancy; he thinks you're his mummy."

While the Quinn family settled into the Portlock community, Bill Quinn was on the move downtown. Congratulations were in order when the newspapers announced in June 1951 that "William F. Quinn, prominent in legal and theatrical circles, becomes a partner today in the law firm of Robertson, Castle & Anthony."

Quinn was particularly proud because he knew of no other Harvard classmate who had been invited to become a partner in just four years. He would have liked his father to have known about the progress of his career but Charlie Quinn had died of cancer in 1950. Bill and Nancy had gone to St. Louis to see him when he was first ill. Charlie Quinn never made it to Hawaii.

Quinn's oratory skills brought dozens of opportunities for speeches to organizations and business groups. In 1950, Quinn took on the hot topic of communism at the St. Francis Xavier Clubs Convention. Hawaii was still recovering from the 1949 dock strike. Almost completely dependent on shipping, the Islands were devastated by the 178-day work stoppage. The strike tied up shipping, forced many small businesses into bankruptcy, caused food shortages and enormous financial losses to industry, and established the ILWU as a power. The ILWU was led by Jack Hall and Harry Bridges, both accused of being Communist Party members, who were labor leaders both in Hawaii and on the West Coast.

At one point during those long months of strike, *The Honolulu Advertiser* ran front-page "Dear Joe" letters charging that the ILWU was serving Joseph Stalin, the Soviet dictator, in a plot to destroy Hawaii's economy. Some readers mistook the "Joe" for Joseph Farrington, the publisher of The Star-Bulletin, but the letters were crudely addressed to Stalin.

The U.S. House Committee on Un-American Activities came to Honolulu in the spring of 1950 to investigate communism in Hawaii. The trial of the "Hawaii Seven" lasted seven months, commanding widespread interest.

At the Xavier Clubs Convention banquet, Quinn challenged the delegates:

> *If you would do battle against the evil force of the hammer and sickle, you must display the overpowering truth and goodness of the Christian life, and not merely try to out-argue communism.*
>
> *You who are special followers of St. Francis should broaden your battleground. Broaden it to encompass a share in the world-wide battle against the evil ideas embodied in communism. However small as you believe the significance of your own battle, remember that by your acts of charity you will be destroying skepticism and choking off communism among your own neighbors.*

Serving the community was a popular theme with Quinn. At still another convention, of the Young Men's Institute, Quinn as keynote speaker stressed the significance of the Catholic fraternal organization's motto, "Pro Deo, Pro Patria...For God, For Country."

The Advertiser reported his address:

"Service of God is measured by charity. Charity...or love of thy neighbor...is founded upon our recognition that our fellow men have immortal souls, that they have a personal relationship with God; in short, it is an appreciation of human dignity."

Mr. Quinn asserted that the forces which are aligned against the individual human dignity must be counteracted by a moral renaissance, regular practice of the Faith and positive contributions in the field of Catholic action.

He urged the members to not limit their activities in Catholic groups but to also spread out through the community in order to sustain a moral sense.

Quinn served as chairman of the Red Mass planning committee assisting the Most Rev. James J. Sweeney, the Catholic bishop. He joined Governor Samuel King and Judge Gerald Corbett on a panel discussing "Mentally Retarded Children and Community Awareness." Quinn was then president of the Honolulu Community Chest.

Law, politics, speeches, family, friends, theater, symphony, community and church work—the Quinns were occupied. Whenever Bill was elected to a presidency, such as The Honolulu Community Theatre or the Honolulu Chapter Society for the Preservation and Encouragement of Barber Shop Quartet Singing in America, Inc., Nancy did her part. She would serve tea or act as hostess or model in a fashion show. She attended official dinners and sometimes acted on Bill's behalf when he couldn't be there. She had her own starring roles singing and dancing for the Holiday Ball, the Honolulu Junior League's annual fund-raiser held at the Royal Hawaiian. She became a cast member of the Junior League's Children's Theatre, a trouping show that played to more than 100,000 schoolchildren around the Islands.

Bill Quinn continued to hit the boards of theater as well. Lacking a suitable auditorium, Hawaii Community Theater, under the direction of Elroy Fulmer, adapted by establishing "Banyan Playhouse" at the Moana Hotel. HCT's version of in-the-round staging opened the 1949-50 season with Moss Hart's *Light Up The Sky*. The comedy opened to a sell-out crowd.

Quinn played the part of the director in this burlesque of show business. According to a critic, "honors were equally divided among the actors."

Fulmer had decided to resign from HCT. As his final production, he put together a top-notch cast for *The Hasty Heart*. Fulmer had given Hawaii a long, distinguished record of excellent theater; he produced some shows on the local stage while they still ran on Broadway. This was one of the good things about being so far away from New York. HCT was never a threat to big-time theater.

The Hasty Heart playbill read:

> "Bill Quinn as Yank will not soon be forgotten in the title role of *Mister Roberts*, a production that HCT recalls with pardonable pride. Bill followed this outstanding success with a part in *Light Up The Sky* which was hardly the plum that *Mister Roberts* was but...well, Bill was a good sport. Back in stride again as the American warrior, Bill has a sympathetic assignment tonight as the stuttering Yank.

Quinn played the lead in the *Brigadoon* production of the Honolulu Community Theatre while serving a second term as president of HCT. One critic said:

> William F. Quinn, as the romantic lead, gave another unforgettable performance such as he played in *Mister Roberts*. In addition to his dramatic talents, he disclosed a pleasant, rich singing voice and beautiful diction.

Ed Mangum, the new HCT director, came up with an innovative musical production. He scaled the show to fit the confines of the Fort Ruger stage, and twin pianos replaced the traditional orchestra in the pit. It was grand, exciting and such a smashing success that performances were extended for two weeks.

Juggling to keep up with his commitments, Bill remembered the advice of Father Dan Lord at the University of St. Louis, when he was so hot to pursue a theatrical career: "Keep singing, dancing and acting for your own enjoyment. But pursue that law career."

Taking that advice had been a turning point in his life. Now he realized that Father Lord's words applied once again. He couldn't carry on his legal profession, tend to his family, accept community responsibilities and do theater, too. When he finished his term of office with HCT, it was a long time before he returned to the stage.

Chapter Eight

Big Time in the Old Town

"I guess I got to be known a little after that."
BILL QUINN

In 1952, Portlock neighbor Ken Conningham, treasurer of the Honolulu Gas Company, asked Bill Quinn what seemed like a simple question. Would he consider being nominated as president of the Precinct Club? Herb Keppeler, a real estate agent with Bishop Estate who later became a trustee, had been president of the Precinct Club for about 10 years, Conningham explained to Quinn, and Keppeler felt that he had been in office long enough.

"Yes, that would be all right," Quinn answered.

The result was a full-blast contest in the Republican precinct that took on the color and ballyhoo of a major territory-wide campaign.

"In those years, the Precinct Club extended from Kahala all the way out to Waimanalo," Quinn recalled. "Aina Haina development had just started, but the Hind-Clarke Dairy (located there) was still in operation."

About 50 people attended the evening precinct meeting. Among them was Elizabeth (Libby) Kellerman, whom Quinn described "a strong, articulate Republican and a very independent-thinking person." When Libby Kellerman, an attorney, spoke, everyone listened.

A slender, stylish woman in blue jeans or linen suit, Kellerman had a southern accent and a warm, gracious manner. Yet her words were direct, succinct. Never minced.

The slate of candidates with Quinn for president, nominated and sponsored by retiring president Herbert K. Keppeler, was announced to the crowd. Libby Kellerman stood.

"This sounds to me like a conspiracy to just put some officers in without anybody having a proper say."

A group, led by Kellerman, nominated its favorite, Harold Conroy, for president.

Before the evening was over, nominations were made for other offices, too. Kellerman herself ran for county committee-woman, and there were 35 candidates for 21 seats in the territorial convention. The next day, electioneering in the precinct began in earnest. Campaigns grew in intensity as organized groups of women staffed telephones and rang doorbells to urge club members to vote.

"What I thought I accepted, a job just to accommodate somebody, ended up as a contested election," said Quinn. "There were motorcades from Portlock going down to Aina Haina and motorcades from Aina Haina going to Portlock and a big battle between Quinn and Harold Conroy for president."

Quinn won the contest, but with the intensity of the campaign, the club had grown to 400 members. Kellerman also won. "Libby was absolutely right," Quinn pointed out. "We now have active and interested members."

At the first opportunity, Quinn invited Joseph Farrington, who was running for re-election as delegate to Congress, to speak at a monthly club meeting in the new Aina Haina School. Joe Farrington was a distinguished figure, not just because of his gray-haired attractiveness. His was an impressive record of accomplishments. He was personally and politically popular; he was president and publisher of the *Honolulu Star-Bulletin* and son of a former governor of Hawaii, Wallace R. Farrington. Joe Farrington was also a strong proponent of statehood. He wanted to identify the Republican Party with that cause. In 1947, at the start of his second term as delegate and on the opening day of the 80th Congress, Farrington introduced House Resolution 49, designed to admit Hawaii as the 49th state.

The Farrington bill was lost in the Senate, Quinn recalled, "largely because of delaying tactics by Senator Hugh Butler of Nebraska. The senator concluded that the Territory of Hawaii should be purged of communism in its political and economic life before being given the prize of statehood."

Quinn had heard Farrington speak and wrote as a reminder to himself one word, "enthusiasm," on the palm of his hand. Now, as precinct president, Quinn introduced Joe Farrington that evening in 1952. Stirred by his own zeal, Quinn gave everyone a bit of a fight talk:

"Here's a man who's trying to get us equality with the rest of the people in the United States...he is our man on the scene...."

Farrington's main theme didn't deviate that night, or any time in his past terms: "...When I go back there, to the capital, I'm not allowed to vote...ever. Hawaii needs a vote. Let me continue to fight for our rights...let me go back and see if we can't get statehood."

While Farrington roused the 300 members who were there, Quinn apparently impressed Farrington. The next day, he called Bill. "Would you take to the campaign trail with me?"

Within that week, Quinn was part of the Farrington team. He found himself at rallies in Waimanalo, Waianae, Ewa, making speeches on Farrington's behalf. Farrington triumphed and returned to Washington to serve his third term as delegate to Congress.

For Quinn it had been quite an experience.

"I guess I got to be known a little after that."

"A little" recognition for Bill Quinn soon turned into soaring in Republican prominence as he continued to support

Farrington and the cause of statehood. From precinct president, Quinn rose to chairman of the Republican District, then chairman of the Republican Convention. He was articulate, compassionate and sincere.

As Winston Churchill said, "Of all the talents bestowed on man, none is so precious as the gift of oratory." Gift or not, Quinn's words were heard by many people: "the cause (statehood) belongs to the people, not just the parties."

The day of the general election in 1952 proved to be an embarrassing one for Quinn in his new Republican position. Nancy's parents, "Noni" and "Daddy," as she called them, had come from St. Louis for a short visit. Mr. Witbeck, a staunch Democrat, was interested in elections and was particularly curious about the territorial process. When Bill went to the precinct voting site, the Witbecks went along. Outside the polling booth, Quinn introduced his father-in-law to Stanley Kennedy, founder and president of Hawaiian Airlines. Martha Kennedy, Stanley's wife, returned from the voting line to say that her name was not on the registered voter list. She was baffled and quite upset. Kennedy chided her about it, then discovered that his name wasn't listed with the registered voters either.

"But there must be some mistake," Quinn said, and stepped up to receive his own ballot. Alas, neither was his name on the list. After weeks of meetings, speeches and knocking on doors urging people to get out and exercise their constitutional privilege, Bill Quinn, Republican leader of the precinct, would not be allowed to vote. According to territorial law, if a voter did not cast a ballot in the general election one year, his registration was canceled and the voter must register again. Quinn and the Kennedys had been together in Washington, D.C., on Hawaiian

Airlines business at the time of the previous general election. They had forgotten the rule.

Daddy Witbeck learned quite a bit that morning about the territorial election laws. Until his death, he never let his son-in-law forget them. He kidded Bill without mercy.

Quinn continued his press to see those territorial laws become state laws. With every speech, he felt that statehood was one step closer in Washington, though the way was littered with statehood opponents—one of their main arguments was that Hawaii's voting population was predominately Asian. Japanese-Americans were now the largest single voting bloc in the territory. There was also the issue of communism and how the International Longshoremen's & Warehousemen's Union (ILWU) had taken such strong control over the sugar and pineapple industries. Extensive publicity by Mainland papers on how the longshore strikes had brought Hawaii to its knees led Washingtonians to believe that Harry Bridges, the ILWU leader, was more powerful than the governor of the territory, who was appointed by the president.

In 1953, a petition for statehood was unrolled down Fort Street. The paper stretched a full block. As evidence of their patriotism and rousing enthusiasm for statehood, a group of young *nisei* organized the day's rally and produced about 116,000 signatures. This "Statehood Honor Roll" was carried by members of the 442nd Regimental Combat Team to Texas, where they met soldiers they had rescued in a famous World War II battle. The two raised more publicity for the cause. Fortified and invigorated, the small band of warriors, their petition in hand, traveled to Washington and asked Congress to grant statehood to the Territory of Hawaii.

Their plea was resolute and honest: "Give us our right, give us our due...we're citizens of our country. We went out and fought and died for our country and we don't even have the right to vote, but still you tax us."

They couldn't persuade the nation's governing body. Hawaii statehood was denied again.

Meanwhile, the shift continued in Island politics. Neal Blaisdell, one of the Islands' native sons, decided to run for mayor against incumbent Johnny Wilson; he asked Quinn to join his campaign.

"It was an unusual time in the history of the Republican Party...(the Democrats) decided to get rid of Wilson in the primary. It was the time to do it because he was running against an unknown fellow who had been around town but who was brash and noisy. His name was Frank Fasi. So the Republicans all went over in the primary and voted for Fasi in order to dump Wilson and that was exactly what happened. Then they came back and voted for Neal," according to Quinn.

Two weeks before the election, Quinn got a call from Blaisdell's headquarters. Nelson Prather, Blaisdell's campaign manager, told him: "Somebody's given us 15 minutes of television. Would you take it for Neal?" Quinn was aghast.

"Fifteen minutes? Five minutes, maybe, but 15 is impossible.

"But I did remember Bishop Fulton Sheen on television and how he worked from his library, sitting on his desk, reaching for a book, etc. There wasn't much time for preparation but using the same technique, I chose 'The Fox and The Lion' out of *Aesop's Fables*, where I could identify Frank Fasi as the fox and Neal as the lion."

Catholic Bishop Sheen's "Life Is Worth Living" was a national prime-time TV broadcast from 1952 to 1957 that brought viewers gentle, homey religious messages.

Quinn took the fable book, cut out the middle pages and placed his notes in there. Next he had the television studio get him a desk and set up a library-like room.

He pulled it off without a hitch. "I did the whole damn 15

minutes." Blaisdell went on to beat Fasi, but Fasi's future had the mayor's office in it.

More change was coming. The sudden death of Delegate Farrington stunned the territory. Still a young man, he died at his desk in Washington. Friends and fans mourned and wondered just who would carry on his leadership in the cause of statehood. With Farrington's passing came an ominous gloom, a foreboding, perhaps, of crushing defeat.

A Political Revolt in Paradise

The Republicans had considered Hawaii their domain for 50 years. That changed in 1954. The new, reorganized Democratic Party trounced the Republicans and became the masters of the territorial Legislature. They won 22 of the 30 House seats and 10 of the 15 Senate seats. Democrats also took the majority of city and county supervisory seats. The leader of the new Democratic Party, Jack Burns, did lose his try for delegate to Congress to Betty Farrington, Joe Farrington's widow.

Battle-scarred GOP veterans licked their wounds and found solace in the fact that the two top positions in the territory were held by Republicans, Governor Samuel Wilder King and Honolulu Mayor Neal Blaisdell. Interestingly enough, as powerful a position as the Democrats held, their efforts were thwarted. Republican Governor King vetoed their legislative reforms.

But for the GOP it was too late: Internal strife, the factions that grew away from the immovable old guard and the closed-door policy that the *haole* elite took against the veteran *nisei*, wrapped together into a fuse that lit a time bomb.

"We could see it coming and almost predicted it to the year," Quinn reflected. "The pity of it was that such disaster could have been avoided...if only the Republicans had invited, encouraged or even just listened to the returning veterans."

Portlock 1954

In the post-war years of the early '50s, there was an insecticide truck that sprayed for the dengue mosquito regularly. It filled the air with a noxious fog, and while it worked and no one complained, people joked about it: "Oh, oh! They're spraying for Quinns again." The Quinns were multiplying again.

In September, two months prior to Blaisdell's election, there was a lot of excitement running up and down Portlock Road. The Quinns had become proud parents of a fifth child, a tiny blonde girl named Cecily.

"When I returned from the hospital, all the kids were standing at the end of Portlock Road waiting and they followed the car all the way to our driveway," said Nancy.

"I'll never forget their expressions and squeals of excitement. Then when I stepped out of the car with Cecily, all of them huddled around us...we couldn't take a step."

"But Stevie, who was pushed back about three or four rows, was yelling, 'That's my sister; can't I see her?'"

Quinn recalled it as "a happy, wonderful time. I even took a couple of days off to enjoy our little blue-eyed miracle. Billy, Stevie, Timmy and Chris were wonderful to watch and dear Nancy was as proud as I."

A long weekend is about all his time off amounted to. Quinn was a man in demand.

"After Neal's successful campaign, he offered me an appointment," said Quinn. "I turned that one down but realized that for whatever it wrought, I was embarked into politics." Quinn had tasted the political apple and found it savory.

"Neal then had another proposal and this time I said yes. The mayor's office was developing a city charter and J. Ballard Atherton had agreed to chair a committee—a Charter Commission."

The Honolulu Charter Commission, including Quinn,

Raymond Y.C. Ho, Allan J. McGuire, Robert G. Dodge, Suyuki Okumura, Thomas D. Murphy, Mrs. Eureka Forbes and Atherton as chairman, was confirmed by the Board of Supervisors and sworn in by Blaisdell.

The commission brought in experts from public administration services and the National Municipal League. One of the "aces" was Murray Seasongood, former mayor of Cincinnati who had helped draft the charter for his city. That charter was credited with changing "one of the most corrupt" cities in America into a model municipal government. The commission had a lot to learn.

"The major question that we had was whether we should have a city manager or a strong mayor. Because we were a territory, and after a lot of debate...we decided that since the people of Hawaii did not elect their governor and did not have any voice in the naming of their judges, they really ought to have some office which is a strong political office that they could elect. We decided on a strong mayor," Quinn said.

Portlock 1955

Between the Charter Commission and his law practice, which had broadened, Quinn was busier than ever. Nancy, who almost never called the office, phoned Bill one morning.

"Bill, I just got a call...Daddy's gone...he died in his sleep last night. It's so hard to believe, I feel like he was just here..." Her voice sagged.

Bill left the office early. He felt sad for her and knew how difficult it was to be such a distance from family.

"At a time like this, Hawaii is a very remote place," they agreed, and then discussed whether she should go to St. Louis for the funeral.

Nancy was sure that would not help her mother. "No, Bill, Noni has her sister and she understands why it's best that I not leave the children." The decision was made.

About a week later a loving letter arrived from Noni. As she read it quietly to herself, read of the burial, the friends who called, what everyone said, the eulogies, the prayers, Nancy could no longer hold back. She cried steadily for a long time, remembering sweet, tender moments, treasured childhood memories of her father.

She felt miserable most of the following day. That evening at a friend's house where they had been invited for dinner, Nancy asked Bill to take her home. She hadn't told anyone that she was pregnant; now she knew she was about to lose the baby.

Bill drove her straight to the hospital, where she suffered a miscarriage. Two heartbreaks, first her father and now her baby. She recovered in a few days, but it was obvious that she needed a rest.

The entire neighborhood rallied, taking shifts and sharing household chores. For after all, the Quinns were quite a well-known and wonderful brood, all seven of them.

Chapter Nine

The New Republican

*"Island politics and the Republican Party have not
heard the last of Mr. Quinn or the policies that he represents."*

GARDINER JONES
The Honolulu Advertiser, 1956

B ill Quinn had a major Hawaii Supreme Court argument
on the calendar. He was in his office preparing for his 10
a.m. appearance when he had a call from Jimmy Glover,
a friendly, outgoing and very successful contractor. His
wife, Barbara "Barbie" Glover, was heir to Cox
Communications, the big publishing empire out of Georgia.

Glover had been a territorial senator for 12 years and
remained a Republican leader. Quinn remembered Glover told
him, "There's a group of us who would like to see you." Quinn
explained he would be tied up in court.

"Then when can I get in touch with you?"

"I'll be up at the Pacific Club playing volleyball about noon.
You can call me there."

At noon Glover's call came: "When can we see you?"

"I have to go back to court," Quinn said. "I'll be available
about three thirty."

Glover told him to come to E.E. Black's office.

Quinn knew it had something to do with politics; it was the

last day for filing for any office in the '56 elections.

E.E. "Johnny" Black, a large man with a 6-foot frame and a deep booming voice, was one of the most successful contractors in Hawaii. Despite his bark, he was charitable, well-respected in the community and a strong, influential Republican.

"When I arrived," said Quinn, "I found not only Glover and Black waiting for me but also Ben Dillingham, the incumbent Republican senator, who had been told by his father, Walter Dillingham, not to run for office again. There were other leading Republicans, including Ed Bryan, party chairman, who had decided not to return to his seat in the Senate."

Ben's withdrawal had left a vacancy on the Republican slate. The two other Senate candidates were long-time incumbents: Joe Itagaki, member of the 442nd, and Mary K. Hart Robinson.

Quinn understood immediately why he was there. They wanted him to run in Ben's place as a third Republican candidate for the territorial Senate.

"How impossible," Quinn recalled thinking. "The Democrats had achieved a clean sweep just two years ago. I'm still a *malihini* after being here only nine years and the territorial Senate is an islandwide race...impossible," he murmured to himself.

"No, I can't do it," Quinn told them.

"Why not?"

"I've got five small children. It wouldn't be fair to them. Not to Nancy, either."

Johnny Black grinned. "Why don't you call her?"

Bill called Nancy and told her what was happening.

Much to his surprise, his wife said, "You're always saying that good people should run for office. Now's the time to make good on your words."

Bill was taken aback, but he wasn't convinced.

"I still can't do it. I'm up to my ears at our law firm now and there's no way I can take time off."

Black replied, "Look, I'm a big client of your law firm. We'll go up and see Garner right now."

He called Garner Anthony, the chief lawyer of the firm, at home on Pacific Heights and said he was coming up. It was around 5:30, with the sun just reaching the western horizon. Quinn continued his objections all the way up the twisting drive.

Black came right to the point, Quinn recalled: "Garner, we want this young man to run for the Senate. He says he's too busy. What do you think?"

"Garner," remembered Quinn, "had always called himself a 'Wilsonian Democrat' and behaved just that way. He really didn't know beans about politics. Garner thought I'd go to the office as usual and then maybe later make a few calls or ring doorbells or something."

Quinn voiced his own objections again, but he said Garner answered, "Of course he can run."

When they returned to Black's office, Quinn made one more try. "I still can't do it....My career is going too well. It just doesn't make sense for me to get involved in running for office. I'll do my bit, but not this."

It was getting late. The deadline for filing was only hours away. Jimmy Glover stood up. "Why don't you go to dinner with Barbie and me and we'll talk about it?"

Quinn met them for dinner at The Tropics, Tony and Peaches Guerrero's popular restaurant a block off Kapiolani Boulevard. All through the meal, Bill's hosts plied him with brandy and arguments. At 10 p.m. Bill finally gave in. "Okay. I'll do it."

There was a whirlwind of action. Jimmy called an aide, who came in with 25 signatures, previously collected and prepared, which were required for filing. Then, with only minutes left, they went directly to the secretary of Hawaii's office and filed Quinn as a senatorial candidate.

The next morning *The Advertiser* reported that the Republican slate had four nominees for the three Senate seats; G. Paul Cooke Jr., popularly known as Peppi, had also filed at the last minute for the territorial Senate. This was Peppi Cooke of the *kamaaina* Cooke family; Cooke's father had been president of the Senate for many years. All of a sudden they didn't need Quinn to fill the ticket. He was in a contested primary. It was going to be tough.

The Advertiser of September 16, 1956, gave the Republicans an editorial tribute headlined "New Faces in the GOP":

> The Grand Old Party pulled some pleasant surprises from within its ranks in the last hours before the roster closed on the 1956 crop of political aspirants.
>
> ...In the closing hours came the entries that will make a dingdong battle of the GOP senatorial primary: G. Paul Cooke Jr. and William F. Quinn. Both can be expected to wage hard campaigns in their first attempts at elective office. Mr. Cooke is a *kamaaina*, a member of a widely known and respected family that has served Hawaii well in past years. Mr. Quinn, a successful attorney, brings unusually high qualifications and well-earned recognition gained in his nine years of residence here. The two will add stature to the Senate race."

The only good thing that Quinn could see was that he didn't have to worry about campaign finances. Between the Glovers and E.E. Black, that problem was well taken care of. He asked Marty Anderson, a young, vigorous lawyer with Anderson, Wrenn and Jenks, to be his campaign manager. Fliers and signs were printed and his small headquarters opened in the Merchandise Mart Building on the corner of Alakea and Hotel streets. Lou Hubbard, a neighbor from Portlock, staffed the office with volunteer Shada Pflueger at her side, and Bill Quinn set out for the first party rally in which he was a candidate.

The old-style rallies were colorful. Normally held in city parks, church yards or school playgrounds, these rallies were casual affairs. A small stage would be decorated with bunting; Japanese lanterns over bare light globes would lend an exotic atmosphere. Grandfathers and little bundled babies and neighborhood dogs would arrive and settle in for the evening. People carried folding chairs, blankets, pillows and sacks of food. Hula dancers greeted the candidates with leis. Musical troupes, speeches, the promises, the singing and dancing made it a gay and happy time, bringing the people closer to the candidate and vice versa.

At the rally at Farrington High School, the candidates were given one and a half or two minutes to speak. Each was introduced by an emcee, Hawaiian music played and the candidate approached the stage.

"First I heard, 'Joe Itagaki, longtime incumbent senator, Joe Itagaki, sergeant in the 442nd, Joe Itagaki,' etc. etc. Then Joe got up and he talked."

"Second, 'Mary K. Hart Robinson, our sheriff, longtime incumbent, from a great Hawaiian family and married to Mark Robinson whose family goes back to the early days of the Kingdom,' etc. Then Mary got up to talk."

"Third, and the music girls really hit the strings...'Peppi Cooke from the great Cooke family, whose father was a longtime president of the Senate.' Peppi got up on the stage with a musician from Molokai and they both sang "The Molokai March" and then he spoke.

"By this time I wanted to crawl under a rock and I hear the announcer start my introduction by saying, 'born in Rochester, New York...' those were his very first words."

"I sank down into my chair. I couldn't stand it."

Nevertheless Quinn went through his prepared talk. He couldn't tell whether or not he had any impact on the audience. A few nights afterward another rally in Aala Park dragged on till late in the evening. The Senate candidates were the last to speak. Quinn saw his opportunity.

"Hardly anybody was there except the musicians, who traveled along with the Republicans from rally to rally. When Peppi was called to the stage, he did his 'Molokai March' and then spoke. When it came my turn, I took the stage and turned to the trio and said, 'Can someone do the soprano in *Ke Kali Nei Au*'?'"

"One of the girls answered 'yes' but gave me a strange look of '*haole* boy, what you talking about?'"

"So I said 'key of C'. So we sang it..."

"That," said Quinn, "was one of the big breaks that I had because that same troupe followed us around throughout the campaign. I'd give my two- or three- minute speech and then she'd step forward and we'd sing, and I'd get that much more time before the audience."

That first reaction from the soprano vocalist, however, proved to Quinn that he was still a stranger in town, a *malihini* (newcomer) telling the *kamaaina* (long-time resident) what to do. He tried hard to justify himself, but each time he passed out cards and shook hands, he saw the look that said, "Who are you?"

"Who are you?" Quinn remembered it well. "I battled that every single time I turned around. I kept asking myself, 'How can I make these people accept me...I've been here almost 10 years?'" Quinn realized that although there had been no such conflict while working with the young *haole* group of the neighborhood precinct in the early '50s, now he was in an islandwide campaign; it was entirely different.

Quinn started to campaign in earnest. There was only one

way to do it. Much to the puzzlement of Garner Anthony, he wasn't in the office; he was out campaigning.

After a couple of weeks, Howard Hubbard, neighbor and friend, pointed out to Quinn that his campaign was going nowhere. Quinn realized it only too well; he didn't know where to turn. Out of the blue, a group of young Japanese-American veterans came to Quinn's headquarters. They had a friend who was running for office in a *haole* district and they were hoping to swap help. Looking around, though, their leader, Twinkle Kawakami, was unimpressed with Quinn's set-up: "You call this a campaign? Nothing's happening."

Quinn knew that their motive was to help their friend, Mike Miyake, running for Republican representative in Moiliili. He realized what Kawakami said about his campaign was true. He'd been out there for three weeks and nothing was happening.

Marty Anderson had been sidetracked with his law practice and couldn't give Quinn the help he needed. Quinn had to make a move, fast. He asked Hubbard to take over the campaign. "After all, Howard, you already have your wife here full time. You might as well work together."

Quinn accepted Twinkle Kawakami's proposal and met with the group to plan strategy. An alliance would help Quinn among the Asian-Americans and help Miyake among the Caucasians. Quinn went with the Japanese men to the public housing areas, to all the neighborhoods in Moiliili, Kaimuki, Kapahulu, Kalihi. Bill cut an impressive figure, his dark hair slightly receded enough to heighten his forehead and balance the wide, open Irish smile. He was tall, slender, with a collegiate, energetic flash. His wrists hung a bit beyond the cuffs, adding a Lincolnesque air.

They worked very well together, Quinn stepping briskly down the middle of the street, with Kawakami's men zipping along each side. They knocked on doors; when somebody came,

Quinn would run over, shake hands and introduce himself.

"No one had ever seen a campaign like that—particularly from a Republican."

"The next fortunate thing that happened was that Gardiner Jones, a political reporter with *The Honolulu Advertiser*, called and asked if he could go with me, campaigning that is. He spent an entire day with us from 6 in the morning 'til 6 in the evening. He even brought along a photographer, and I got publicity like you couldn't buy. There was a full page, pictures and story, and the headline was 'The New Republican.'"

Quinn won the primary and Peppi was out. Then came another month of hard, door-to-door campaigning against the Democrats.

Quinn lost in the general election, but he showed well at the polls. He ran well ahead of Joe Itagaki and Mary K. Robinson and came very close to knocking off Herbert Lee, a Democrat who was the incumbent president of the Senate. The polls closed at 6 p.m.; the ballot count had gone on until the early morning hours. Quinn vs Lee. The *malihini haole* boy had done all right. It had been a fight to the finish.

The Japanese-American men who had worked the streets with Quinn remained his good friends. The election was a double disappointment for them because Mike Miyake didn't get elected, either. However, they also knew that by hard work and strategic planning, they had become veteran Republicans.

Still reeling from the '54 election, the Republicans faced even more changes as the Democrats kept their control of the '56 Legislature. Two years before, John A.(Jack) Burns lost his bid for delegate to Congress; Republican Betty Farrington, widow of Joe Farrington, went to the capital. In 1956, Burns defeated her and became the first Democrat elected to that office in 24 years.

Gardiner Jones in his December 31, 1956, "Year In Review" in *The Advertiser*, wrote this prophetic glimpse:

Some of the faces that will figure prominently in that new era were glimpsed briefly in the 1956 campaign, the most notable being that of William F. Quinn, who made a convincing if unsuccessful race for the Senate. Island politics and the Republican Party have not heard the last of Mr. Quinn or the policies that he represents.

≈Chapter Ten≈

An Auspicious Time

*"Our people are equal in every respect to all people who
live on the Mainland. The truth is that they are
deprived of their rights to govern themselves."*
                                        WILLIAM F. QUINN
                        Hawaii Statehood Commission, 1957

Wat Bill Quinn thought would be just another
business reception turned into a surprising
encounter with Hawaii Governor Samuel Wilder
King. The governor took Quinn aside and asked
him if he would be willing to be on the Hawaii
Statehood Commission. U.S. District Judge C. Nils Tavares had
been chairman of the commission for three years and felt that it
was time for new Republican voices to be heard.

"The governor reminded me that the Statehood Commission
was far more important than the Charter Commission. He also
said that the delegation was hard at work preparing its presenta-
tion to Congress, which would reconvene in January 1957, just
a few weeks hence, and that a full nine-member commission
should participate."

Governor King, appointed by the president, as all U.S. territory governors then had been, was a strong backer of statehood;
Quinn felt honored and accepted the nomination. To do this
important work, he resigned from the Charter Commission.

Although his appointment to the statehood group needed territorial senate confirmation, he started in right away.

Hawaii had been fighting to become a state ever since formal annexation to the United States in 1898. In 1919, Prince Jonah Kuhio Kalanianaole, Hawaii's delegate to Congress, submitted the first bill calling for statehood. Through the years there followed dozens of congressional investigations, reports and recommendations:

As Lawrence Fuchs wrote in *Hawaii Pono*:

> ...But Hawaiian statehood, a symbol of the right and ability of the peoples of the Islands to govern themselves, was always blocked...

Quinn traveled with the commission to Washington in January 1957. The spirited group was ready to meet the anti-statehood forces. The commissioners were surprised, though, to find that opposition to statehood had shifted from claims Hawaii was "over-populated by Japanese" to allegations that communists had taken over the Islands.

"We had many supporters in Washington," said Quinn, "but almost to a man, we'd get the same question: 'Doesn't Harry Bridges run Hawaii?'" Bridges' influence through the ILWU was strong.

"We went around seeing lots of senators and congressmen. There were three or four of us who would talk about something specific, then I would do the wrap-up," explained Quinn. His spiel went like this:

> "We have judges there but we have no voice in their selection. Our judges of the Circuit Court are appointed by Washington and occasionally we'll get one who hasn't even

lived in the Islands before, ever. It's the same thing with the governor."

He'd pause then raise his voice:

"It's part and parcel, this almost unconstitutional thing...that we should be kept in this secondary position. We pay our income taxes, we don't have any voice, we don't have any vote in Congress, and we can't name our top judicial and administrative officers."

His finale, addressing the Congress:

"You may think of us as a little South Sea island but we have some major industries and people interested in new businesses out there. Our people are equal in every respect to all people who live on the Mainland. The truth is that they're deprived of their rights to govern themselves."

Quinn also went to the Department of the Interior and met Tony Lausi, who was head of the Office of Territories, and his assistant, Ted Stevens. Stevens later became a U.S. senator from Alaska.

Bill returned with the delegation from Washington's cold winter scene, totally, enthusiastically dedicated to the cause of statehood. He could see it coming.

Three months later, the Hawaii Statehood Commission, chaired by Lorrin P. Thurston, publisher of *The Honolulu Advertiser*, returned to Washington and was received in the Oval Office by President Eisenhower. With Thurston and Quinn were Commissioners Jack M. Fox, Ward Russell, former Governor Oren E. Long and Katsuro Miho. Quinn, already a familiar face and effective spokesman for statehood, became the object of political speculation. While Quinn was still in Washington, a rumor appeared in the Hawaii newspapers.

> *Washington, April 8* (UP) Hawaii Statehood Commissioner William F. Quinn has been introduced to some Republican congressmen as the candidate who will oppose Delegate John A. Burns in the 1958 elections, the United Press learned today.

In Honolulu, Nancy Quinn answered queries: "Bill never mentioned it to me. I think it's scuttlebutt."

Bill Quinn's popularity probably cost him his commission seat. When he got back to Hawaii, even more confident that statehood was imminent, a phone call from Governor King punctured his mood. The governor didn't think he could now get the required territorial Senate confirmation for Quinn's appointment to the Statehood Commission.

"Bill, you know you ran against these fellows in the senate," Quinn recalled King's words, "and there's no way they're going to confirm you for the Statehood Commission. So I'm not going to submit your name."

Bill argued: "I wish you would, Governor. I really enjoyed serving on the commission and I don't know for sure that they would not confirm me."

The governor repeated, "They're not going to. I don't want to send your name down and have it rejected."

In Quinn's place he named O.P. Soares.

Bill went back to practicing law. The same week, he received a call from somebody in the governor's office asking if he would be the chairman of the Hawaii Library Commission.

"I had to laugh at the absurdity...I replied, 'Yes, I'll serve any way I can.'"

Spring rolled into summer. As the days got longer, the

amount of legal work facing Bill increased. He even worked Saturdays.

Mid-morning one Friday, Quinn got a call.

"Is this Bill Quinn? Is this the Bill Quinn who's on the Statehood Commission?"

"Well, I was on the commission but I'm not any more," Quinn answered.

"This is Tony Lausi from the Office of the Territories." Bill recognized his voice. "Secretary Fred Seaton wonders if you can come back to see him."

Why the heck does he want to see me? Quinn wondered. Puzzled and resenting the interruption a bit, he shot a glance at his date book.

"What's this all about, Tony?"

"The secretary wants to talk to you about number one and number two out there," Lausi said, referring to the political leadership.

"I'm very busy. Two of my partners are away at the American Bar Association meeting in London." Bill paused. "Let me think about it. Call me tomorrow...I'll be here."

The more he thought about his clients, the case load he was committed to, and the 24 hours that flying to the East Coast took, plus the time required for meetings in the capital, and the 24-hour trip back, the more impossible the proposition became.

It appeared he was the only one who thought so.

When Nancy heard about the call, she said: "I don't understand why you would turn down a call from a secretary, a Cabinet member. After all, he is a spokesman for the president."

Malcolm MacNaughton, president of Castle and Cooke and an influential Hawaii businessman whose intelligence and wit Bill respected, left no doubts about his feelings.

"Bill, you gotta go. What are you waiting for?"

Quinn remembered that Howard Hubbard, his close neighbor and former campaign manager, a quiet, bright and sensitive friend, said: "You have a short memory. I'll tell you why Washington needs your advice. You organized our Precinct Club. You rallied 400 new members into the Republican Party. And don't forget how you fell only 3,000 votes short of breaking the all-Democratic slate in the general election...and that was less than a year ago. I watched you come from behind and lead the Republican ticket. You were the dark horse."

Bill's horn-rimmed glasses bridged a double frown as he listened. Then Hubbard, in an unusual burst of enthusiasm, leaped to his feet. "Come on, Bill, you're the only one who knows what's going on. If you ask me, I think they want you for governor."

Quinn, piqued by what he considered a ridiculous remark, fired back in his resounding voice: "You've got to be out of your mind."

≈Chapter Eleven≈
Command Performance

"I don't mean to interrupt you, Mr. Secretary, but I want you to know that I didn't come to Washington seeking a job and I don't want one."

WILLIAM F. QUINN
to Interior Secretary Fred Seaton
July 1957

The next morning Tony Lausi called again. Quinn agreed to go but made it clear that he would turn around and fly straight home after he met with Seaton. "I won't be in until Monday evening," he told Lausi. "Get me a place to stay."

"Will do. Count on meeting with us at lunch on Tuesday."

On Sunday evening, July 22, 1957, Quinn took an overnight flight into San Francisco, connected with an east-bound plane and arrived in Washington at about 9 p.m. Monday.

Walking to the Capitol Tuesday morning, he was very conscious of the sticky summer heat. Vapors of steam rose from the city's streets and a dismal fog hid the sky. His navy blue suit, white shirt and tie, D.C.'s traditional attire regardless of weather, wasn't the coolest of apparel.

He went first to the Office of the Territories to see Tony Lausi, whom he remembered from his statehood barnstorming days, and Secretary Seaton.

"What's this all about?" Quinn asked Lausi.

Lausi said he didn't know, but Quinn recalled Lausi weighed his words and said, "but I'll tell you what I think. Fred Seaton is going out to Hawaii in another three weeks. Here it is July and Governor King has been holding over since January. Secretary Seaton wants that governorship settled before he gets to Hawaii. Perhaps it means a reappointment for King and a younger man named as secretary of the territory."

Secretary of the territory was the second highest office in the Islands.

Quinn said nothing. Together they went to meet Seaton in the secretary's dining room.

It was obvious from the moment the three were seated— Seaton, Quinn and Lausi—that the group of 25 assembled assistant secretaries gathered around the large oval dining table were there at the invitation of Secretary Seaton.

They started firing questions Quinn about his experiences in the Navy, his law years, his arrival in the Islands, the major election he had been in and other political situations.

"You ran for election in the local Senate. What happened? Why weren't you elected?"

Bill had been on stage and under a spotlight many times, but this was different.

The questions continued: "You were here last year testifying in Congress for Hawaii's statehood. Why aren't you on the commission now? What happened out there?"

"When did you finish law school?"

"What was your opinion of the governor's veto on the tax bill?"

To that, Quinn replied, "I thought he made a mistake."

Just then Secretary Seaton, who had remained silent throughout the meal, turned to Quinn and asked him to go into his private office for a cup of coffee.

Their departure was abrupt.

What next? wondered Quinn as the two men sat down. The secretary, a Kansan, started talking. Like Quinn, he had the nasal twang of the Midwest.

"As he's talking," said Quinn, "it's very clear to me that he's leading up to a job; so I said, 'I don't mean to interrupt you, Mr. Secretary, but I want you to know that I didn't come to Washington seeking a job, and I don't want one.'"

Seaton, senior to Quinn by 10 years but known as "the baby of the president's Cabinet," pondered the statement. Then he looked directly at Bill for a long moment.

"Well, you can say that to me, but I would challenge you," he said, turning toward the window and pointing at the Capitol dome, "to say NO to the president of the United States."

"This is crazy," thought Quinn as he followed Seaton's gesture. "My law practice is starting to boom, I've got five little kids with another on the way...the last thing I want is a number-two job in government."

Firmly he repeated, "Sir, I do not want and would not take the job of secretary of Hawaii."

The secretary was silent.

Although this was Quinn's first meeting with Seaton, he had heard Seaton was a person who said what he wanted to and wasted no words.

After a long pause, Seaton looked Quinn straight in the eye. "What about governor?"

After several moments in shock, Quinn gasped, "I don't believe this...governor?" He regained some composure and admitted, "I can't say no to that."

Seaton followed up sternly, "Is there anything in your background that would militate against this appointment?"

Escapades of Quinn's youth, the wear and tear and problems of just growing up flashed across his mind. Then came the most recent and vivid thoughts of all—those late evenings upstairs in the Barefoot Bar at Queen's Surf, where Quinn was known as the *malihini* Irish politician who would sing "*Ke Kali Nei Au*" or "Danny Boy" with little urging. Not the best image for a top executive, grimaced Quinn. But not a serious liability, either.

"No sir," he gulped.

"Well," said Seaton, "You'd better be right or you're dead. Because I'm going to suggest that the president announce your appointment as governor before there's an FBI field investigation. When are you leaving?"

"Tonight," Quinn replied.

"Cancel your plans and have dinner with me tonight. Tony will join us. I want to know who you think ought to be secretary of Hawaii. We can talk more about that at dinner."

They shook hands. When Quinn walked from the secretary's suite to the exit hall, Lausi stepped up and asked him what had happened in there.

"He asked me to be governor."

Lausi was flabbergasted. His chin fell, his shoulders dropped back and his face registered astonishment. Lausi, Seaton's confidante, worked closely with the secretary on all interior and territorial matters. But in this case, it was obvious that he had not been informed of Quinn's possible nomination for the top job.

Quinn went to his hotel room, canceled that evening's return flight, then penciled a wire to Nancy.

"HEARING SUCCESS MAY GET FAVORABLE DECISION TOMORROW TELL PADG CANCEL DEPOSITION"

In their spousal language the message said, I'm delayed another day. "Padg" was his partner, Frank Padgett, who was covering Quinn's clients in his absence.

He was concerned, too, about publicity and the protection of his family. Five children and another due in November.

He had not seen a Hawaii newspaper since leaving home, but Quinn knew that back there speculation probably peppered the newsprint. Reports on his presence in the capital had been moved up from the back page to Page One. He learned that pictures of the nine Republican contenders as "best bets" for governor appeared under the caption "In the Running."

What he didn't know was that just as he was preparing for his meeting with the president, three of those contenders were in the capital campaigning for their own choices for Hawaii's governor—Randolph Crossley, a good friend of Eisenhower's, Harold Kay and Art Woolaway. Woolaway, chairman of the Republican Party of Hawaii, was seeking the reappointment of Governor King.

Quinn was busy pondering Seaton's request about the person he felt best qualified for secretary of the territory. The first one to come to mind was Alex Castro, his good friend who had played Ensign Pulver in *Mister Roberts*. Alex was a local boy and prominent in the younger community of successful businessmen.

"But I started to realize how wrong that would be. Appointing me when I had lived in the territory only 10 years was bad enough. It was going to be such a violent change that I'd better get some continuity and stability. I felt that very strongly, and it was part of my passion for statehood."

Finding himself the nominee for appointed governor of the territory was a diabolical twist of circumstances. Quinn had long argued against the territorial system of appointed rather than elected officials. Now he was the one being imposed upon the people without their having a choice.

He could imagine mutterings of protest: "...too young, a *malihini* who hasn't even lived with us very long...named as the chief executive officer of our territory."

He was 38 years old.

His nomination showed very clearly how right the statehood cause was, he thought.

"It was then that I realized that Farrant Turner, the holdover secretary of Hawaii, who was old enough to be my father, had been a colonel with the 442nd and was a much-admired figure in the community, was my man. That's who I decided upon."

That evening at dinner, Quinn gave Seaton and Lausi his reasoning and conclusion about Farrant Turner. They agreed. Seaton told Quinn he was set to meet with President Eisenhower the next morning.

The Oval Office

On July 24, 1957, at 9 a.m., six days since he had first received Lausi's call, Quinn, Seaton and Lausi walked quickly around the side lawn to the back entrance of the White House. Their visit was to be hush-hush and they must not be seen either coming in or going out. They were taken to an elevator and up to the president's office.

Quinn recalled Eisenhower "was just recovering from a minor heart condition. His speech was slightly slurred, but he was beaming, very pleasant, a wonderful gentleman. What a thrill for me."

The president talked about Hawaii and its bid for statehood. Referring to what he had heard on the Hill, Quinn said Eisenhower commented, "When you get to be governor, I hope you can do something about that communist influence out there."

Bill knew from his own years of promoting statehood exactly what the president was referring to. The biggest remaining aspect of opposition to statehood for Hawaii was the rumor that the movement was led by communists and communist-inspired people in the Islands. There had been widespread publicity about Harry Bridges, an admitted communist; also about Jack Hall, the

ILWU and leftists charged with Smith Act violations. In many eyes Hawaii and communism appeared synonymous. Eisenhower's comment reflected what he heard from congressmen, senators, his department heads and others.

Quinn was well aware of the communism fears, but he also knew that a growing number, perhaps even a majority, in both houses of Congress were now favorable to Hawaii statehood. He was convinced the movement couldn't be stopped much longer.

Shaking hands with the president, Quinn answered, "I'm going to do my best to serve you, Mr. President."

Outside the president's office, Seaton warned, "There's nothing that you are to say to anybody. This announcement has to come first from the White House."

The newly appointed governor hurried back to the hotel, the stifling Washington climate forgotten. He called Nancy, of course, told her what had happened and swore her to secrecy. He changed his travel plans and routed his way back through St. Louis, to visit the family home and his widowed mother.

Repacking his overnighter, he found a gift enclosure that he had neglected to open taped to a pint bottle of Scotch. The card read, "To our dark horse, good luck, Howard."

Quinn chuckled at his friend's prophetic note. "Some horse race," he murmured to himself. "I never knew I was in it."

≈ Chapter Twelve ≈
A Tumultuous Day

*"No man has ever had a more meteoric rise in Hawaii
politics than 38-year-old William Francis Quinn, the
man announced today as President Eisenhower's choice
to be Hawaii's 12th territorial governor."*

JACK BURBY
San Francisco Chronicle
July 26, 1957

Nancy stayed calm as the whole neighborhood buzzed
with speculation. The week Quinn was gone, the
newspapers were filled with articles regarding his visit
in the capital. From the time Bill called Nancy after
his meeting with the president the previous
Wednesday until the news was officially released by the White
House, she knew she must put their secret out of her mind. She
did.

From Washington, the *Star-Bulletin's* bureau had reported
that it was improbable that both incumbents, Governor Samuel
King and Secretary of the Territory Farrant Turner, would be
reappointed:

It is apparent that either the 70-year-old King or the 62-
year-old territorial secretary, Farrant Turner, will not be reappointed.

By contrast, Alaska has a 38-year-old governor in Mike
Stepovich and a territorial secretary who is in his early 50s.

Quinn's being summoned by Secretary Seaton left everyone at home guessing. Seaton just wasn't saying, even to his top staff, what he planned to do about the Hawaii governorship. Rumors and some news stories thought Quinn to be a dark horse candidate for the governorship but, as the *Bulletin* quoted one source:

> ...It is more likely that he is under consideration for secretaryship in view of his *malihini* status.
>
> It is known, however, that Seaton was impressed with William F. Quinn, 38-year-old attorney, who conferred with him here Monday.

Then the *Star-Bulletin* headlines caught everyone by surprise:

IKE DITCHES KING FOR 'YOUNG BLOOD';
QUINN LEADS FIELD FOR TOP T.H. POST

Islanders were stunned to learn that King had resigned as governor of the territory. The article said King received a radiophone call from Secretary Seaton notifying him that he would not be reappointed by the White House.

The *Star-Bulletin's* Gardiner Jones wrote:

> ...Ed Bryan, territorial Republican chairman, said the news shocked him.
>
> Ed Johnston, Oahu Republican chairman, said he and Mr. Bryan had lunched together yesterday and had agreed that the odds seemed to be swinging toward the governor's reappointment.
>
> One of the governor's bitterest critics, former Democratic National Committeeman Frank Fasi, said it is stupid, shortsighted and ungrateful for the Republican administration not to reappoint the governor.

"I've had a lot of fights with him," Fasi said. "But so long
as we have to have a Republican governor, it's fair to say that
he has courage and has earned reappointment."

Early Friday morning, July 26, 1957, the same day that Bill
was flying from St. Louis to the West Coast, Mildred Kashiwa, a
precinct Republican, called Nancy Quinn and asked, "Did you
know that Bill was named governor?"

That afternoon, the *Star-Bulletin* headline read:

WHITE HOUSE SELECTS WILLIAM F. QUINN AS
GOVERNOR

On Friday, reporters caught up with Quinn when he landed
in San Francisco on his way home from Washington and St.
Louis.

"It was already dark," Bill recalled. "I looked out the window
and there was a group at the bottom step with a couple of cameras. I knew they were reporters. All I could think of was my
blabbermouth mother, who had promised not to say a word."

"I walked down and didn't look left or right. Then somebody
said, 'How do you feel, Governor? Hi, I'm Jack Burby,' he
smiled.

"I remembered that Burby was formerly with the *Honolulu
Star-Bulletin*, an energetic young man whom I had known over
recent years."

Burby and three or four other newsmen walked with Quinn
into the terminal. Burby's account was released by the *San
Francisco Chronicle* via radiophone:

Attorney William F. Quinn threaded his way self-con-
sciously through his first airport press conference as Hawaii's
new governor and headed straight for an airport motel to

catch some needed sleep.

"Is this Hawaii's new governor?" asked one outspoken member of the welcoming party. Quinn squared his shoulders and squirmed a little while the stranger sized him up.

"First governor I ever saw who looked human," the man said.

It was reported, too, that Quinn had no idea the word was out when his plane arrived from St. Louis and relaxed only after learning the White House had made its announcement.

"I feel very humble about it," he told reporters, looking a little trapped in his white summer suit.

"It's a big challenge and an awful responsibility. I had no idea it was coming. But I've got enough Irish in me to tackle it."

No man has ever had a more meteoric rise in Hawaii politics than 38-year-old William Francis Quinn, the man announced today as President Eisenhower's choice to be Hawaii's 12th Territorial Governor.

Portlock

Once the news was on the radio and headlined in the papers, the celebrating began. Portlock neighbors were excited and their children were caught up in the frenzy. Nancy's attempts to keep her family calm and on a level routine were futile. The telephone never stopped ringing. Friends, acquaintances and even strangers, mostly Republican fans, called with good wishes and offers of assistance.

One of the many calls was from a stranger, who asked to speak to the governor.

A little surprised, Nancy said, "He's not here."

"Are you the governess?"

Just then a stampede of 8-year-olds raced through the front

door to the kitchen; Nancy answered, "I sure am."

Good, practical help arrived when Bam MacNaughton, Malcolm's wife, sent her maid down to the Quinn house to tend to the children's supper and give Nancy an hour's rest.

Bill's arrival in Honolulu on Saturday afternoon was tumultuous. Neighbors turned out at the airport with leis, flags, banners and signs. By the time Bill had been hugged by his family and greeted by officials, and had met with the press, Danny, the governor's chauffeur, was waiting to drive the Quinns home. Forty-five minutes later, at the entrance of Portlock, a cavalcade of cars, a rush of neighbors, children and pets flanked the old black Packard limo as it slowly threaded its way through a shower of streamers, flags and plumeria petals. The dark horse had returned a winner.

Now it was time to wait. Each day, requests for appearances, speeches and invitations jammed the mailbox. Bill and Nancy faced it with smiles and a brief explanation that Bill's office was not official until the U.S. Senate confirmed his appointment.

In a letter to Bill's mother, Nancy wrote of the surprises and tensions that arose as they awaited Bill's confirmation:

> Tuesday Aug. 13
> Dearest Mother Q.
>
> Know you are anxious for news of happenings but they are happening too fast to compute...
>
> We receive so much correspondence it takes all our free time to read it, much less sort it, which is all so gratifying, pleasing and humbling.
>
> At present being housewife, mother, plus potential governor's wife makes life difficult...plus being 6 1/2 months pregnant, which I kept quiet from you and Mother because I felt you sometimes worry about me and I'd rather save you that and just tell you when it was over, but now our lives are open books.

Mr. Secretary Seaton and party of five arrived at 3:00 yesterday. Bill and I and other officials met them at airport...chatted a short time at their hotel. Today at 3:00 Bill called and said, "Could we cook a steak or two for five this evening?" and he meant Mr. Secretary Seaton and party...

I called the housekeeper who has been coming in a couple of hours a day to come and feed Ceci, Chris and Tim, got a cateress...went to the market...home at 5:00...they came at 6:00...had a typical Quinn evening on the patio with noisy T.V. and kids, Ceci spilled a coke all over the punee, Snuffy snuggled up to Mr. Sect/y of the Interior Office of the United States...aloha shirts...good dinner...no protocol...far as I know, operation success!! Gov's chauffeur came and took them all to their plane departure at 9:00. Secretary Seaton was charming, sweet and considerate. I had never met a cabinet member before but my fears were wiped out.

Betty Farrington and Betty Wilder are trying to run me a little but I am doing my best to hold my own and let them think they are doing it. I can't afford to alienate anyone but I refuse to lose my independence.

Our friends are all wonderful and think the whole thing is grand and hope we'll stay "Bill and Nancy" so the heck with the few "old guard" that want us stuffy.

The celebrity euphoria gave way to a letdown.

Bill had been waiting to hear for word of confirmation ever since his return on July 27; by mid-August he was jumpy.

"When Seaton and his party came through here on an official trip to the Trust Territories, I learned that Seaton had hired a former Republican congressman to lobby for my confirmation, but nothing had happened. I was stuck. I couldn't practice law, I couldn't act in any official capacity and the waiting was awful," Quinn recalled.

Quinn knew that Seaton, a round-faced, pleasant gentleman, had the ear of the president and spoke with authority. Bill also knew that he had to be patient.

"Finally, with only about two weeks to go before Congress adjourned for the year, I was called back to Washington, and Seaton's man took me around. I saw in an instant why nothing had happened. Seaton's man had no real sense of the situation," Quinn said.

Quinn returned to Honolulu discouraged. A few days went by and still nothing. Then Seaton, still on his tour of the Pacific Territories, called and Quinn described to him what he had experienced.

"Your guy took me into a Senate hearing. It was a hearing involving the Teamsters and Jimmy Hoffa. Lyndon Johnson was presiding....It was a packed room. Every senator was there, all the lights were on, everybody was very busy...and this guy starts to take me around and introduce me to all these people!" His timing was all wrong.

There was no time to waste. "Maybe you'd better go back to Washington," Seaton told Quinn.

Behind the Scenes

Lorrin P. Thurston, president and general manager of *The Honolulu Advertiser*, recognized the gravity of the delay and spared no words in his blast of the Washington Democratic senators. In an editorial on August 25, 1957, he wrote:

> DELAY IN CONGRESS ON HAWAII
> GOVERNOR NO JOKE TO NATION
>
> ...This sorry situation appears to have been created initially because some senators are peeved over Secretary Seaton's delay in appointing an assistant to further minerals legislation in which they're interested. Others appear to find

amusement in an opportunity to heedlessly embarrass the Eisenhower administration.

It seems incredible that such trivialities could persuade national legislators to disregard the seriousness of a continued vacancy in Hawaii's governorship. But things like this do happen at the national capital, as will be recalled by those who remember the long period that many vacancies existed in the courts here.

The people of Hawaii cannot afford to remain silent while the Senate "jokes" with their governorship.

By the time Quinn got to Washington, August was nearly over. "First I made my inquiries," he said. "I found that Senator James E. Murray of Montana was the chairman of the Senate Committee on Territorial and Insular Affairs, the hearing committee. I also found out that Murray had had a battle with Eisenhower over an entirely different matter, had left town in a huff and would probably not be back.

"I went to see Murray's son, who was the clerk of the Senate committee, but he could do nothing. He was sure that his father would not even be back for the end of the session."

That left Quinn in a political no-man's land. No amount of pacing the floor would help, yet he could not give up. "What am I going to do?" he asked himself.

He searched the membership and saw that the number-two man on the Senate committee was a prominent Democrat, a longtime leader in the Senate, Clinton Anderson of New Mexico.

"I made an appointment to see him and told him my sad story. I said, 'I can't get a hearing. It's just been completely destructive of my professional life...'"

Anderson wasted no time. He called Murray on the phone. Quinn recalled Anderson's side of the conversation: "I want a hearing tomorrow morning at 9 o'clock. Don't say it. Just call the hearing."

At the hearing, the committee recommended approval and Quinn was confirmed by the Senate as governor of the Territory of Hawaii. The procedure took 14 minutes.

The August 27, 1957 headline in *The Honolulu Advertiser* read: LABOR DAY INAUGURATION SET FOR QUINN

Two days later, Hawaii's delegate to Congress, John Burns, addressed to Lorrin Thurston a blistering letter about Thurston's angry editorial:

> Dear Lorrin,
>
> Your lead editorial of Sunday, August 25, "Delay in Congress on Hawaii's Governor," shocked and astonished me. The tone of your editorial—in complete disregard of the facts—libels the conscientious, dedicated, overly burdened and knowledgeable senators of the United States, particularly those who are members of the Interior and Insular Affairs Committee of the U.S. Senate.
>
> I certainly believe an effort should be made to rectify as far as possible the grave injustice done to the great and distinguished members of the Senate Committee on Interior and Insular affairs.
>
> Kindest personal wishes. May the Almighty be with you and yours always and in all ways.
> Sincerely,
> John A. Burns

Lorrin Thurston replied:

> Sept. 3, 1957
> Dear Jack,
>
> I don't know just what your purpose was in writing me that self-righteous letter, Jack, but it doesn't ring the bell.

Through your help, through our editorial, through the efforts of a lot of people, Bill Quinn was confirmed. It could have been the case that without this combined pressure, his confirmation might easily have dragged on until January—with disastrous results to the progress of the Territory.

Don't make the sad mistake some of your predecessors have. "Big Shot-itus" is a devastating disease, in politics particularly. The voters detect it far more quickly than the average politico.

Your letter indicates to me that in eight short months you have been bitten by the disease. Upon how you handle this malady may indeed depend the life and extent of your political leadership.

Kindest personal regards. May the Almighty grant you the power to analyze yourself, your actions and your words with increasing clarity.

Sincerely,

Lorrin P. Thurston

PART THREE
≈Chapter Thirteen≈

The Inaugural

*"No one feels more strongly than I that we, the people of
Hawaii, should select our own governors and enjoy
equal rights with our Mainland brothers."*
                    WILLIAM F. QUINN
                    Inaugural Address
                    September 2, 1957

As had the 11 governors preceding him, William Francis
Quinn took the oath of office in the ornate coronation
stand on the grounds of Iolani Palace where a king was
once crowned. David Kalakaua, the second to last of
the Hawaiian monarchs, had the eight-sided pavilion
of Victorian architecture built as part of the elaborate ceremonies
surrounding his coronation in 1883, nine years after he actually
became king.

Years later, the pavilion was renamed the "Bandstand," as it is
still known. Beneath its blue dome on September 2, 1957,
Quinn was inaugurated as governor of the Territory of Hawaii.
He would be the last governor of the territory, the last governor
of Hawaii appointed by a President.

The sudden summer showers that greeted Governor Quinn's
inauguration were a good omen, according to Clarice Taylor, an
authority on Hawaiian culture and mythology. "A gentle rain is
considered a blessing from the gods," Mrs. Taylor said. "Rain
brings fertility, not only biologically but in the realm of ideas and

achievement."

Another Hawaiian authority remarked that "Governor Quinn, being non-Hawaiian by birth, wasn't affected one way or the other by the rain. For him it was just some water on his back."

Quinn's inaugural marked a new page in Hawaii's political history. *The Honolulu Advertiser* editorialized that day:

> Territorial politics got a severe shakeup in 1954 when the Democrats for the first time in 50 years won control of the Legislature....In recent months the younger element of the Republican Party has taken a firmer hand in the organization and has been speaking with a louder voice.
>
> This remodeling of the Republican Party is not confined to Hawaii. It has been going on across the nation, and in some sections the struggle between the new and the old elements has been quite bitter.
>
> The new governor is a personable, able attorney, highly respected by his associates in the law. He already has shown himself to be a powerful candidate in the elective field. He is a man of human warmth, mature judgment and understanding. At 38 he has the vigor of youth and the habit of sober, cautious thought of the man of experience.
>
> William F. Quinn brings many excellent qualities to the governorship. While he has little background in the day-to-day operations of government, this need not be a handicap. He has pronounced himself ready to rely on the judgment of men more experienced then he in this area.
>
> Mr. Quinn's appointment, of course, was not dictated because of any outstanding skill in government. He frankly was chosen in the hopes that he could lead the Territorial Republicans in a rejuvenation.

The rain stopped. Moist, heavy air saturated the crowd. A throng estimated at 4,000 assembled quietly around the Bandstand. Off to one side, a large platform had been erected especially for television and news camera crews, placed at an angle that would permit clear shots of the historic scene.

The best of plans can go amiss, however. Four, 8-foot-tall *kahili* with their 2-foot-high crowns of pink and white plumeria blossoms surrounded the octagonal pavilion and blocked the line of vision from the platform. At the last minute, just before the bugle trumpeted the start of the rites, workmen hurriedly dug new post holes, the *kahili* were moved and finally the cameras began to roll.

Led by stalwart Republican Senator Wilfred C. Tsukiyama, Senate majority leader, well-respected by *haole* and *nisei* alike, the official party marched from the palace steps to the bandstand. Interior Secretary Seaton and Territorial Republican Chairman Ed Bryan followed; then Governor Quinn and Farrant Turner, who would continue to serve as secretary of the territory. First Lady Nancy Quinn and Mrs. Turner, both wearing hats and gloves, were escorted to the first two seats of the front row.

The Air National Guard Police honor guard, in their crisp uniforms, white hats, cartridge belts and gloves, stood at attention. Bishop James J. Sweeney, in purple vestments, gave the invocation. The Kaahumanu Choral Group in black *holoku* came forward and, led by Bina Mossman, sang "The Queen's Prayer." Then Secretary Seaton took the rostrum. He said he carried word from President Eisenhower: "You have his complete and unqualified support for statehood."

After Turner received his commission of secretary of the territory and Chief Justice Philip L. Rice read the Oath of Allegiance, Bill Quinn came forward and repeated the oath.

Then the new governor, tall and confident, began to speak. The sun popped from behind a heavy cloud and seared the crowd. Programs fluttered as hundreds fanned the stifling air. One in the honor guard adjacent to the Bandstand wobbled, then buckled to the ground. The governor continued to read his address:

> *...No one feels more strongly than I that we, the people of Hawaii, should select our own governors and enjoy equal rights with our Mainland brothers. The realization that I assume this office not by the will of the people prompts me to vow that I shall meet all the people of our Islands and shall in fact be their Governor to the best of my ability....*
>
> *...I ask for your encouragement, your help and your prayers in this undertaking and I hope that I may merit your congratulations when the job is done. Aloha and mahalo.*

The *Honolulu Star-Bulletin* editorial that day read:

> ...Governor Quinn in a ringing inaugural address laid down a six-point basic program for his administration. It had all the fire and optimism of a young man in his first big political job...

The next morning, *Advertiser* columnist Bob Krauss wrote:

> It sort of did my heart good to hear young Bill Quinn get up there in the Iolani Bandstand and launch himself into history yesterday. He stood there in a new blue suit and a shirt with a collar that was too big for him and talked about Hawaii's destiny and our expanding economy and the challenge of the future as if he were a 70-year-old veteran instead of a 38-year-old beginner. I stood there and thought to myself, heck, he's only five years older than I am. Maybe I'll be up there soon myself....

During the hour-long ceremony, one photographer concentrated on the five Quinn children; in *The Advertiser* a full-page spread of 11 pictures was entitled:

QUINN-TUPLETS ENLIVEN DAD'S INAUGURAL

Eight of the shots were of Chris, dressed in coat, long trousers, white shirt and striped tie, wiggling and twisting as a 7-year-old is likely to do. The other pictures showed his three older brothers dressed in coats and ties, with baby Cecily in organdy.

"Putting a wardrobe together for four boys, ages 7 through 15, for both the inaugural and the school year was no easy task," remembered Nancy. "Coupled with the move from Portlock to Washington Place (the governor's mansion), which was postponed until after the inaugural, made it hard on the children, too. It was an enormous adjustment for everyone."

At the final words of the governor's address, the U.S. Army Band played the National Anthem. Then Senator Tsukiyama invited everyone to a reception at Washington Place, across the street from the palace.

Washington Place

Four thousand well-wishers jammed the grounds and the house for the inaugural reception.

The governor, in a dark business suit, a boyish grin and many strands of *ilima*, stood in the receiving line for four hours. As each guest came through the line, Quinn would say "and this is my wife, Nancy." The Quinns received with Secretary of the Interior Fred Seaton and Secretary of the Territory and Mrs. Farrant L. Turner.

Through the spirited day, the first lady kept her natural, friendly manner and winsome smile. She wore a soft, rich, Chinese damask redingote dress and coat, created by Anna of

Vienna, a Honolulu designer. Named "Nancy green" for the occasion, the ensemble was appropriate for the time of day yet had a certain formality. Her turban of the same material was designed by Elsie Krassas, Honolulu modiste.

She wore high-heeled amber shoes, and after standing in the receiving line at Washington Place for two hours, her pregnancy forced her to accept some relief; she sat on a high stool. There was no let-up in the reception line; the governor wiped his perspiring brow and his lipstick-smeared cheeks. He had learned his first lesson: The chief executive of Hawaii needs a strong right hand.

Flowers were everywhere. In the reception rooms and on the covered terrace fragrant *maile* lei filled the air. They hung from the tops of all the doors, festooned pillars and the rosewood piano. *Kahili* of white plumeria stood at each end of the receiving line, their trailing lei hanging to the floor.

Finally it was time to say aloha. As the last guest stepped through the front gate, the Quinns headed to Portlock Road and a final night in their own home.

The governor's vow "to meet all the people of our Islands" was already scheduled for partial fulfillment. The official party would fly by Hawaii National Guard plane to Kauai and Molokai in the morning; they would then visit Maui and Hawaii during the four-day tour. Secretary Seaton; Tony Lausi; Farrant Turner; Arthur Woolaway, territorial Republican committeeman; and Ed Bryan, chairman of the Territorial Republican Central Committee, would travel with the governor.

And there was an announcement: "On Monday, September 9th, the governor will open his office in Iolani Palace for business."

Chapter Fourteen

A Day in the Life

"William F. Quinn is taking to governorship like a small boy to chocolate ice cream..."

GARDINER JONES
The Honolulu Advertiser
September 1957

The first two days of a Neighbor Island tour included eight airplane trips, four banquets, a couple of political meetings and a series of minor controversies. "In my inaugural address, I swore publicly that I wanted to go out and meet the *people* of the Islands, shake their hands, and say, 'I am your governor, even though you had nothing to do with my getting there.'

"Despite my wishes, there wasn't much time left to go out to the plantations, or make stops along the way," said Quinn, "I didn't want the way paved or prepared; I wanted to meet them at work."

Quinn was wound up like a racer in a derby, always ready to go. When others in the party thought to call it a day, Governor Quinn was still eager to hit the road.

"You've read about me. Now here I am....I want to talk with you," he'd say. At one of the plantation garages, "his honor" got down on his hands and knees to speak with a mechanic working under a cane-haul truck.

"I did all I could in that short time (on the trip) to introduce this strange and unusual *malihini* who had become their governor," Quinn recalled years later.

For all of his efforts, Quinn felt resentment against him, the same kind that had dogged him in the '56 campaign. This time, not only was he a *malihini* but he replaced for their part-Hawaiian governor, Samuel W. King. Governor William Quinn's appointment had revived the tensions between the two Republican groups, the dominant *haole* and the Hawaiian.

Bill Quinn returned late Friday afternoon to find the household move from Portlock to Washington Place had been completed.

"Good timing, Bill," Nancy laughed.

Their second-floor family quarters were spacious and completely private. A small room adjacent to the large master bedroom had been converted especially as a nursery for the expected baby, and the boys were bunked in two large bedrooms. Cecily had her own room, and there was a family room overlooking the back terrace.

The family was comfortable enough, but the children missed their friends and playmates.

"Bill and I talked about that and decided we would try very hard to keep Sunday as our family day and spend it out at Portlock," said Nancy. "I also made that the cook's day off and I fixed dinner on Sunday evenings."

Nancy worried about the small elevator that burrowed its way from the downstairs hall to the second floor. She was afraid that it would be such an attraction for the boys that they would run it to death. Many years later, Nancy still remembered the housekeeper's reassurance: "Don't worry, Mrs. Quinn. That elevator is so slow that after one ride they'll call it boring and never bother with it again."

A photographer from *The Advertiser* caught the spirit of the youngsters with his feature photo of the three little Quinns sliding down the banister, entitled: WASHINGTON PLACE WILL NEVER BE THE SAME.

Secretary Seaton dined with the first family the evening he and Bill returned from the Big Island. It was the last day of his month-long visit in the Trust Territories. He was to return to the capital early Saturday morning.

After that the new governor's job really began.

Iolani Palace

The governor's office, situated on the second-floor *mauka-ewa* corner of the 19th-century Victorian-style Iolani Palace, looked back across the lawns to Washington Place and beyond to Punchbowl Crater. The palace, a symbol of the monarchical years of old Hawaii, was built for King David Kalakaua in 1882. Following his death, his sister, Liliuokalani, took the oath of office as queen in 1891. Her reign of a little less than two years was troubled almost from the very beginning. A chain of events led to the abolition of the monarchy and the annexation of the Hawaiian Islands to the United States.

When the Hawaiian Islands were annexed as a territory, the palace became the seat of the government offices. The Legislature convened in the former Throne Room, with the executive offices upstairs. As the government grew, so did the demands for office space. Wooden appendages jutting out from the ground floor lanai were built; add-ons marred the majesty of this historical edifice.

Later, after statehood, the palace would be returned to its splendor and a new Capitol would house government offices.

During his first days in his palace office, Quinn was in his stride, taking it all in with zestful energy, savoring every day.

First, Quinn named Bob Ellis as his administrative assistant. Ellis had managed the Honolulu Chamber of Commerce governmental and municipal affairs. He named Larry Natsatsuka as press secretary and Lucille Hubbard as acting appointments secretary.

He set the date for his first press conference. "I was nervous," Quinn admitted later. "I was thinking about all these pressing things, statehood was very much in my mind, as was the Highway Act and my search for a city planner. And what do I hear?

"'Governor, will you revoke the territory's policy against aloha shirts?'" Public employees were not permitted to wear the popular, casual shirt style in those days. Gardiner Jones reported:

> ...Political analysts argued that if Mr. Quinn intended to continue the aloha shirt ban, he would have said so without hesitation. Instead, Mr. Quinn fenced adroitly: declining to be pinned down.
>
> "This is not the time for an announcement," Quinn said soberly.
>
> Then he laughed.

Quinn did lift the ban.

There was good coverage on the governor's priorities. It was stated that 30 of the 193 authorized Territorial projects were set. "Top of the high-priority list," the governor said, "is construction of the new Honolulu International Airport terminal facilities."

He announced that for the time being he would retain Governor King's cabinet and act later on their resignations, submitted as usual at the end of King's administration.

"I did one thing as soon as I became governor, I made that cabinet a working unit...just because a guy was head of prisons didn't mean he shouldn't hear about water or something else. We met frequently and it worked well, as everybody was trying to formulate policy.

"I really didn't know anything about government," admitted Quinn. "It was September and in the following February of 1958, just five months away, the Legislature was scheduled to have a budget session. The first thing I did was to try and find out how the territory operated and how the legislators put the budget together."

Quinn was astonished to get a book about two inches thick that had been prepared or assembled by his predecessor, Governor King.

"I learned that King had presented a budget that followed the same form as previous budgets, ever since we had been a territory." Quinn explained, "Apparently every department just put down whatever it was they wanted and the executive division hadn't done a thing about it in terms of ordering priorities, nor was there any editorial analysis of any of it. It was submitted as it was...just piled up and sent to the Legislature.

"I decided that was where I would start and learn what it was all about. I owe what was really a fine education in the operation of the territorial government to Paul Thurston and Richard Takasaki—who were the budget director and deputy director— Bob Ellis and my staff."

Quinn went to the budget office and asked to see the long list of items—one at a time. Together, he and his staff started analyzing and began to see where the conflicts and excesses were. From there came the ordering of priorities.

"We worked at night and right through the holidays until finally we put together a good budget document along with a narrative of what we were doing and why."

Meanwhile

Receptions, luncheons and dinners honoring the Quinns filled the social calendar. Among the many community organizations was the Filipino Civic Club, where the governor delighted the guests with a song and then danced the rumba at their Aloha Serenade. The Japanese Chamber of Commerce hosted a tea house testimonial dinner, where Quinn wielded chopsticks and offered introductory remarks in Japanese.

One by one the community associations like the Chinese Chamber of Commerce, the Business and Professional Women and the Republican Women followed, scurrying to honor the new governor and first lady. There was a United Nations Day banquet with representatives from Korea, the Philippines, Japan, China and Great Britain.

The Army, Navy and Marine bases staged reviews, receptions and banquets for Quinn with military formality usually awarded a three-star general. On his first official visit to Fort Shafter, headquarters of General I.D. White, commander-in-chief of the Army's Pacific Command, the new governor was greeted by a 17-gun salute, ruffles and flourishes. The ceremony ended with selections by a 36-piece band, including "When Irish Eyes Are Smiling."

Protocol prevailed at each function, military or civilian. Without a secretary or official adviser on such formalities, Nancy purchased her own book on the subject. It proved to be her trusty, stalwart friend.

Gardiner Jones of *The Advertiser* wrote of the seemingly tireless governor and his grueling schedule:

> His second week in office and already everyone has observed that the new governor is getting into his job with leaps and bounds. William F. Quinn is taking to governorship like a small boy to chocolate ice cream.

The demands on the governor's time and thought have been enormous. Yet he appears absolutely untouched by fatigue. He whips into the palace and bounds up the staircase in vigorous strides. Callers get a big Quinn grin, a booming hello and a powerful handclasp.

In his evening public appearances the governor has been making speeches, singing in his celebrated baritone voice, entertaining at Washington Place or being entertained at testimonial dinners. As one government official said about the affairs, "The food alone would kill me."

≈Chapter Fifteen≈

How Do You Keep Them Down on the Farm
or
When Sugar Was King

"The sugar strike was one of the most dramatic things that I have ever been involved with in my entire life."

GOVERNOR WILLIAM F. QUINN
February 1958

Even the Democrats were surprised by the Republican governor's reaction to Act 150 of the 1957 territorial Legislature, the centerpiece of the Democrat's legislative program. The Territorial Planning Act was foremost among their accomplishments. They were convinced Quinn would never implement it.

"It so happened that I got quite enthusiastic about it myself. I not only embraced it, I enhanced it and enlarged it beyond their wildest dreams," said Quinn later. "It was planning at the territorial level, which was an entirely new concept even nationwide."

The governor knew that such a plan had everything to do with Hawaii's ultimate destiny. The more immediate, major concern facing the Islands, he believed, was to try to win statehood. Statehood was uppermost in his mind.

"I was encouraging the Statehood Commission," Quinn recalled, "and I was trying to keep track of what was happening in Washington. I was prepared to go back and testify."

When Quinn's enthusiasm for the Territorial Planning Act became known, he was accused publicly by the Democrats of stealing their territory-wide economic development program.

The governor responded quickly, calling the charge "absolutely asinine." At a Republican testimonial dinner in his honor on Maui, he made his position clear: "The welfare of the people of Hawaii cannot possibly be a partisan platform."

The Maui News of Wailuku reported:

> The governor's speech highlighted his two-day tour of Maui, a tour during which he took the island by storm, visiting sugar mills, a pineapple cannery, talking with merchants, meeting people on the street. The young governor even sang for Maui school children.
>
> In his speech, the governor strongly supported development of tourist resorts on the Neighbor Islands to strengthen Hawaii's total economy.

"One of the early things that we did in the Territorial Planning Office was to try to find a solution to what was a major, major problem," Quinn said. "Honolulu was going along: The tourist business was growing at a nice, steady pace, but on the Neighbor Islands, it was disaster."

Since World War II, sugar and pineapple had become more mechanized; more and more people lost their jobs; people were leaving the Neighbor Islands; unemployment ran to 12 or 13 percent. Young people were leaving the farm communities to seek their future elsewhere.

On the Big Island, in a speech given at the Hilo Country Club, Quinn told more than 400 Hawaii residents that their island could make or break the economic development program of the entire territory.

Talking like a "Dutch uncle" to the islanders, he stressed his theme that the Big Island residents had to solve their economic problems.

"Here, as nowhere else in the territory, you have the land which is so vitally needed for development," he said. "Unless you people can develop a climate for progress, this whole program will fall flat on its face."

Quinn added, "The territory can and will do a great deal more," he said, speaking of the development of agriculture, timber resources and industry, "but it's up to the Big Islanders to take the initiative themselves."

The governor started a "save the farm" program to head off economic disaster on the Neighbor Islands. He was lauded by _The Honolulu Advertiser._

VIRTUE AND GOVERNOR QUINN

A recent achievement of virtue on the local scene is the forthright action by Governor Quinn in taking upon himself to invite the Neighbor Islands to work out a concrete device through which they could accelerate economic development, both separately and jointly.

The governor made it clear that he wasn't proposing another government committee or commission, rather a broadly representative development committee on each island and a coordinating Council of all islands, all of which will be the result of private volunteer action.

Following the Council of Islands' first meeting, the governor named Boyd MacNaughton, president of C. Brewer, chairman of the newly formed Neighbor Island Development Council.

Boyd MacNaughton, older brother of Malcolm, shorter in height but no less impressive, lent what was known as the "MacNaughton touch" to Hawaii's oldest _kamaaina_ firm, C. Brewer & Co."

MacNaughton was determined to expand Brewer's sugar interests in new and different ways."

Hawaii Pono, L. Fuchs

The governor's search for the right man as territorial planning director extended to California. During the first two weeks of November, Quinn was traveling as an official guest of the City of San Francisco. He interviewed and hired Frank Lombardi to be head of the Planning Office, Territory of Hawaii. Lombardi, 39, was chief of the projects planning division of San Francisco's Department of City Planning. He began his new $14,000-a-year job in the Islands in January 1958.

Quinn completed his speaking engagements in San Francisco and flew to Washington, D.C., to take up legislative matters affecting Hawaii. When he got to the capital, he learned of the birth of their sixth child, a girl. This was the second time that Bill became a father in absentia; he was in the South Pacific when their second son, Stephen, was born.

The baby's name was announced when the governor returned from his two-week, coast-to-coast journey. He spoke with the press: "With Mrs. Quinn's approval, we've chosen the name Mary Kaiulani Quinn. We figured it would mean a lot to her when she grew up to have a Hawaiian as well as a Caucasian name and Princess Kaiulani was a very lovely young lady. Besides," Quinn added, "Mary Kaiulani goes well together...it has a musical ring, don't you think?"

Through the Christmas holidays and into January, the governor worked on the budget. Quinn asked the assistance of the Legislative Reference Bureau at the University of Hawaii. The bureau delegated Jess Walters to assist in developing a legislative program.

"I was assigned to that project," Walters recalled, "and when the governor seemed sufficiently satisfied with my work, he offered me a job. So I went with him in '58."

Walters was a positive, soft-spoken, self-effacing man. His sandy-blonde hair and ruddy complexion enhanced his youth, but he was knowledgeable and exacting with numbers.

"As budget liaison," Walters said, "our office developed the budget, but the governor himself became personally involved. He took great delight in the mass of detail, and he arrived at the point where he knew the departmental budgets better than many department heads."

Finally they moved into the budget session.

"I called a meeting of the legislators at Washington Place, a week or so prior to the session, and I handed out this budget...something that had never been done," Quinn recalled. Up until then, he said, the governor had taken the budgets each department prepared and handed the thick packet over to the Legislature.

"I gave them a budget that was consolidated and about one-half-inch thick. I spoke to them about what we were doing and why," Quinn continued, "what the priorities were and why. They asked me questions and we had quite a lengthy exchange...that was fruitful."

Walters said Quinn "viewed the budget as a principal instrument to carry out his policies and therefore he became very much involved....The governor, in effect, put the legislators on notice that they had better be able to answer to his requests."

After many discussions between the governor and Frank Lombardi, the planning chief, on the problems of the Neighbor Islands, the conclusion, at least in the short term, was to generate some tourist activity on the other islands.

"At that time," Quinn said later, "there was only Kona Inn on the Big Island and Wailuku Hotel on Maui. Pioneer Inn in Lahaina was too far in the country to be counted."

Under Lombardi's leadership and Quinn's direction, a blue-ribbon study was commissioned.

Headed by Walter Collins of Belt & Collins, a major firm of planners, the study commission had economists, architects and others interested in destination areas.

Within six months, the report listed 21 potential resorts throughout the territory, all of which were rated as prime destination areas; each was larger than Waikiki; most had no water, roads or other improvements.

"That's when I started a program that I carried through my entire time as the territory and state governor," Quinn said. "I developed my statewide capital improvement programs. They dealt mainly with roads, water, harbors, airports and parks.

"I put these things in to open up the resort areas, primarily," Quinn said.

In Quinn's administration, funds were apportioned based on the priority of the project. Priorities were determined by what could be done first and lead to the best advantage. Money was not doled out on the basis of so much money for each island.

"In the territorial days, every single legislator had his pet projects for his own district," Quinn explained. "However, even then the governor had line-item veto power, and I used it."

Quinn would put his administration's capital improvement program before the Legislature and most of it would pass. But the legislators would "also pass all these cafeteria, gymnatoria, auditoria and et cetera; something for just about every district. I'd just line-veto them out. I'd take the blame; they were perfectly happy....The legislators got to tell their constituents they'd tried and we got these major projects going."

In February, Quinn made the last leg on his get-acquainted tours when he traveled to the Garden Isle of Kauai. He continued his back-to-the-farm theme, met with farmers, pineapple growers, fruit packers, taro and rice growers, businessmen's associations and high school students. He planted seeds for further development of land and resources, visitor attractions and statehood.

When he returned to Honolulu, he was stunned to receive the desperate word from drought-ridden Kona that it should be declared a disaster area.

"The drought was of such magnitude that they just ran out of water," said Quinn. "We were called upon to ship water from Oahu over to Kona and pump it into their schools and hospitals because they just didn't have any. I remember that we used a Navy barge to take the water to Kona. From there it was trucked to the various towns and farms."

The *Honolulu Star-Bulletin* reported on February 8, 1958:

> *TANKER ARRIVES WITH WATER FOR KONA*
> ...336,000 gallons shipped for drought disaster relief.
> ...The idea for shipping water to Kona by barge was broached last week to Governor Quinn by County Chairman James Kealoha.

The governor was not satisfied. He found the situation unbelievable. He called in hydrologists. "Can't we go and find water over there?"

He reasoned that since Oahu was overflowing and Kona had the same geological structure, it must have water, too.

"They went over there," said Quinn, "and they tramped around, they listened and looked and finally started drilling up *mauka* Kona. They found some all right, but it was 600 parts per million salt.

"Immediately some of the press and public dubbed it 'Quinn's folly.'"

"Quinn's folly" became the big joke in Kona. But those hydrologists weren't laughing. "Now we know exactly where to go," they said, and about a quarter of a mile away from the first, they dug another well. The water they brought in was about six parts of salt per million parts of pure water.

"To this day, Kona has the purest water in the state," recalled Quinn with a prideful grin.

When Sugar Was King

At the turn of the century, about the time Hawaii was annexed by the United States, sugar was "king." In 1958, the sugar industry remained the major mover of Hawaii's economy. Except for the federal government, sugar was the major employer, the major generator of revenues, wealth and jobs. Pineapple was second, followed by tourism.

Until 1947, the "Big Five" was the dominate complex controlling the financial and industrial structure of the territory. The Big Five was an unusually large series of interlocking directorates in territorial corporations. The ILWU has been credited with breaking that control.

In 1946, the International Longshoremen's and Warehousemen's Union had called a strike of all sugar plantation workers. Sugar companies were divided in their reactions to union demands. After a 79-day impasse, costing the plantations millions of dollars and much suffering among the families of the workers, management agreed to a wage increase that was even higher than what had been asked for in early negotiations. The ILWU claimed major victory.

Lawrence Fuchs wrote in *Hawaii Pono*:

> Harry Bridges, ILWU chief, telegraphed from the West Coast that Hawaii "is no longer a feudal colony."
>
> The strike settlement, printed in English, Filipino and Japanese, established the ILWU as the bargaining agent for a large percentage of Hawaii's laborers. It also brought an end to paternalism.

Now, early in February 1958, the union-management contract expired and within 48 hours an Islandwide sugar strike loomed. The ILWU had rejected as "completely unrealistic" and "ridiculous" the industry's offer of 4 cents-an-hour wage increase. The union was demanding 25 cents.

After a futile last-ditch negotiation session and with the words "She's on at midnight," Jack W. Hall, ILWU regional director, shut down the sugar industry. Hall was a hulking giant of a man—tough, ruthless and an alleged former active Communist Party member.

Lawrence Fuchs, *Hawaii Pono*:

> By 1950 Jack Hall had abandoned his strong Communist sympathies: Hall sought power for himself and his union, regardless of the consequences.

"The sugar strike was one of the most dramatic things that I have ever been involved with in my entire life," Quinn said. "I knew that a prolonged strike would batter Oahu's economy...the effects could be far more serious on the Neighbor Islands where the economy to a large extent is based on sugar."

The negotiations were deadlocked. Quinn called in federal mediators.

"Well, they tried, but after 18 days of futile acting as 'go-between' the two men returned to the Mainland."

The future was grim. Neither the ILWU nor sugar management had retreated from its original position. Quinn warned that until both were willing to make concessions, the mediators would not return.

Days then weeks went by, and at first it seemed no one cared. The sugar was growing; workers were not badly needed.

"Then things started to get tougher," said Quinn. "Almost three months had passed and the cane fields needed weeding....They needed to begin the harvest. Violence began on the picket line. They were hiring scabs to come in and it got to be worse and worse."

The governor tried again.

"I brought in a nationally recognized mediator who tried for about a week and then left, saying at the airport, 'A plague on both their houses.'

"Finally, I felt that we had reached a court of last resort." Quinn called for round-the-clock negotiations that he would conduct himself.

"I told both union and industry I didn't want their professional negotiators." Quinn told the sides he wanted Boyd MacNaughton, the Hawaii Sugar Planters Association president and head of C. Brewer, and Harry Bridges, ILWU chief from San Francisco. They each asked to bring two others.

"I was attempting, according to the press, 'a summit meeting.'"

The marathon began in the governor's second-floor Iolani Palace office. It wasn't actually round-the-clock. They did break for sleep. The conferences continued and gradually both sides began to move. Then, when they had almost closed the gap, they both stopped.

Calm, gentlemanly, normally soft-spoken Boyd Mac-Naughton shouted, "Not another goddamn thing, Governor. That's it. FORGET IT!"

"Harry Bridges said almost the same thing: 'We've moved much further than we ever thought we would and that's it. NO MORE!'

"They were so close," said Quinn, "and that was after being around the table for hours and hours and long into the night. We finally broke up and the mediators walked out. I left in despair..."

But the governor wasn't out of ideas. He went to the radio stations.

"I told the public that 'this is what these people are doing to you...look what's happened to our jobs, to our territory's economy, and all because people won't budge even one quarter of one cent.' I guess I made them look a little ridiculous when I told everyone about it. About 4 o'clock that morning I got a call that they had reached an agreement."

Final negotiations dragged through the deadline, and 11th-hour talks continued, with the union still demanding a 25-cent-an-hour raise. The other points such as separation, pension and vacation pay had been agreed upon. Quinn recommended a three-year contract with an immediate 16-cent-an-hour wage boost, reopening after two years.

It was another week before the final settlement was signed and the sugar field crews were back to work. But it was the governor's compromise proposal on the basic issue that brought them together. Quinn insisted later, however, that his radio broadcasts to the people of the Islands, when he accused both the union and management of "destroying the Territory of Hawaii," actually shamed them into settlement.

Amid all the headlines of accusations, barbs and blasts, and in what was to be a long, often trying and continuously eventful public life, some days for William F. Quinn would stand out always as moments of great personal satisfaction. One such time was a Saturday in June 1958.

126-DAY SUGAR STRIKE SETTLED
VICTORY FOR QUINN TOO

...The governor today, barely in the tenth month of his administration, is tasting the sweet fruits of success.

...Whatever may be said...it will appear in the eyes of most people that Governor Quinn was the man of the hour in the settlement of the 1958 sugar strike.

This job proved to carry a grueling schedule, leaving Quinn little or no time for his family. Nancy confessed that there were occasions when she felt very much alone, "especially in the evenings when he worked late. The demands of the office were relentless, but Bill continued to have enormous energy, curiosity and enthusiasm."

Sometimes there would be an unusual respite.

"Our first celebrity visitor was England's queen mother," Quinn said. "The only rough part was that she and her entourage arrived at the airport at 4:30 a.m.

"It was not an official visit and the State Department said we were not called upon to do anything. Nevertheless, Nancy and I decided we'd meet her and see if she wanted anything during the layover. I'm so glad we did."

Queen Mother Elizabeth, mother of Elizabeth II, queen of England, came off the plane in the rain and asked if she could "sightsee" and buy something Hawaiian for her grandson Charles. Conditions were not ideal for sightseeing, not in the dark and rainy predawn. But she rode with Governor Quinn and her secretary, Colonel Martin Gilliat, to the grounds of Iolani Palace, then to Ala Moana Park and Kewalo sampan basin.

"We found an open store where she bought some postcards and then we went back to the Aloha Lounge at Honolulu Airport," Quinn said.

Nancy Quinn followed in another car with Lady Gene Rankin, one of the ladies-in-waiting. The queen mother's entourage included two ladies-in-waiting (each having a maid), a secretary, a second secretary, physician, comptroller, two dressers, a hairdresser and two footmen. They were en route to New Zealand and Australia from Vancouver and flying in a BOAC airliner.

Honolulu Advertiser Columnist Bob Krauss wrote:

> Governor & Mrs. William F. Quinn nearly missed the arrival of the queen mother of England Thursday morning

because their radio-alarm clock didn't go off.

Their driver woke them up at 4:10 (ETA 4:30).

"We got there in time," said First Lady Nancy Quinn, "but I'd rather not think about how we did it."

A week after the queen mother's visit, word came of yet another royal visitor about to arrive—the Shah of Iran. The Shah came for a three-week stay at oil multi-millionaire Ed Pauley's retreat, Coconut Island in Kaneohe Bay. The governor was at the airport to greet the Shah. A reporter at the ceremony described the meeting of the Iranian leader and Governor Quinn, father of four sons as, "ironical." The 38-year-old monarch, His Imperial Majesty Mohammed Reza Shah Pahlavi, a handsome, eligible bachelor, had divorced his stunning wife, Queen Soraya, because she failed to provide him with an heir.

The Pan American Airline plane flew the Iranian colors, a tri-striped flag of green, white and red. There were only five others in the shah's party.

When asked about the shah's appearance, Quinn replied, "Yes, he wore a great, big diamond ring...a cravat? Well, maybe both. He was sparkling!"

Following the shah's arrival, Hawaii greeted President Carlos P. Garcia of the Philippines, his wife and daughter. He arrived en route to Washington, D.C., on a mission he termed vital. It was his first trip away from home since assuming leadership of his country in March 1957.

Honolulu Advertiser:

> Representing his 22 million people, Garcia is frank to admit that he will ask the United States for a $600 million loan to help offset the Philippine recession.
>
> The Garcia party's official welcome was held at Hickam Field complete with a Marine band, a review of troops from each U.S. armed service and 21-gun salute. The following

morning the party boarded President Eisenhower's plane for the flight to Washington, D.C.

⪢Chapter Sixteen⪡
Skullduggery and Politicians

"Wela ka hao...strike while the iron is hot...now is the time to grant statehood for Hawaii."
LIFE MAGAZINE
Lead Editorial, 1958

"I t was early in 1958 when Jack Burns, Hawaii's Democratic delegate to Congress, and I talked about Alaska and its chances as a future state," said Quinn. "It seemed to me that we were on the same track: i.e., whichever one gets statehood first, Alaska or Hawaii, would give momentum to the other. I was opposed, however, to linking Hawaii and Alaska in one bill."

Alaska had just come along as a statehood candidate, while people in Hawaii had worked for statehood for more than 50 years. Since 1903, there had been at least 17 petitions from Hawaii to Congress for statehood.

Quinn didn't believe that Alaska was qualified to be a state in those days.

"They were so spread out and they had rather sparse resources. They didn't have the oil then and my feeling was that many congressmen would say, 'If I have to accept Alaska because I'm accepting Hawaii, then I don't want Hawaii.'"

Quinn realized later he didn't think about the political implications: Alaska was strongly Democratic. Hawaii, although things were changing, was still thought to be a Republican stronghold.

In early June, the Senate Policy Committee reached agreement on Alaska statehood, and on July 1, 1958, President Eisenhower signed the Alaska bill.

"On the same day, the president asked for immediate Hawaii statehood. We were all elated, whereupon we started to put the wheels in motion to get statehood for Hawaii. Strike while the iron is hot...that type of thing," Quinn said.

"Hawaii's State Constitution had been adopted in the 1950s as additional evidence of Hawaii's readiness. We also sought consultants to advise us on how to set up the Hawaii State government, and most Island leaders were optimistic over the prospect of statehood in '58."

Unfortunately, Washington chicanery was under way.

Said Quinn, "Suddenly I bumped into this coolness from Jack Burns' office and from the local Democratic Party."

Congress accepted Alaska because it had strong Democratic politicians, while Hawaii was still under the considerable influence of Harry Bridges, an alleged communist. As Senator Norris Cotton, Republican of New Hampshire, said, "I'm voting for Alaska because there are no Harry Bridges in Alaska. There are no communist cells in Alaska." Republicans boasted, too, that they supplied 33 of the 64 votes for passage of the Alaska measure and that only seven from their side were among the 20 opposing.

What about Hawaii? Opposition voices kept saying, "No, no, no. No Hawaii statehood this year. Next year will be better."

"My thinking," said Quinn, "was that next year might never come. There were so many civil rights bills pending in the Congress, and there were a lot of southern Democrats who thought that any representative from the state of Hawaii, no matter what party, would be in favor of civil rights for the minorities and that, the southerners did not want."

While Hawaii Republicans, Democrats and the Statehood Commission were pressing to find out what to do about the position shifts of long-time statehood supporters in Congress, it became apparent that both parties in Washington had played politics and that even Hawaii's Delegate Burns had had a role in stalling the Hawaii bill, Quinn said.

Antagonism toward Burns existed among independent voters. Many voters said that if Jack Burns felt the statehood issue as deeply as reported, he had a strange way of showing it. Many people found Burns an imperious personality, cold, aloof, inflexible and dictatorial.

Fuchs, in _Hawaii Pono_, wrote:

> "The delegate (Jack Burns) had agreed to a deal in Congress separating the questions of Hawaiian and Alaskan statehood. Tying the two statehood bills together in the past united the opposition to each measure and meant defeat of both. Burns agreed to push Alaska first, while Hawaii waited its turn."

Governor Quinn and Territorial Secretary Turner charged that Hawaii had been betrayed.

Honolulu Star-Bulletin June 7, 1958:

> ### BURNS STALLS STATEHOOD, SAYS QUINN
> Governor Quinn today accused congressional Democrats, including Hawaii's Delegate Burns, of conspiring to stall Hawaii statehood.
>
> Speaking to the Oahu County GOP convention at the University of Hawaii, the governor emphatically called

Democrats to task for working out a "dark compromise" to push Alaskan statehood while abandoning Hawaii.

He said he was angered by creeping criticism of GOP congressmen who are being labeled anti-statehood because they voted against admission of Alaska in the House.

"Statehood for Alaska and Hawaii are separate issues," the governor said. "The Republican Party has been and always will be strongly in favor of Hawaiian statehood."

He blamed the House Democratic leadership for abandoning Hawaii in favor of Alaska.

Quinn received a hurried call from Seaton. Quinn said Seaton ordered him to: "get a group back here, but I don't want that Statehood Commission of yours. I don't want Lorrin Thurston. I want some good, solid Republicans."

"I knew that he meant new faces, a stronger representation of Republicans for statehood," Quinn said. "I also knew that any change such as that would put me in the hot seat. How could I send people other than the Statehood Commission to Washington and not have it look politically motivated?"

Quinn had another dilemma, too. One of the battles going on in Washington was over who was going to get credit for statehood. The president favored statehood for Hawaii; the administration was for it and so was most of the Democratic-controlled Congress; but each party wanted the full credit.

Quinn pondered and arrived at a solution. He asked Betty Farrington, former delegate to Congress, and Samuel Wilder King, former governor of the territory of Hawaii and ex-delegate to Congress, to join him as a vanguard to go back to Washington and espouse the statehood cause. The Statehood Commission would then be the follow-up. King's record on statehood was particularly outstanding: In 1935, King, supported by the sugar industry and the Hawaii Equal Rights Commission, had introduced a statehood bill in the House of Representatives. King, one-eighth Hawaiian, a kindly man and friend of the *haole* elite, had never showed any resentment toward his replacement, Bill Quinn.

"I felt that both Betty and King would carry some color of authenticity and could be effective since both had served in Congress and had a lot of friends on the floor," said Quinn.

Quinn, King and Farrington left for Washington and "all hell broke loose," according to Quinn. Bill Richardson, a part-Hawaiian lawyer who was Jack Burns' protégé in the office of Chairman of the Hawaii Democratic Party, charged, "The governor is just trying to make this whole thing a political animal."

Charges and countercharges flew. Burns, on a Washington newscast, said "that we were a 'politically partisan delegation that would harm Hawaii's chances for statehood," Quinn said.

A few days later, the Statehood Commission arrived; each member was assigned to various members of Congress. Quinn was to see Leo O'Brien, chairman of the critically important House committee.

Quinn recalled his conversation with O'Brien: "I'll tell you. Your delegate is not encouraging the passage of the statehood bill," said O'Brien, "I happen to think that you've got to pursue it and pursue it right now and you'll have my firm and full support. But, you've got to do something about it because if Jack Burns isn't in there really pushing for it right now, it's going to be very hard to get."

Washington newspapers reported that the Island statehood bill had been stalled and that angry words had been exchanged in the House Interior and Insular Affairs Committee. An unsuccessful attempt had been made to break the parliamentary logjam bottling up the Hawaii bill.

"With the postponement of our bill for at least another week," said Quinn, "I knew that I must get to the majority leader, Lyndon Johnson, a close friend of Jack Burns."

Quinn got help from Jim Rowe, an old friend whom he had known in Air Combat Intelligence during the war. Rowe had worked in the White House under President Roosevelt and was a good friend of Lyndon Johnson.

"Jim and I had a good visit and I told him that I'd like to see the majority leader and hopefully, I can urge him to lend his support to statehood. Jim agreed to arrange a meeting.

"My date at the majority leader's office was set for 6:30 that very evening. I was there on time and I guess I waited almost two hours before Johnson walked in."

Quinn remembered his conversation with Johnson this way:

"I'm glad to meet you, Governor," drawled the Texas Senator. "Jim Rowe says that even though you're a Republican you're not such a bad guy."

Quinn said, "Well, Senator, I come seeking your support and your assistance on the statehood for Hawaii bill this year."

Johnson frowned, "You know we've got a very busy session, and we haven't got that much time left. Furthermore," he pointed, "You see that red phone over there? That's the phone that I talk to your President on, and your President wants to have a mutual assistance pact and I'm trying to work to get his mutual assistance pact for him, and I haven't got time to put all these other things into our agenda. You are not on the agenda."

Quinn, in preparation for his time with Johnson, had brought with him the lead editorial of that week's Life magazine.

"*Wela ka hao*...strike while the iron is hot...Now is the time to grant statehood for Hawaii."

"But, Senator," Quinn said, "there's so much support throughout the country for this. We've been waiting so long...to show you the support; look at this editorial."

Quinn didn't have a chance. Johnson got mad. "I mean he got mad," Quinn said.

"I was seated opposite him at his desk. He got so mad that as his face came closer and closer to mine, it got redder and redder and the veins on his neck stood out. Then he yelled, 'Listen to me, young man. I'm the majority leader in the Senate and things will move in the Senate when I say they're going to move, not when anybody else, not you, not your president, not anybody else, only me. Do you understand that?'"

Quinn couldn't believe what he'd heard.

"I'm sorry, Senator; I appreciate your giving me a chance to visit you. "Quinn got to the door and turned around. "Maybe, Senator, you could make some positive statement that you think that statehood for Hawaii would be on the agenda in the next session or something like that?"

"I'll say whatever I feel like saying," was Johnson's reply as the governor went out the door.

Still campaigning for the cause, the governor flew to New York, where he made several TV and radio appearances. He managed to "stump the panel" on the popular television quiz show "What's My Line?"

"They were trying to find out what I did and when they heard me say that I was from Hawaii, they asked, are you a planter? A professor? Have you ever been elected? Finally time lapsed and no one had asked if I was the appointed governor....I did manage to make a pitch for statehood and that made it worthwhile."

Besides making public appearances in New York, Quinn also wanted to get General Douglas MacArthur's endorsement for Hawaii's statehood.

"I arranged to meet with MacArthur at his suite in the Waldorf Towers. I will never forget when he walked through the door. He came to about my chin. I had seen his pictures all during the war and, for a time, our fleet air wing was under his command. The pictures always showed him with his pipe in his mouth, his hat pulled down, broad shoulders and I thought, gosh, this is a tremendous man, you know. Actually, he was about 5-9 or -10."

As soon as Quinn and the renowned general sat down, MacArthur started to talk "and he never stopped talking."

"But he spoke beautifully, with complete sentences, like it had all been written in advance. He was that bright and that articulate and at the end he said, 'Absolutely, you write a statement, and I'll sign it, and it can be used whatever way you wish.'"

"I wanted another endorsement, and that was from Eleanor Roosevelt. She was living in New York at the time and writing her columns. She was very gracious and said, 'Of course, I've always been in favor of statehood for Hawaii. Just give me the endorsement and I'll be happy to sign it.'"

They'd done all they could do. The delegation went home. "That was the end of it for 1958," admitted Quinn.

Jack M. Fox, a member of the statehood Commission, wasn't happy about it. He accused Delegate Burns of balking statehood. *The Honolulu Advertiser* quoted him on his return from Washington:

> "Unfortunately," Fox said, "Burns chose to raise the red herring of partisanship the day our delegation arrived in Washington. He chose to wash Hawaii's political linen in the streets of Washington instead of making an all-out pitch for statehood."

Fox was also quoted as saying that if Burns had thrown his weight behind the statehood drive immediately after Alaska's success, "our chances would have been very good, indeed."

Governor Quinn claimed Burns's political decision was to put the Democratic Party ahead of his Isle constituents.

Quinn told a seminar of Republican candidates at GOP headquarters that the national Democratic Party had decided that Hawaii should not get statehood this session.

The governor said that Burns faced a real dilemma...either contradict the wishes of the Democratic leadership, or contradict the wishes of his Isle constituents.

"He chose the second course," said Quinn.

Excerpts from a lengthy editorial in *The Advertiser* of July 27, 1958, shredded Burns's credibility and placed the blame for Hawaii's failure to obtain statehood in the last session of Congress squarely on Delegate John Burns.

...Delegate Burns sought to place obstacles in the way of Governor Quinn's efforts to revive statehood to Congress after Burns had agreed to a deal surrendering Hawaii's established precedence to Alaska.

...He failed the people of Hawaii at a time when it had the best opportunity to win statehood.

...He failed them again when, after Alaska had won statehood, he did not press Hawaii's right for equal and immediate admission to the Union.

...The people of Hawaii are not asking for statehood as Democrats or Republicans. They are demanding admission to the Union by right of their American citizenship. They want none of the partisanship and self-service that are apparent in the attitude of Delegate Burns.

In the midst of all the political flap, there was a small article in the *Honolulu Star-Bulletin* about the New York TV quiz show, "What's My Line" in which the governor was a winner and how he had donated his prize of $50 to the Honolulu Community Chest, making the governor the first contributor to the Chest's fall fund drive.

The big news at Washington Place when the governor arrived home from his three-week journey was that Mary Kaiulani, age 9 months, had "popped another tooth."

≈Chapter Seventeen≈
Winding Up Their First Year

*The Islanders, however, were not finding Bill Quinn so
ordinary. "The sugar strike of 1958 alone was enough
to set him apart from the ordinary man."*
HENRY WALKER, JR.
Chairman of the Board
Amfac, Inc.

I t was after the governor's return from Washington and in
the middle of the night when a sudden, brilliant light blasted across the southern horizon; a frightening, penetrating
glow of concentric red, yellow to orange rings like a giant
mushroom afire.

This was no dawn; still, the city awakened with hysterical cries
of "nuclear war"..."fire ball"..."enemy attack"...piercing the
night's shroud.

"The only reassurance was not to hear any air-raid warnings,"
said John Barkhorn, a resident close to the Coast Guard
Lighthouse on Diamond Head.

The military had failed to warn Hawaii's citizenry of the
Johnston Island nuclear rocket explosion. The Hawaii population
erupted en masse, incensed.

Three months before, when Governor Quinn had received
notice of the future blast, he met with Admiral Stump, commander-in-chief, Pacific Fleet. "I asked for reassurances that the safety of Hawaii's people would not be endangered," said Quinn,
"and that an announcement of the impending test be made in
advance."

The governor was told that Hawaii was in no danger but that Atomic Energy Commission regulations prohibited such an announcement.

"In the future," the governor said, "if there are going to be any further tests as perceptible as last night's, I will urge again that I be given authority to give advance notice."

Territorial Senator Dan Inouye told the reporters, "This is no joke. People actually thought that Pearl Harbor had been blown off the map."

The officers of ILWU Local 142 called upon President Eisenhower to halt the tests.

"We protest the nuclear explosions being set off so near our Islands. Self-preservation, sanity and self-respect impel us to demand an immediate stop to this reckless poisoning of the atmosphere," demanded the ILWU.

Within a week's time, a letter was sent to Governor Quinn from the Pacific commander-in-chief that pledged advance warning of any nuclear test on Johnston Island. The voices of the Islanders had been heard.

Also that summer, Farrant Turner, secretary of the territory for five years, announced his resignation from his post to run for delegate to Congress on the Republican ticket.

Turner, the man who organized the 100th Infantry Battalion and commanded it with the rank of colonel during World War II, said, "I am running for delegate and may I say that I hope to be the last delegate from Hawaii in its territorial status."

During his years in office, Turner had switched from Mr. Secretary to Mr. Acting Governor 16 times for a total of 233 days. Finding Turner's successor was not going to be easy.

"Besides," said political analysts, "it calls attention to one of the few inadequacies of Hawaii's Governor W.F. Quinn."

Said *The Honolulu Advertiser* in August 1958:

...The governor's job is not an easy one. To succeed in it, he must do more than successfully administer the affairs of the government, even if he does this outstandingly well.

He must also, somehow, successfully function as the head of his party. Success in this latter function must at times seem impossible without impairing success in the former function.

Succeeding to both functions would seem to call for genius, but that is what Americans demand of a chief executive in government.

Quinn immediately sent the names of his two top choices for the $16,000-a-year position to Interior Secretary Fred Seaton, who oversaw territorial affairs. The president, acting with the advice of the secretary, would make the appointment. Quinn nominated Alex H.F. Castro and Ed Johnston. Johnston was an insurance executive and chairman of the Oahu Republican County Committee. Castro, Island-born, was a Realtor and active in the Republican Party. He'd been elected to the Constitutional Convention and had a grass-roots edge. He was also a personal friend of Quinn's.

Turner's announcement of his candidacy was made at the same time that the press was reviewing Quinn's first-year performance as governor. It had been a year of testing, planning; a year full of strike, statehood, speech and song. It was noted that the number of speeches he made and songs he sang, while plugging statehood and tourism, was astronomical.

Looking back over the year, analysts recognized Quinn had not shirked crisis. He came face to face with the Kona drought; he acted as self-appointed mediator in the sugar strike as he paved the way for a solution between the ILWU and the sugar industry; he avoided a potential conflict with the City and County by releasing funds to advance new school construction, and he pressed for agricultural cooperatives to aid the territory's farmers.

An editorial in *The Advertiser* addressed his future:

> Governor Quinn's appointment to the governorship was a surprise to almost everyone in Hawaii, including himself, we suspect. Thus far it has proved to be a pleasant surprise and there is good reason to anticipate that it will continue to be so.

On September 18 the official word came from the White House that Ed Johnston had been named secretary of Territory of Hawaii to succeed Farrant Turner. Johnston took the oath of office September 19, and served his first stint as acting governor the next day. Quinn left for San Francisco to be the keynote speaker at the city's Pacific Festival.

Honolulu Star-Bulletin:

> The appointment of 40-year-old Edward Johnston as secretary of Hawaii - and acting governor when 39-year-old Governor Quinn is out of the territory - gives Hawaii an administration with a forward-looking drive....But historians will have to look far to find a younger team than that which now guides the territory.
>
> There will be widespread regret that Alex H.F. Castro was not appointed the secretary. He also has youth, drive, fervor and varied and valuable community service. In addition he is Island-born, his roots are in Hawaii and the service he gives is to the land of his birth.

After the announcement of Johnston's appointment to replace Turner, caustic Isle Republicans said that the Interior Department had little regard for the opinions of local GOP leaders. Old resentments flared; some recalled the manner in which the interior secretary unceremoniously dumped former

Governor King to make room for Quinn.

Neither the president nor Seaton sought the opinion of any of the GOP leaders, including Quinn, Farrington, King, Turner or Ed Bryan, chairman of the Republican party.

The Democrats, including Jack Burns, made the accusation that the territorial administration had been taken over by *malihini* officials and that the two top jobs were given to Isle newcomers, Quinn and Johnston.

Quinn bristled at the insinuation aimed to discredit Illinois-born Ed Johnston. "It is regrettable that people would attempt to make out that some in our midst have been strangers here because they have been in Hawaii only a third of their lives," he said. "We became Hawaiians when we came here to make our homes and to take an interest in society and to participate in its activities. Citizens who love Hawaii are deserving of a full part in running the government."

Almost everyone knew that Quinn was born in Rochester, New York, raised in St. Louis, and was a 10-year resident of Hawaii when he was appointed governor. Not everyone knew, however, that Jack Burns, Hawaii's delegate to Congress, was born in Montana.

While the political maelstrom filled part of the newspapers, Bob Krauss reported on the Pacific Festival in his *Advertiser* column *In One Ear* :

> Contrary to all predictions, Gov. Bill Quinn did NOT sing *Ke Kali Nei Au* at the Pacific Festival in San Francisco. In fact, he was so busy he didn't sing at all.
>
> But Hawaii Day at Union Square drew the biggest crowds of the week and all the free pineapples were snatched away long before the noon hour show was over.

It was campaign time. The GOP chose to air the Republican issues on a special series of telecasts. The governor and three other speakers, Tad Kanda, Hebden Porteus and Bob Fukuda attacked the Democratic Party and its program as dominated by big labor and partisan narrowness. Quinn once more zeroed in on Burns. "Mr. Burns, himself, was one of the chief reasons we didn't get statehood in the last session."

After the primary election the governor and the speakers' team enthusiastically stumped the GOP's four-point program: recovery of non-essential military lands, concern with excessive taxes, increase of the minimum wage and extension of unemployment benefits.

Turner's campaign for the delegate position was doomed from the beginning. Quinn and other GOP members tried to help by giving speeches for the Turner campaign. Nevertheless, the incumbent Burns piled up the biggest vote ever amassed by any Isle Democratic candidate.

It was a crushing defeat for Turner, who was motivated by the belief that the Japanese population could be won back to the Republican Party. He was bitter and claimed that the money and help that he had been promised for his delegate-to-Congress campaign did not materialize. He began to conclude that he "had been thrown to the wolves."

Fuchs in *Hawaii Pono* wrote:

> To Turner, Quinn was another Eisenhower. Genial, able, undoubtedly popular, he was too much of a New Dealer and not interested in building the Republican organization. Quinn, it was often repeated in the corridors of Iolani Palace, acted more like a Democrat than a Republican, as did Honolulu's popular Mayor Blaisdell. Turner was known to have asked of Blaisdell, "Is he a Republican or a Democrat?"

Governor Quinn and Delegate Burns set aside the cross-fire and finally reached an agreement on statehood. Together at the Hawaii Statehood Commission meeting, the governor and the delegate swapped gracious compliments and confirmed their dedication to a bipartisan campaign aimed at statehood in 1959. With political considerations laid aside, the two leaders joined a united Hawaii to drive ahead and put the 50th star on the American flag.

The annual Western Governors' Conference was held in Hawaii on November 23 to 26, 1958. It was the first event ever where Hawaii was host to the top executives of 14 states and territories. The governors—along with a battery of staff assistants and press representatives—focused national attention on Hawaii just when statehood efforts were being accelerated.

The Islands needed that kind of publicity. "It was," in Quinn's words, "an indication that Hawaii is taking on the stature of a state. It is very important that we keep working at getting statehood. After losing our chance this past session, I'm even more convinced that by working together we will achieve our goal in early '59."

Washington Place

It had been a good year for the Quinn family. Nancy accomplished her task as first lady with remarkable graciousness. The social calendar was filled with tea and coffee hours, concerts, receptions, luncheons and sparkling black-tie dinners. Nancy had no secretary and organized the events herself, creating everything from table and seating charts to menus and receiving lines.

The children adjusted to the big house, but when it came to Danny, the chauffeur, dropping them off at school each day, they objected. They didn't want to be driven into school. They chose to be dropped off a couple of blocks away so as not to be, as the boys put it, "so showy."

"In the golden days before the governorship, I used to do a lot of reading at home. I read to the children," Quinn said. "They'd gather around and I'd read. But that just went by the boards. We, or I, had to go out just about every night. So I was pulled away from my children during this period."

Nancy added that "Ceci, even at the age of 4, had her moments of loneliness. Washington Place was a beautiful downtown mansion but it was no neighborly playground and Ceci longed for playmates. She used to sit on the backyard wall and watch the young girls of St. Andrew's Priory play during recess."

In December, Mother Quinn arrived for a two-month visit. On the day of her arrival, Secretary Seaton flew in from Washington to address the Western Republican Conference. The Governor quipped, "Now I have my two bosses right here..."

Grandmother Quinn, blue-eyed, her blonde hair set in deep waves close to her head, with her bright smile, was just what the little ones needed.

The following morning, *The Honolulu Advertiser's* Bob Krauss interviewed "Mom":

> Governor Quinn will probably shoot me when he reads this, but I have just discovered that he wore bangs until he was 5 and knickers until he went to high school.
>
> The source of this confidential information is his mother, Mrs. C. Alvin Quinn of St. Louis, from whom he obviously got his good looks and Irish charm.
>
> The bangs, she explained, were called Buster Brown haircuts and were the common hair style among boys until they started grade school.
>
> He was a marble champion...an avid reader...he liked to climb trees but never once broke a bone...
>
> Her son "was just an ordinary boy, happy-go-lucky," she said.

Islanders, however were finding Bill Quinn more than ordinary. There was wide agreement that he was meeting the problems of his office with courage and skill.

"The sugar strike of 1958 alone was enough to set him apart from the ordinary man," said Henry Walker Jr., chairman of the board of Amfac, Inc. "Bill was very instrumental...to finally get it settled. That strike almost finished off the industry. Had Bill not stepped in at that moment we might not have gotten ourselves a settlement. It was the last time a strike like that was ever to be called."

≈Chapter Eighteen≈
Getting Ready

"Hawaii...as an internationally famous meeting place—a center of learning for the advancement of the philosophies, cultures and arts of the Pacific and Asian world."

GOVERNOR WILLIAM QUINN
New Year's Message, 1959

Greeting islanders on New Year's morning, 1959, were the bold and optimistic predictions of the Territory's governor. *The Honolulu Advertiser* that morning said:

QUINN: STATE MEANS FABULOUS FUTURE
By William F. Quinn

Hawaii is growing and prospering. That, more than any other fact, generates the confidence the people of Hawaii have in the future of their island community.

Hawaii, now on the threshold of statehood, is already getting a preview of things to come. We are embarked on an era of growth and expansion, but it is only a start.

Throngs of Americans can be expected to flock to Hawaii, to see at firsthand these Islands fabled in songs and stories, an insular community deeply imbued in American traditions and loyalty, yet unique in its ability to harmonize the Occidental, Oriental and Polynesian cultures.

The governor wrote that Hawaii's growth opportunities included:

> Hawaii...as a new economic center of opportunities in commerce, communication and carriers;
>
> ...as a world-famous vacationland for hundreds of thousands of visitors;
>
> ...as an internationally famous meeting place—a center of learning for the advancement of the philosophies, cultures and arts of the Pacific and Asian world.

Washington Place

The governor's optimism was contagious. The executive mansion, usually resting in composed, luxurious quiet, was ringing with the festive, happy sounds of music and laughter.

The Quinn charm reigned as the governor in a slate-gray suit and the first lady in a royal blue lace *holoku*, both wearing strands of fragrant Big Island *maile* lei, greeted 1,500 guests at their New Year's Day open house. The five Quinn children darted in and about the adult party. After thirty gallons of brandied eggnog were consumed and the last chorus of "Auld Lang Syne" sung, the executive mansion emptied just about as fast as it had filled two hours earlier.

The rest of that first day of the New Year found the seven Quinns together and alone. It was a peaceful, fun family time of the type that had become rare in their busy lives.

The Advertiser reported on January 5, 1959:

QUINN ASKS $200 MILLION T.H. SPENDING

> The governor will send a record budget request of more than $200 million to the Legislature this year.

...It will be "Quinn's budget" in every sense of the word. The governor even plans to break precedent by taking his budget message in person to the Legislature.

Quinn started work on the budget last spring. He didn't know how other governors had handled the chore, and wanted time to familiarize himself with past procedure. He also wanted to be able to justify personally the recommendations his report will contain.

"I learned pretty quickly when I started that one of the finest ways to get a real grasp of the programs of the departments is through the budget process," he says.

Quinn's record capital improvement budget included priorities for construction of highways, harbors, public buildings, tourist attractions and a tax-slash plan. At the same time, the governor officially proclaimed the imminence of statehood and called a conclave of community organizations from all islands to meet and plan for a year-long Hawaii 50th State celebration.

The *Honolulu Star-Bulletin* reported:

Governor Quinn has called a pre-statehood convention for this Saturday. The reason being is that statehood may go through Congress at unprecedented speed and Hawaii must get ready now for that event.

We hope that rather than just a revival meeting or rat race, out of it will come a planning committee that will move with efficiency.

Asked in a televised press conference if he would be interested in being the first elected governor, Quinn said "yes," that he would run when Hawaii became a state. He faced 25 reporters for a half-hour of unrehearsed questions and answers on current topics.

"I feel that I have a responsibility to run for office. I believe that if the opportunity presents itself, I would attempt to continue the job I am now doing," he replied.

A half-hour later, reporters contacted former Governor Samuel King, who said he would still run for governor as a Republican regardless of Governor Quinn's intentions. There were rumors that Republican Mayor Neal Blaisdell was also interested in the 50th State post.

Democrats were quick to call Quinn's aspirations premature.

"I think we ought to concentrate on helping Delegate Jack Burns get statehood before we start running for office," said territorial Democratic Chairman William Richardson. Richardson was a close friend of Burns. Burns, his political mentor, had helped to establish Richardson as one of the major supporters of the Hawaiian people.

Robert E. Cates, Oahu Democratic chairman, predicted a "bloody" primary fight between King and Quinn, with Quinn the winner.

"Since Quinn is being charged with adopting Democratic programs and with being more of a Democrat than a Republican, it looks like a real ding-dong battle between him and King," Cates said.

In the meantime, the one-day, 2,000-person, statehood planning convention rallied with gusto. Honolulu business executives brushed elbows with Hilo housewives as delegates from hundreds of Island organizations, answering the call from Governor Quinn, gathered at McKinley High School. Even Walter F. Dillingham, Hawaii's most powerful industrialist of the '20s and long-time opponent of statehood, was there.

A. Grove Day in *History Makers of Hawaii* said this of Dillingham:

> Walter F. Dillingham, a confirmed Republican who never sought office, is regarded as the leader of the anti-statehood

forces that for many years were able to defer the granting of full citizenship to Hawaii residents.

Dillingham, with his traditional red feather lei around the crown of his dark hat and a small bow-tie at his chin, came prepared to fly his new colors as a Hawaii 50th State supporter.

In the executive offices, planning for statehood proceeded. Consultants were hired to work out how the state government should be organized to fit within 20 major departments, as required by the Constitution.

"In the territorial days we had over a hundred boards, commissions and agencies," said Quinn later, "with the effort being made to stay independent from the federally appointed governor. It was quite a job."

Various different functions had to be melded into a smaller number of departments, Quinn said. "We formed a committee with some legislators to look at this so we'd have some advance work done with the Legislature."

About 50 boards and commissions needed to be transferred or reorganized. Among them were the boards of health, massage, pharmacy, photography, prison inspectors and barbers, and the tax appeal court, to name a few. Another 50 were to be abolished, including the boards of loyalty, voting machine and appraisers, the committees on disposal and on fishery advice and the authority on water. In many cases the heads of the various boards were either transferred or dropped altogether.

Congress began hearings on Hawaii's statehood. Quinn got a call from George Abbott, general counsel of the Interior Department in Washington.

Abbott asked Quinn to come back to the capital.

"When?"

"Right now. The secretary would like to see you here as soon as possible," Quinn recalled Abbott said.

Above:
Young Billy Quinn, 1923

Above Right:
Bill Quinn and Nancy Witbeck are married in St. Louis, July 1942.
(J. Gregg Puster photo)

Right:
The Quinn family at the airport after Bill Quinn was appointed governor in 1957.

Above:
Honolulu Community Theatre's 1948 production of Mister Roberts *starred William Quinn (left.) Also featured were Jim Wall and Alex Castro.*
(Kroshaw Studio photo)

Right:
Bill Quinn played with Jan Burriss in Honolulu Community Theatre's production of Brigadoon *in 1953.*
(Sula White photo)

Right:
*Victory cele-
bration at
Quinn head-
quarters on
Kapiolani
Boulevard,
July 28, 1959.*
(*Honolulu Star
Bulletin* photo)

Below:
*Bill Quinn sought Douglas MacArthur's support for statehood. Photo taken
in New York, 1959.* (*Honolulu Star Bulletin* photo)

Right:
Cecily Quinn curtsies before Madame Chiang Kai-shek at Washington Place, 1959.

Below left:
West Germany's Willy Brandt is greeted by Governor Quinn and Monty Richards (center), February 1959.
(*Honolulu Star-Bulletin* photo)

Below right:
Governor Quinn with Prime Minister Ikeda of Japan, 1961
(Pacific Command photo)

Left:
Crown Price Akihito and Princess Machiko, with Governor and Mrs. Quinn, 1960

Left:
Governor and Mrs. Quinn flank Princess Takamatsu and Prince Takamatsu of Japan, 1960.
(*Honolulu Star-Bulletin* photo)

Below:
Pre-statehood days, Quinn with Lucy Blaisdell and Ferrant Turner, Secretary of the Territory.
(Takashi Umeda photo, *Honolulu Advertiser*)

Left:
*Statehood!
Governor Quinn
receives word that
President has signed
the bill, August 21,
1959.*
(*Honolulu Star-Bulletin*
photo)

Above:
*The photo of William F.
Quinn that appeared on the
cover of* TIME *Magazine,
August 10, 1959.*

(Werner Stoy photo,
Camera Hawaii)

Below :
*Governor Quinn welcomes an
important guest, his mother, Mrs.
C. Alvin Quinn, September, 1959*
(Pan American Airways photo)

Right:
Governor Quinn and President Eisenhower, walking at center at Honolulu Airport, June 1960.
(Ollie Fife photo)

Below:
Governor Quinn with Barbara Eisenhower, President Eisenhower, Tim, Steve and Billy Quinn, Nancy Quinn, John Eisenhower, and in front, Cecily, Chris and Mary Quinn.
(Ollie Fife photo)

Above:
*In 1962 Governor Quinn (left)
welcomes astronaut Walter
Schirra at Hickam Air Force on
his return to American soil after
his six orbits around the earth in
spacecraft Sigma 7.*

Below:
Harry Lyons, Honolulu Advertiser *cartoonist, depicts climate between Governor
Quinn and Legislature, 1961.*

Below:
*Quinn family, 1983, left to right,
sons Christopher and Billy, William F. Quinn, and his wife Nancy, sons Tim
and Steve. In front, daughters Cecily, Mary, and son Gregory.*

Fortunately, Quinn was able to get a plane to Washington that day. Abbott met him, rushed Quinn from the airport to the Old Senate Office Building and into the Supreme Court chambers. The room was filled with microphones, extension cords and news reporters. Quinn and Abbott waited a few minutes and then down the hall came a roar of excitement, flooding the staid, dark-walled tribunal. Members of the Senate, including Washington state's Scoop Jackson and other leaders, accompanied by Jack Burns and the Democratic national committeewoman, Dolores Martin, burst in.

"They were all set to have this big Democratic celebration of statehood for Hawaii passed by the Senate; it hadn't been passed by the House yet," said Quinn.

"Can you imagine their consternation when they walked into this room and there I was?"

Of all the pictures taken during those historic moments, there was one that was published across the nation—Governor Quinn receiving an orchid lei and a kiss from graceful, part-Hawaiian, part-Portuguese Democratic National Committeewoman Dolores Martin.

"She saw me, her eyes lit up, she came running over, threw her arms out, gave me this big hug and all the cameras flashed, and that was the picture that was used all over the country showing the Republicans were there," Quinn said.

The story of just how the Senate moved with such alacrity on Hawaii statehood, especially when several southern leaders were ready to speak against the bill, was reported in *LIFE* magazine a few days after the vote.

Quinn described it: "I understand from reading the *LIFE* article that Lyndon Johnson whispered to each member as they came forward to voice their opposition, 'That young son of a bitch from Hawaii is on his way here, and we want to get this through before he ever gets here, so we'll put it in the record as a Democratic accomplishment.' And that's a true story," said Quinn.

On March 12, 1959, a single day after the Senate acted, the U.S. House of Representatives passed the statehood bill. Governor Quinn called Acting Governor Ed Johnston in Honolulu and set off the biggest celebration the Islands had seen since the end of World War II...Statehood Day.

With the signal from the acting governor, 52 air-raid sirens screamed; virtually every church bell in town pealed; students were released from school at noon; at the university a 50-star American flag was hoisted; and by evening, radio newscasters announced:

"There'll be spontaneous dancing in the streets; musicians have donated their services, pianos and instruments have been borrowed and sound systems have been installed; a-two-and-a-half-story-high "international bonfire" on Sand Island will be lit; and off Waikiki, U.S. Navy destroyers will fire their guns; light Army aircraft will drop flares offshore, and a million candlepowers of light will be shimmering in the dark. Finally, it's to be a two-day celebration, concluding with a crashing 50-gun salute on the grounds of Iolani Palace."

The Saturday *Star-Bulletin* :

QUINN CONFERS WITH IKE ON SIGNING
Washington, March 14: President Eisenhower will sign the Hawaii statehood bill early next week.

Hawaii's Governor William Quinn visited the White House to thank the president on behalf of the people of the Islands for the part the administration played in pressing for admission of Hawaii as the 50th state.

Quinn said Hawaii wishes to perform as a "Hub of the Pacific" in creating greater understanding between the East and West and the peoples of Asia "whose friendship we are trying to nourish."

Quinn will have 30 days after formal notice of Eisenhower's approval to issue an election proclamation. The primary could be held no less than 60 and no more than 90 days after the proclamation. A general election could be held no later than 40 days after the primary.

En route back to the Islands with a presidential admonition to speed the statehood transition, Quinn read with great interest Jack Teehan's account of the closing ceremonies of the Statehood Day celebration.

COLOR AND PAGEANTRY CLIMAX CELEBRATION
by Jack Teehan

Hawaii's two-day celebration came to an official end last night in a splash of color and pageantry on the historic grounds of Iolani Palace.

Thousands of Oahuans packed the grounds before the brilliantly illuminated palace, festooned in the regal purple of the monarchy. There they were serenaded by the Royal Hawaiian Band.

Moonlight and Rain

Beneath the silver crescent of a moon and the lightest of showers from errant clouds, members of Hawaii's last territorial Legislature filed to their seats on a raised platform before the front palace stairs.

There was a roll call of famous names of Hawaii:

Victor S.K. Houston, 82, delegate to Congress, 1927 to 1933. A man who fought for statehood 30 years ago.

Former governors: Ingram M. Stainback, Lawrence Judd,

Senator Oren E. Long and Samuel Wilder King.

Mrs. Joseph R. Farrington, herself a former delegate, was honored both for her statehood efforts and those of her late husband, Joseph R. Farrington, a man who, in the words of Ed Sheehan, master of ceremonies, "Literally gave his life to the cause of statehood."

Said Sheehan: "His father before him, Wallace Rider Farrington (a former governor), is also being honored tonight by her presence here."

Distinguished Guests

Mrs. William F. Quinn, wife of the Governor, Acting Governor and Mrs. Edward E. Johnston and consular officials from 16 foreign countries were among the distinguished guests.

And then the pageant began. The production portrayed the history of Hawaii from the laying of the palace cornerstone in 1859 through the crowning of King Kalakaua and the annexation ceremony.

Iolani Lauhine opened the production with an old Hawaiian chant high atop the palace roof. The show ended with a burst of applause as the American flag was raised with the Hawaiian flag beneath it to the strains of "Hawaii Ponoi."

A group of Maemae students led the crowd in the Oath of Allegiance as the Royal Hawaiian Band played the National Anthem and a 50-gun Marine salute boomed out across the makai side of the palace grounds.

Dropping the newspapers at his side, Governor Quinn reflected on the dramatic happenings of the past couple of days with satisfaction, pride and a feeling of accomplishment. He might have missed the grand celebration at home, but he didn't miss the big performance in Washington. Topping it off, he thought, was his visit with Eisenhower. Bill Quinn smiled when he remembered the president's parting shot and how Ike flashed his famous grin, shook hands and said, "Get out there now and get to work."

≈Chapter Nineteen≈
Transition

"Nothing endures but change."

PLATO

The governor's arrival from Washington was that of a triumphant warrior returning home from battle. Fans, officials and family heaped leis around his neck, smeared his cheeks with kisses and cheered. A statehood banner and "Welcome Home Governor" signs waved throughout the crowd.

Reporters and greeters asked the obvious question. The governor replied, "If I decide to be a candidate for political office in this great state of Hawaii, then at that time I'll decide whether to resign the office of governor."

Quinn predicted that elections would be held by mid-summer and that Hawaii's eventual entry into the union "would probably be in late July or the middle of August."

Mayor Neal Blaisdell wasted no time announcing his intentions that he wanted to be Hawaii's first state governor. He said, "I'm prepared to take on and beat anyone who wants to make a contest of it."

A small news item beneath the spirited headlines quoted Nancy Quinn; she was expecting another child. The Quinns' six children, four boys and two girls, ranged in age from under 2 to

16 years. As to when the child was due, she said, "It might be the first baby of 1960."

Quinn returned to a busy calendar. Visiting dignitaries were frequent in the Islands; the governor's office had to work in appropriate greetings. On the same day that President Eisenhower signed the Hawaii statehood bill—March 18, 1959—King Hussein of Jordan arrived in Honolulu.

Sanford Zalburg wrote in *The Honolulu Advertiser* :

> King Hussein of Jordan arrived yesterday for four days of rest and relaxation from the burden of being the youngest ruler in one of the most troubled spots in the world, the Middle East.
>
> The handsome 5-foot, 3-inch, 23-year-old monarch told reporters in fluent English, "My country is in good shape."
>
> He said that this time he had no trouble flying out of Jordan. Last November two Syrian Russian-built MIGs chased him home while he was flying a royal plane bound for a vacation in Europe.
>
> Hussein and his entourage of 14 Jordanian officers, ministers and court members were greeted at Hickam Air Base by high military and civilian brass, including Governor Quinn, Mayor Blaisdell and Admiral Harry D. Felt, Pacific commander-in-chief.

The next morning the king addressed the Legislature. The members and a large crowd of spectators jammed the House chambers in Iolani Palace.

He congratulated Hawaii on becoming the 50th state, "which you fully deserve," he said, "and on becoming members of the noble American nation."

He told the assembly that this was his first visit to the United

States, and he said, "The Hashemite kingdom of Jordan and its people adhere to the same principles of freedom of nations and world peace as the United States of America.

"We had to struggle to preserve our Arab nationalism and to save our homeland. So far we have succeeded, but a great task still lies before us. With support of the free nations, this task will be fulfilled."

A highlight of Hussein's visit was a poi supper at Washington Place. "When we first met, the king was very down," says Quinn, "but at dinner he warmed up and really had a good time."

Hosts Bill and Nancy Quinn were well aware that King Hussein was a devout Moslem who didn't eat pork. Hence the dinner in his honor was a luau served up in traditional Hawaiian fashion except that the king was served a squab stuffed with wild rice and wrapped in ti leaves instead of the pork everyone else received.

"He tried everything on the menu," Nancy said, "including the lomi lomi salmon, poi, broiled lobster, broiled kumu, chicken luau, haupia, coconut cake and orange juice. I know that he really enjoyed the meal...he even ate island-style with two-finger poi and managed very well."

Two days later the governor drove to the Royal Hawaiian Hotel to have a parting visit with the king. Quinn found Hussein's staff seated on the terrace.

"I asked where his majesty was and they pointed to him, saying, 'He doesn't want to leave.' Hussein was seated in a chair all by himself, overlooking the ocean. His dark eyes, deep in meditation, appeared mesmerized by the rolling surf. As we chatted, I realized that he was overwhelmed by the beauty of this place and he really did not want to leave. But soon it was time and we drove to the airport, said goodbye and parted as friends."

≈

It seemed as though Governor Quinn had scarcely had a chance to unpack from his last journey to Washington, D.C., when he was called to return.

"When the president of the United States says come up and see me, you go. Especially," said Quinn, "if he has given you a major job and just made you a full-fledged American citizen."

Quinn was one of nine governors invited to the White House to discuss ways to strengthen the federal-state unemployment compensation program.

The Advertiser March 19, 1959:

> Quinn, who has an aching back (suffered on the volleyball courts of the Pacific Club) and is so tired he was in bed before 9 o'clock Monday night, would just as soon not go.
>
> But the governor was so concerned about leaving at this crucial time that he sounded out legislator leaders. "Nobody indicated I shouldn't go," he said.

His immediate concern was with Frank Lombardi, territory planning director, whom he had appointed a year before. He knew that Frank was in serious danger of losing his job. The governor had learned that in a caucus, 16 Democrats had agreed to be bound by the "unit rule" on appointment confirmations, and that the majority favored the ouster of Lombardi from the cabinet post. The "unit rule" would pledge all Senate Democrats to vote as a body in accord with the caucus majority when Quinn's appointments reached the floor.

"He (Lombardi) comes to our island to hold meetings," one Neighbor Island senator was quoted as saying, "and he doesn't even bother to call us to let us know what he is doing. He seems to have forgotten that we wrote the act that created his job."

The governor argued that long-range planning could not be done on a short-term basis. "I think Lombardi is the target of criticism because of the impatience of many people to get the planning job done. But it can't be done in a year and that's all the time he's had," Quinn responded at the time.

Only one Democratic senator spoke out against the caucus. Frank Fasi said he would never be bound by unit rule and that he was disgusted by their decision. "Each senator should vote according to his conscience and reach a decision based on the qualifications and moral character of the appointee," Fasi was quoted as saying.

Before his departure to see the president, Quinn once more backed all his appointees and named another 250 people for short-term appointments. Quinn was hopeful, but he knew that crafty, and sometimes unscrupulous, vote-getting tactics could defeat even the best of candidates.

Hawaii would soon have a new chief executive who would name his own appointees; that meant it was possible that Quinn's proposed appointees might not last out the year. The governor hoped the senators might see little or no reason to oppose their confirmations. However, some might expect more cooperation from an appointee kept on tenterhooks, dangling in the hot political air.

Quinn left for Washington braced for a long and uncomfortable flight with his aching back. With the governor was his oldest son, William Jr. "He'll be a big help to me carrying luggage and such," the governor said, referring to his injured back.

At the same time, a political surprise flashed across the horizon. After several days of frantic activity among GOP leaders, Mayor Blaisdell dropped out of the governor's race.

Blaisdell, a *kamaaina* and veteran politician, reportedly acted in part out of loyalty to ex-Governor Samuel King. King had given him his first big break in government when he named Blaisdell territorial welfare director. Blaisdell knew how badly King wanted to be the first elected governor. The Republican Party was relieved not to face a three-way primary fight pitting Blaisdell against Quinn and King.

When Quinn returned from his meeting with the president, he announced the primary would be held in mid-June. That gave rise to a flood of calls offering free advice. Lorrin Thurston, president and general manager of *The Honolulu Advertiser* and chairman of the Hawaii Statehood Commission, came into the executive office one morning and said, Quinn recalled later, "Of course you must resign your position." Then, unabashed, he added, "and I think I should be appointed governor in the interim."

The governor politely declined, saying he had no intention of resigning at the moment.

Speculation around Iolani Palace was that Governor Quinn might run for the U.S. Senate if Jack Burns, who was Hawaii's delegate to Congress and the major Democratic hopeful, announced his candidacy for the gubernatorial post. The rumor was that Interior Secretary Fred Seaton would like to see a Senate seat filled by a Republican. Both political parties were "caught in a logjam," as reported by the evening press, waiting for Burns to make up his mind.

At this time, sad news hit the community in two jolts. Farrant Turner, admired *kamaaina* business and community leader who'd served as secretary of the territory, died of a heart attack. Hundreds of mourners attended services at Central Union Church where they heard Reverend Thomas L. Crosby's eulogy: "...Remember his unostentatious spirit and that there was no place in his life for unnecessary show, ambitious display, pretense or sham."

Within the week, islanders were shocked again. Their beloved Samuel Wilder King, age 72, had suffered a fatal heart attack after undergoing colon surgery. King was laid to rest at Punchbowl National Cemetery near the grave of Turner, who preceded him in death by five days.

A retired Navy captain, King had served Hawaii as a supervisor, delegate to Congress, governor and member of the Legislature. He had lived just long enough to see his Islands granted statehood.

The Primary

"The word politician means different things to different people. Some people consider a politician a dirty person who connives and makes deals, makes promises he never keeps, etc. That's one definition. Another definition is one who brings people together, who works with a materialistic society with people of all different persuasions and exercises leadership to get these people together to do things. That's the high quality of a politician. We see evidences of both," Contributing Editor Bud Smyser wrote in The *Honolulu Star-Bulletin* that spring.

In *The Advertiser* on April 5, 1959:

> QUINN TO RUN FOR GOVERNOR
> SUGGESTS KEALOHA FOR #2 POST
>
> Governor William F. Quinn formally announced that he is a candidate for election for Hawaii's first state governor.
>
> In his prepared statement to the press, he said, "My experience suits me for the job. My sense of duty impels me to try to complete programs now under way for the benefit of our new state."
>
> In addition, he said, "I chose the governorship because

the only position I should run for, grounded in logic, is the position I now hold...I know the job better than anyone else."

Quinn said that he was issuing the statement to end speculation about his nomination. He did not elaborate on the question of resigning from office: "The question is under serious study and I will abide by the decision made."

Although Delegate Burns had not formally announced his candidacy, many knew it was a matter of time. The media and the voters expected a rough battle between Quinn and Burns.

Quinn was faced with other tough assignments at the same time. Voters do not always have the opportunity to see a candidate as an ordinary guy, or as the executive who has to make tough decisions on the spot. Those who worked closely with Governor Quinn faulted him sometimes for being too soft-hearted. The day Quinn fired one of his nominees on the Liquor Commission, they were astonished. Here was a Bill Quinn they had not seen before.

QUINN FIRES COMMISSIONER FOR REMARK

Harry Kronick, a long-time member of the Honolulu Liquor Commission, was fired today by Governor Quinn for charging that Hawaii's Filipinos are dangerous when drinking.

Governor Quinn stated that he had withdrawn Harry Kronick's nomination from the Liquor Commission. "His singling out one of our racial groups as prone to violence was wrong.

"It does not reflect my opinion and has brought disgrace upon my administration."

James Kealoha, Big Island mayor and county chairman, announced at the end of April he would run for lieutenant governor. On the same day, Wilfred Tsukiyama, silver-haired elder legislative statesman, joined the Republican slate as candidate for the U.S. Senate.

"I urged Jimmy to run with me," the governor said. "He's a very popular Hawaiian politician and had been around for a long time. He brings a good balance, being from a Neighbor Island. Furthermore, there won't be two *haoles* seeking the two top jobs."

The barrage of criticism launched by Democratic chiefs against Quinn for not resigning his position continued. The Interior Department had cleared Quinn on the Hatch Act, meaning he could run without resigning, but the Democratic leaders jumped all over him.

William Richardson, chairman of the new state's Democratic Party, said Quinn was being unfair to the people of Hawaii by "spending his time campaigning and neglecting the official duties of this position except those that pertain to his campaign. I deplore his use of Washington Place and Iolani Palace as his virtual campaign headquarters."

Quinn remained silent on the matter, focusing on his legislative agenda. In the session's closing hours, the Democratic-dominated Legislature failed to confirm the appointments of more than 300 nominees to department posts, boards and commissions. The Senate, it was reported, feared saddling the first state governor with officeholders selected by the territorial governor. Quinn accused the Democrats of meddling and interfering with proper administration.

"It's a pity," he told the press, "that actions of this importance should have as their motivation politics rather than the public interest."

Finally Delegate Burns returned from Washington to

announce he had made up his mind: He would open his campaign to be the state's first elected governor. Burns would suffer somewhat from his late arrival. One week before the primary was very little time to get his party organized. However, Burns, a former Honolulu police captain, was reported to be in great spirits and supremely confident that he would wind up in Washington Place two months hence. He took a crack at Quinn:

"He should have resigned. My best information is that he is violating the Hatch Act," Burns said.

Combined *Star-Bulletin* and *Associated Press* dispatches, May 6, 1959 :

Senator James E. Murray, D-Mont., chairman of the Senate Interior and Insular Affairs Committee, challenged the right of territorial governor Quinn to remain in office while campaigning for election as the first governor of the state of Hawaii. Murray called on President Eisenhower to remove Quinn because he refused to give up his $19,000-a-year job as territorial governor when he became a candidate.

The final decision was reached 10 days later:

U.S. RULES QUINN CAN STAY IN OFFICE

The opinion, issued by the Department of the Interior, held that the Hatch Act provisions against partisan political activities of federal employees do not apply to the governor of Hawaii. The governor is a territorial officer.

The Interior Department held further that the Hawaii Statehood Act provides without qualification that all the officers of the territory shall continue to discharge the duties of their offices until the territory is admitted to the Union, including a provision that they may seek election to state or federal office without relinquishing the offices they hold.

That didn't quiet Quinn's opponents. Name-calling began. Over on Maui at a Democratic rally, Deputy County Attorney Kase Higa, speaking on behalf of Burns, said:

"This man Quinn has only been here about 12 years....He is a *malihini*, a *kolea* bird (the plover, a migratory bird) and a carpetbagger.

"If he is elected governor, he will continue to represent the big interests of the Dillinghams, the Castles and Hawaii's other people of great wealth."

At the final count in the primary election, Burns beat Edward Hitchcock for the Democratic nomination and tallied some 20,000 more votes than Bill Quinn, who won the Republican primary. But this was only the prelude. Everyone was waiting for the big one—the general election four weeks away.

The gubernatorial race was expected to be the most exciting in Hawaii's political history. Quinn and Burns hadn't even warmed up. The Republicans conceded that the governor would have an uphill fight to overcome Burns's 20,000-vote primary lead.

The primary votes had barely been tallied when both Burns and Quinn were called to Washington. The governor went for a three-day conference with President Eisenhower on the complex problems involved in easing the Hawaiian Islands into the Union as the 50th state. Burns went to explore complications in the Agricultural Act that could cost Island sugar growers millions of dollars in federal support.

The General Election

An early surprise came when the AFL-CIO endorsed Quinn. Most had assumed that labor naturally voted the Democratic ticket, and had taken for granted that other unions would join the ILWU in backing Burns.

WHY QUINN?
An editorial by the AFL-CIO-IBEW
Local 1260, Electrical Workers Union:

Imagine, if you can, a government in which all these offices are filled by hatchetmen of the ILWU. Imagine a government that condones every act of that organization. In view of the plans which Harry Bridges and James Hoffa have for Hawaii, is that not a frightening thought? Doesn't it seem obvious that we would be cutting our own throats by putting Burns in office?

There is another reason for backing Quinn. The COPE investigators (Committee On Political Education) have found reason to believe that certain Big Business interests, which would like us to believe they are backing Quinn, have actually joined forces with the ILWU faction secretively— and are out to put a knife in Quinn's back. The implications of that alliance should be enough to chill your bones.

"On one of my return flights from Washington, D.C.," Quinn said, "I was planning a talk on fair and reasonable distribution of a tremendous number of state-owned lands. My flight was about to arrive in the Honolulu terminal; I planned to fly right on to Hilo for my scheduled speech, when the thought came to me that this is really a second *mahele*, an attempt again to distribute the land out to the people.

"So instead of 'Land Reform,' as the plan had already been named, I called it 'Second Mahele.' I didn't really think about how many people were bitterly opposed to the Great Mahele because it had not worked. Unfortunately it had put the land into the hands of the wealthy *haoles.*"

Democratic State Chairman Bill Richardson dubbed Quinn's proposal a meaningless pie-in-the-sky plan; Burns called it an "insulting gimmick." Said Burns, "The Hawaiian people, by the *Great Mahele*—Kamehameha III in 1848 issued permission that land could be purchased by private persons—eventually lost all the land they had. Now all the people will be fleeced by this one."

Quinn's brainchild, the "Second Mahele," was so unpopular that experts called it a blunder likely to cost what little chance he had to be elected. The harder Quinn tried to find support for his land division, the more opposition he met. The Democrats called it "unrealistic," "a slick trick," "a fantastic dream," "out of the question."

"I tried to get support to amend the Hawaiian Homes Commission Act because there was a huge backlog of Hawaiians waiting. There were 200 one-acre lots, not particularly good farm country, but only a few a year were awarded. I wanted to amend the act so that we could get some of that farm land for land exchange in metropolitan Oahu where many Hawaiians lived and worked. As soon as I suggested that, there was enormous opposition from the Hawaiians saying, 'Don't you touch a comma in that Hawaiian Homes Commission Act; that was Prince Kuhio's gift to us and we don't want to change a thing.' This, even though the program hadn't served the Hawaiians at all."

On July 13, the headlines read: *BILL QUINN STARTS LIFE AT 40...*with a big smile, a few more gray hairs and a heavy schedule:

> 7 a.m. Talk to workers at American Factors warehouse.
> 9:30 a.m. At Iolani Palace for routine official business, including a press conference where Quinn outlined a pro-

posal for construction of a jet runway over water.

11 a.m. Door-to-door campaigning at Palolo homes...within a half-hour he made 75 front-door visits.

2 p.m. Back to Iolani Palace, then back to Palolo homes.

6 p.m. TV broadcast.

7 p.m. Meeting at private home in Kahala.

10 p.m. Meeting with Honolulu growers.

The general election was just days away when Lawrence H. Fuchs, writer and historian from Brandeis University, insisted on interviewing the governor. Bill finally made time for him that Saturday morning at Washington Place. This was to be one of Fuchs's last interviews before his book, *Hawaii Pono*, was sent to the publisher.

The two talked for a couple of hours. Fuchs stood up to leave. "Well, Governor," Quinn recalled he said, "I'll tell you one thing, based upon my studies. I think you're the best governor the territory of Hawaii has ever had. But you haven't got a chance at winning this election."

The day before the election, the governor, with a final campaign swing on his Monday morning agenda, was scheduled to take a 7:30 a.m. flight to Hilo. Early in the morning *TIME* magazine called and asked if it could get a picture right away. Almost instantly the photographer appeared at the front steps of Iolani Palace. The *TIME* writer, to insure a good story, hopped aboard and flew with Quinn to the Big Island. He told Quinn that he had been in town for several days, that the magazine had a portrait of Burns set for publication. In the last day or so, however, the reporter said he had heard that Quinn might win; hence the last-minute pursuit.

The Advertiser the day before had commented that Burns, on the basis of his strong primary showing, was the favorite. Other observers now agreed that Quinn had made rapid strides and was

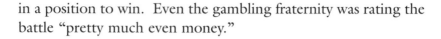
in a position to win. Even the gambling fraternity was rating the battle "pretty much even money."

Election Night

"Nancy and I were at a small gathering in a suite at the Royal Hawaiian Hotel listening to the returns on the radio. It was around 8 o'clock at night and the report began to sound more and more like I had lost," Quinn recalled.

"We left shortly after to go to my headquarters and concede the election to Jack. However, as we drove along with the car radio on, it sounded suddenly like things were changing—changing enough for me to realize that it might not be the proper time for me to concede. Instead, we passed headquarters and drove on home."

"I will never forget our arrival at Washington Place," Nancy said, "There was Josephine Santos, the children's nurse, running down the stairway, arms waving and shouting, 'You won! You won! Governor, you won!" I was stunned. Was it true or not? I had never seen Mrs. Santos so excited. She was always calm and soft-spoken even during the children's rackety times.

"Just then our housekeeper called Bill to the phone. 'Governor, Mr. Burns is on the phone.'"

Quinn added, "Jack Burns was conceding to me. It was such a surprise."

The Quinns headed back to campaign headquarters. As they approached on Kapiolani Boulevard, a black limousine came from the opposite direction. A victorious Hiram Fong emerged. Fong had bested Wilfred Tsukiyama in the primary, and now had defeated Democrat Frank Fasi to become one of the state's two first U.S. senators. The newly elected governor and the newly elected senator embraced in the middle of the boulevard amid cheers, honking horns and flashing cameras.

Quinn's election was a great surprise to many. Even with influential endorsements and great personal popularity, Quinn was always considered the *malihini* who didn't have a chance against Jack Burns. Although he'd been governor for two years, Quinn was still only a 12-year resident of the Islands; the Democrats, assuming that Burns was a shoo-in, put their campaign efforts elsewhere. Quinn came from behind to win the election by 4,500 votes.

On Tuesday, July 28, 1959, William F. Quinn, the last appointed governor of the territory of Hawaii, became the first elected governor of the state of Hawaii.

⪻Chapter Twenty⪼
The Autopsy

"It is morale that wins the victory."
                                    GEORGE C. MARSHALL

Vocal and written commentaries on Hawaii's first state election by political analysts flooded the presses and jammed the air waves, in the Islands and across the nation. Accolades to the new state governor poured like the rains in the valley that sweep from the mountains to the sea.

The evening before the inaugural The *Star-Bulletin* published a "Portrait of Quinn," a "Man of Energy and Decision:"

> Governor Quinn will step out of office tomorrow and step right back in again. He's a battle-tested man in a difficult position, responsible to the people instead of to the president.
>
> The men around Quinn say the immediacy to campaign hard before the general election brought several facts about the man to the fore.
>
> First, he wanted the governorship as fervently as anybody ever wanted anything.
>
> Second, he displayed almost phenomenal energy.
>
> Third, an absolute must in Quinn's campaign was meet-

ing the people wherever they were and regardless of fatigue:

Quinn talked in a gathering of garbage collectors at sun-up. He hiked through housing areas and Chinatown in the heat of the day.

At night he stumped before bowling leagues, attended weddings, dropped in at cocktail parties, and oftentimes broke into a busy evening to do his television stint.

At 10 p.m. or even later, he'd go into session with his strategy committee and hash over problems—sometimes until the wee hours.

And seasoned onlookers say, he's serious about the "Second Mahele." He wouldn't have raised the point, they say, unless he intended to follow through on it.

Author James A. Michener, who had vigorously supported John Burns's candidacy for governor, called Quinn's political instincts a "major state asset." He cited as an example how Quinn handled firing Liquor Commissioner Harry Kronick, the man who spoke disparagingly of Filipinos. To replace Kronick on the commission, Quinn immediately appointed a Filipino-American, a Democrat.

"Mainland politics is played this way," Michener wrote in the October 23, 1959 issue of The Honolulu Advertiser and continued:

> Quinn was quite correct in making this spectacular move. I know, of course, that he had to appoint a Democrat, but his choice of Alfred Laureta, Hawaii's first Filipino barrister, was inspired politicking.
>
> Like Mark Hatfield, who won his (Oregon) governorship against odds, Quinn conducted his campaign on the basis that Kahala (strong *haole* Republican district) had to vote for him, whereas if he worked hard in the bowling alleys and in the cane fields he could pick up a lot of otherwise

Democratic votes. And he was right. It was Democrats who provided his margin of victory.

NEWSWEEK stressed the overall Republican Party triumph:

> To the Republicans who had tightened their belts for a meager diet of political poi, it was a rich and heady Hawaiian feast, complete with the suckling pig of patronage.
>
> Burns's ILWU backing became a political millstone. The specter of a Bridges-Hoffa alliance under a friendly state administration was too much for most Hawaiians.
>
> Aside from the Bridges issue, the results seemed largely dictated by personalities. Republican Quinn, for example, turned out to be a far more effective television personality than Democrat Burns.

TIME magazine's cover featured a smiling Quinn with a pink carnation lei and devoted eight pages to color photographs and five pages to election commentary and Hawaiian history:

> The new Hawaii, building on the strong foundations of education and tolerance left by the old, knows that it already has survived upheavals in the economy, politics and racial structure that would have rocked many another land....Bill Quinn and the 50th state never share a moment's doubt that they are heading toward a whole new future bright with alo-has.

On Monday, August 3, 1959, *The Advertiser* listed the reasons for Burns's defeat:

> Question: What beat Jack Burns?
> Answer: A lot of things.
> 1. Jimmy Hoffa's announcement of the tie-up between the ILWU and the Teamsters to "carve up" unorganized

labor in Hawaii.

2. Bill Quinn's personality. His ability clearly shown in the two years he held the governorship.

3. The split in the Democratic Party ranks, which was aggravated by the rebel Democratic and Republican coalition in the territorial House of Representatives.

4. Burns's personality. "They're starting to call him Old Stoneface," said a friend. "I melted when Bill Quinn smiled at me on television. Jack Burns was like a solemn portrait...seldom smiling," said a woman voter.

5. Burns's mistakes—a fairly long list and rather odd when you consider what a seasoned and how masterful a politician he is. For instance, his speech at the ILWU convention in April giving the ILWU credit for bringing democracy to the Islands.

6. Quinn made mistakes. The "Second Mahele" was a debatable campaign pitch. He may have lost as many votes as he won. But Quinn fought an aggressive, constructive type of campaign. He didn't threaten. He didn't knock down his opponent. He cleverly refused to make capital out of the ILWU-Teamster tie-up. He didn't even mention it.

The Honolulu Advertiser :
    HAWAII TELLS THE WORLD

The voters of Hawaii (population 570,000) Tuesday gave a dramatic demonstration of democracy in action to fellow Americans and to the world.

They did it by:

* Turning out 98 percent of the registered vote, reaffirming that Hawaii takes its political rights and responsibilities seriously.

* Performing maturely and independently, with party labels running second to personalities and performance in the

choice of officials. And it lies in the cosmopolitan, bipartisan delegation which goes to Congress:

Hiram L. Fong, Republican, American of Chinese ancestry, U.S. senator.

Oren E. Long, Democrat, former governor, U. S. senator.

Daniel K. Inouye, Democrat, American of Japanese ancestry, U.S. House of Representatives.

(The fact that Daniel Inouye, a descendant of Japanese immigrants, became the first man in history to win a Hawaii election by more than 100,000 votes should ring around the globe.)

These men in Washington will make not only that capital but all of Asia and the world take notice.

OLD GLORY NOW HAS 50 STARS
Honolulu Star-Bulletin

On Friday, August 21, 1959, President Eisenhower signed the Hawaii Statehood Proclamation, ending the Islands' long history as an American territory and beginning Hawaii's full partnership with the other 49 states.

A phone call from the Oval Office flashed the historic words to Governor Quinn, who moments later took the oath of office and was sworn in as the first Hawaii state governor. Two minutes later James Kealoha was sworn in as lieutenant governor.

The oaths were administered by Associate Supreme Court Justice Masaji Marumoto at an informal swearing-in ceremony held in the governor's office at Iolani Palace. Only the families of the two top leaders were invited to attend, and the formal inauguration was scheduled for Saturday, August 29, 1959.

UA MAU KE IA 0 KA AINA I KA PONO
"The Life of the Land Is Preserved in Righteousness."

A large photograph of the Hawaii state seal engraved with these Hawaiian words and an editorial in *The Advertiser* asserted that as Hawaii's first state governor, William F. Quinn would have power, opportunity and responsibility of a magnitude seldom given to an elected state official anywhere in the United States:

> "The power lies in naming an entirely new state administration and a entirely new state judiciary—about 460 jobs in all.
>
> "As governor, his obligation is first to all the people of Hawaii: Republicans, Democrats, independents, businessmen, wage earners, teachers, doctors, civil servants, men and women.
>
> "And all of Hawaii will be watching to see that he meets this obligation. Governor Quinn has an opportunity to perform great things and great things are expected.
>
> "With great power goes great responsibility."

PART FOUR

≋Chapter Twenty-One≋

The First Inauguration

"I pledge all my talents and energies to the common good."

WILLIAM F. QUINN

The new state of Hawaii saw its first elected governor inaugurated on August 29, 1959. Contrasts marked the beginning of a new era for Hawaii and her people. The inaugural stage was at the foot of Iolani Palace's stairs. Five thousand guests were seated in the wide-entrance drive. The Hawaii Air National Guard's 119th fighter squadron thundered across blue skies, signaling the start of the historic ceremony.

Governor and Mrs. Quinn were escorted to the stage; an honor guard stood at attention and a military band played "Blue Hawaii," the tune that had became Quinn's campaign song. At different stops along the political trail, there'd be a request for him to sing the song.

When Lieutenant Governor and Mrs. Kealoha were escorted to their seats, the band switched to Jimmy Kealoha's hometown song, the "Hilo March."

With a glance and a wink, the governor and first lady smiled at their six children and "Nana" Quinn, Bill's mother, seated in the front row.

Also in the front row was Aunt Jennie Wilson, widow of former Honolulu Mayor John H. Wilson.

"I was 8 years old when they built this palace," said Aunt Jennie. "It was a kingdom then and now it's a state...I don't know if I can sit here or not; they might run me out," she laughed.

"Hawaii Ponoi," the official anthem of the monarchy, the territory and now the state, opened the formalities. Reverend Abraham K. Akaka of Kawaiahao Church gave the benediction. After Quinn and Kealoha were sworn in, state Senator Wilfred C. Tsukiyama stepped to the podium. The audience rose to its feet.

"...The first governor of the state of Hawaii, the honorable William Francis Quinn."

Bill Quinn was not quite as tall as the eight royal kahili flanking the podium, but he was as colorful, bedecked as he was with flower leis. His words rang clear and strong, holding the attention of the multiracial crowd:

> Our state government should and will draw its character from the crucible of mixed races, which is our strength.
>
> ...We of Hawaii of whatever ancestry should drink deep of the cultural heritage that is ours from all of the many races that make up our people."
>
> Now the time has come...now the solemn hour is upon us...for the first time America has enfolded its people of Polynesia and Asian ancestry in its warm embrace.
>
> The banner of man's equality in a free world has been lifted high for the enslaved worlds to see.
>
> Excerpts: Selected Addresses and Messages
William Francis Quinn
Hawaii State Archives

He called for providing the poor, the disabled and the aged with sufficient care and aid. He noted the need for more educational and economic opportunities for Hawaii's young people, and ended his address with a pledge:

> "...All my talents and energies for the common good...I ask for your encouragement, your help and your prayers."

Throughout his speech the spectators, many of whom had deserted their reserved seats to stand in the shade of the trees on the palace lawn, applauded.

Nana Quinn had tears in her eyes. "Every mother kind of dreams of this," she whispered. "It's thrilling."

William L. Kanakanui, 71, watched Governor Quinn's inauguration from almost the same spot where he had stood in 1898 to watch the American flag go up over the newly annexed Hawaii.

> Kanakanui said, "I was only 10 years old when I watched the flag ceremony," he said. "There were two warships in the harbor. Their sailors walked up to the palace and I saw the Hawaiian flag come down and the American flag go up.
>
> "It was a bright day like this one. There was a platform built onto the palace just like today and Sanford B. Dole was there as head of the Hawaiian government. Later in the day there was dancing—mostly hula—and singing and many luaus."

Washington Place

Quinn proceeded to the inaugural reception. Thousands of people extended their congratulations to the Quinns and the Kealohas. Guests massed four and five abreast down the walkways in front of the official residence, waiting to pass through the reception in the front hallway.

Honolulu Star-Bulletin, August 29, 1959:

> The afternoon's reception to which 5,000 islanders are flocking to felicitate the governor they elected, has another familiar setting, Washington Place, the American Georgian-style mansion which was the home of Hawaii's last queen, Lili'uokalani, until her death in 1917 and which has been the official residence of Hawaii governors for nearly 40 years.
>
> Strands of maile and flowers from the Neighbor Islands, *kahili* of white and yellow plumeria blossoms flank the entrance while pure white *kahilis* stand in the living room.
>
> On the queen's piano is a superb arrangement of orchids in varying shades of purple and lavender from the H. Alexander Walker gardens. Acting as junior hosts and hostesses are the Quinn youngsters, six this time, instead of the five who were present for the last reception. Mary Kaiulani, the youngest, was born just a couple of months after their father's last inauguration.
>
> She and 5-year-old Ann Cecily have matching frocks of white pique, trimmed with piping of red and blue.
>
> Another small Quinn will join the family this winter and Mrs. Quinn's costume is therefore a smart, straight-line anticipation dress of gray and white checked silky cotton, topped with a matching street-length coat of organdy. The coat features a soft collar effect with a bow. Gray and white plaid pumps complete the afternoon outfit.

Once inside, the crowds moved to the lanai and out to the spacious lawn. There the punch, cookies and cakes were served while musicians and dancers paid tribute to the new governor and first lady.

After the second hour of standing in the receiving line and with hundreds of guests yet to meet, Nancy slipped off her high-heeled shoes and breathed a quiet sigh. Bill, understanding her weariness, immediately placed his left hand on her lower back. After six children and their seventh on the way, he knew where a little support might help. At that moment a shutter behind them clicked at their backs.

The next day the picture was published as part of the coverage of the historical day. As usual, readers responded. One handwritten note said:

> "Dear Governor and Mrs. Quinn, I found this adorable picture and just had to send it to you! Congratulations to the governor for the wonderful work he's doing. Our thoughts and prayers are with both of you. Aloha from two amateur tennis players.
>
> "Lu & Danny Wong"

In the same mail came another letter that, if it hadn't been so cruel, might have been amusing. The writer compared Nancy's loose maternity dress and shoelessness with a second picture, published on the same page, of two inmates dressed in the baggy uniforms of the Women's Detention Home. Their dresses resembled wrinkled flour sacks. The typed note, filled with abusive language, deplored the appearance of the first lady, and said she didn't deserve to stand next to the governor. The letter claimed she inflicted embarrassment on the "good people of our new state." It was signed, "Disgusted male."

⤜Chapter Twenty-Two⤛
The New State in Business

"...We share an historic task."

GOVERNER QUINN
To First State Legislature, 1959

Monday morning, August 31, 1959, Iolani Palace opened its beveled glass doors for business and launched its first special session of the state Legislature. Among the milling spectators, entertainers and legislative employees, there was an air of urgency, mixed with the gaiety of myriad Hawaiian colors. While the palace's downstairs corridor teemed with humanity, Governor Quinn and his aides were busy in their second-floor offices, winding up work on Quinn's speech to be delivered before the joint session that afternoon.

"The special session was to deal with the reorganization bill," says Quinn, "the same bill developed during the past sessions. Oh, such things as the state flower were thrown in there, but mainly it dealt with the formation of the state government. Of course," he added, "this was a massive bill full of great changes, I mean, some changes were really quite controversial."

The day before the special session opened, three head-shot photos spread dramatically across *The Advertiser's* editorial page.

193

The headline read:

DESTINY IN THEIR HANDS...QUINN, HILL, CRAVALHO

The first state Legislature convenes tomorrow. Its major job will be to design the machinery for a new state government.

This is a complicated, technical job. It is so complex that many of the problems have not yet come to light, will not until the lawmakers are right on top of them.

The Senate is controlled by Republicans under President William H. Hill. The House of Representatives is controlled by Democrats, led by speaker Elmer F. Cravalho. In the governor's chair sits a Republican, William F. Quinn.

Despite the division of power politically, each of these men has emphasized the need for a nonpartisan approach. There is absolutely no doubt of their sincerity in this.

Political sniping will be out of place. The state's need at this critical time makes it imperative for each and every legislator—and the governor—to conduct himself as unselfishly as is humanly possible.

The Big Island's William "Doc" Hill called the Senate to order at 10:02. Hill, the Senate president-designate and its senior member, was known for his talking mynah birds, bushy sideburns and unpredictable hearing aid. A self-made millionaire, Hill exercised political influence proportionate to his financial power. His domain was primarily in Hilo and East Hawaii on the Big Island. With his large real estate holdings, a theater chain, a laundry business and an automobile dealership, he employed at least 600.

Elmer Cravalho, the Maui representative, was named by the 33 controlling Democrats to be the House speaker. Youthful, despite his thorough political seasoning, Cravalho would in a few years be elected Maui's mayor.

The two bodies of the Legislature came together in a joint

session to hear the governor's speech. Quinn called for a non-partisan approach to compressing the sprawling government into not more than 20 major departments. He urged the lawmakers to go slow, not try to do the whole reorganization in the one short session. He called on the Legislators "to specify the broad outline of the new government and leave the executive to fill in the details."

The governor stressed that he was not submitting independently a plan for reorganization. Instead, he accepted the work of the legislative interim committee, formed by the last Democratic Legislature, as a point of departure.

As The *Advertiser* said, "This alone is strong evidence of the governor's sincerity on the points of nonpartisanship and cooperation with the Legislature."

An important job facing the Legislature was to figure out what were the duties of the lieutenant governor. In Article IV, Section 2 of the state Constitution, there was only one specific task: The lieutenant governor will take over the duties of the governor when the official is out of state or is unable to carry out the duties of the office. The lieutenant governor should then perform such other duties as might be assigned by law, thus tossing the final word back to the legislature.

Even before the inauguration, newspaper stories said that the governor and the lieutenant governor, James Kealoha, disagreed on the distribution of patronage. Kealoha was quoted as saying that before he agreed to be Quinn's running mate, he had laid down certain conditions. "They included an understanding that this was to be a joint-venture...that if elected we both would participate jointly in the organization and administration of the government. I assume," Kealoha said, "this joint-venture understanding will include appointments to the various judicial, cabinet and commission posts...."

Quinn had urged Kealoha to run with him. Kealoha was the

popular mayor of the Island of Hawaii, part-Hawaiian with an affable personality and a great smile. It looked like a good balance for the two top executives. "Jimmy was the best representative of the Big Island and as such he was needed in the position," said Quinn.

"At that time you voted for the governor and the lieutenant governor separately. You did not cast just one vote. Jimmy was well supported by the ILWU, which was opposed to me...and as it turned out Jimmy got more votes overall than I did in the general election."

Quinn continued, "In one of our first meetings Jimmy thought that we ought to spilt the appointments 50-50. He came to me and said, 'As your lieutenant governor I got more votes than you did, Governor...I think that we should share all the appointments.'

"I told him, 'I'm sorry, but there is no way I can do that. I'm the governor. I have the responsibility. You can stand up when I'm out of the way but I cannot turn over the chief executive's powers of appointment to you.' He got very angry," said Quinn.

Reporters from both newspapers wanted a statement on the rumored "Quinn-Kealoha feud."

> Governor Quinn and James Kealoha announced yesterday they have reached a "mutually satisfactory" understanding on patronage matters.
>
> The announcement was made jointly by the two men after an hour-long closed-door session in Quinn's office. It followed a week of speculation that they were feuding on how to distribute the hundreds of available jobs.
>
> The governor told newsmen that all appointments to boards and commissions would be made with the "knowledge and consent" of Kealoha.

But things got stickier. Quinn tried to placate Kealoha; still they ended up in a donnybrook.

Kealoha had made a promise to a former territorial judge on Oahu. The judge, Quinn said, "was from the Big Island and a very good friend of Jimmy's."

Quinn had made commitments too. Bert Kobayashi, a classmate of Quinn's at Harvard Law School who later would become Jack Burns's attorney general and then appointed to the state Supreme Court, was head of the Hawaii Bar Association. Quinn had promised Kobayashi and the Bar Association that he would submit all judicial names to them "and if they found the person was not qualified they would tell me that they didn't think them qualified, and I wouldn't appoint them.

"The Bar Association's decision on Jimmy's friend was both speedy and decisive," said Quinn. "They replied, 'Nothing doing...this guy's been handing out masterships and it's been a crooked deal.' I talked to Bert and the committee and explained that we were just starting a new government with a lieutenant governor (where we'd never had one before) and that I had to try and make things work with him.

"Then I asked if I were to appoint this fellow a judge, but put him on another island where he couldn't do as much damage as where all the litigation was, would they agree to the appointment? That's the way it was settled."

Things didn't get better between Quinn and Kealoha, however. About the same time, there was a testimonial honoring the lieutenant governor. Two thousand gathered at the St. Louis College Alumni Association Clubhouse for a "Welcome to Oahu" luau. At the last minute, Governor Quinn had to cancel his plans to attend. Jimmy took it as a personal affront, Quinn said.

"Things were just bad from the day it started," said Quinn. "Since he got more votes than I, he thought that he would run the next time. It started off that way and it was never any better; he was just sitting over there trying to undercut and top me all the time.

"Then I had the real problem," said Quinn. "We're now a state; I have to make about 550 appointments. All of them! All the judges, all the department heads, deputy department heads, all the commission members, everybody else, starting right from scratch." Quinn shook his head at the memory.

"I decided, right off the bat, that the first thing I was going to do was appoint the Supreme Court. I decided, being as naive as I was, that I was going to try to set an example for those to come. I was going to try to get as objective and as bipartisan a court as I could."

Before inauguration and before appointments were made, the newly elected U.S. representative, Dan Inouye, a Democrat, said during a Washington, D.C., radio talk show that he could envision Quinn building a personal political empire. "In six months after he has completed his appointments, he will have a vast political machine." Inouye said that Quinn could appoint about 750 people to government jobs. Some of those in turn would appoint underlings. "This pushes towards 1,000 the number of persons expected to be loyal to the Republican governor." Inouye ended his broadcast with, "The election of Governor Quinn is a great threat to the Democratic Party."

If the governor heard Inouye, he paid no attention. He was too busy lining up justices. "I got some very fine people," said Quinn. He named Cable Wirtz, a Democrat and an experienced circuit judge from Maui; Rhoda Lewis, whom Quinn viewed as a truly nonpartisan lawyer; Charlie Cassidy, a Republican and a leader of the Bar; Wilfred Tsukiyama, lawyer and longtime senator in the territorial Senate, and Masaji Marumoto, another lawyer who was a veteran of the 442nd infantry.

"It was a marvelous group; it had a high level of integrity and legal capability," Quinn said.

The days that followed were wired with problems. "When I was about to send those names down, I got a call from state Senator Vincent Esposito," said Quinn. "Vince was a dynamic and volatile lawyer and one of the *haole* leaders of the Democratic Party."

Esposito said a small group of Democrats wanted to see Quinn. With Esposito, Quinn said, were Tom Gill and Nelson Doi. Gill was Island-born and Quinn thought perhaps the most brilliant of the new Democratic leaders. Doi later was to become lieutenant governor under Jack Burns.

They came to talk about the appointments. Quinn said Esposito told him that as members of the state Senate, "We have the power to advise and consent, particularly the judges." Quinn said Esposito told him the Democrats represented 11/25ths of the state Senate "and we believe we are entitled to name 11/25ths of the appointments, starting with the judges." Quinn said Esposito told him, "That's what the Constitution means, Governor, that the Senate advise and consent, the majority names a majority, the minority names a minority."

Quinn said he countered, "Vince, you must be out of your mind. There's no way I can do that. I'm going to send you good names and you can act as you see fit. I think you owe it to the public to judge these people on their merits and if they're good you should confirm them."

The three stood aside and caucused for a couple of minutes, then, Quinn recalled Esposito said, "Well...here's fair warning to you, Governor. We, all 11 of us, are going to vote against all of your appointments."

"And they did," said Quinn.

The Republican state senators arrived next. That conversation, according to Quinn, ran something like this: "Governor, what we'd like you to do is name all your judges. Send them all down at once; both the circuit judges and Supreme Court judges, because we might want to..." Quinn said they rocked their hands, indicating they may want to switch the appointments around.

Governor Quinn said, "No. I'm going to send you the Supreme Court. After you act on the Supreme Court, then I will send you the circuit judges."

At first the senators objected strenuously; finally they agreed.

Quinn sent down his five names "and the vote was 14 to 11 on all five judges...but not before the Democrats had publicly blasted my appointments. Then I started making cabinet appointments."

Quinn's press secretary, Larry Nakatsuka, was an experienced newspaperman who'd been a labor reporter. "I decided that he would be a good man to head the Department of Labor because he was so knowledgeable, fair and a liberal thinker."

Quinn sent Nakatsuka's name down, and of course the 11 Democrats voted against him. But this time, "two Republicans joined and Larry's name was defeated 13 to 12....The ILWU didn't want Larry and in those days they were strong, a real power." Quinn said the ILWU leadership didn't like Nakatsuka because a decade before, Larry, as a newspaper reporter, had written some stories about the big shipping strike of 1949. "They didn't like the way he wrote that and they carried that grudge to defeat him 10 years later," Quinn said.

Quinn sent Bob Ellis' name down to be commissioner of land and natural resources. "Bob was a sterling public servant, had been my administrative director and had done an outstanding job." Quinn had big plans for the land department: "I had a whole program to make use of some of our state lands for public and social purposes with Hawaiians and others." Republican Randy Crossley was angry with Ellis over the reorganization session of the Legislature. Crossley got fellow Republican Bernard

Kinney to vote against Ellis. They joined the 11 Democrats, "making it 13 to 12 and Bob was defeated. This is what was happening," Quinn said.

"That went on for a while," Quinn said, "and the man who first broke that pattern, who said, 'I just can't do this anymore; I'm not serving the public,' was George Ariyoshi, one of the famous 11."

The special session was coming to a close. Toward the end of October the governor got a visit from the president of Chevron, Ted Peterson.

Quinn remembered Peterson said to him, "Governor, I know this is late, but Vice President Nixon was supposed to come to our Business Advisory Council meeting in Pebble Beach, California."

The council was made up of some of the major business executives of the country. He said that the vice president had been scheduled to address them the following Saturday night and had been forced to cancel.

"I've been asked by our executive committee to ask you if you would address our Business Council," Peterson said.

Quinn answered, "I've got this first special session here and I don't see how...but I'd like to talk to these people on Hawaii's economic development...to come over here and invest now."

"I knew it was a golden opportunity to promote Hawaii," Quinn recalled, "if I could do it. I first talked with Elmer Cravalho, speaker of the House, and "Doc" Hill, president of the Senate. They both said, 'By all means go. This session is just being wrapped up now. No problems.'"

James Michener, one of the most successful authors in the world, wrote a series of articles appearing in the evening *Star-Bulletin*. He evaluated the political workings of Hawaii and called Quinn's political instinct "a major asset":

While performing his chores at home, Quinn has not overlooked the national scene. He has made judicious public appearances and statements. His public relations people have whipped up releases linking him with the vice-presidency.

And it is not ridiculous to discuss him for some national position, perhaps as a future secretary of the interior.

Before going to Pebble Beach, the governor went to the Midwest and delivered the Navy Day Address to the Chicago Council of the Navy League on October 27, 1959:

> *This is my first Mainland speech since I became the first elected governor of the 50th state. I have had to decline numerous requests—I guess the first governor of a new state is a rare attraction, particularly if he is a Republican—but I had the strongest inclination to accept this one even though our first Legislature is about to adjourn after grappling with problems of becoming a state and there's much to be done at home.*
>
> *I accepted not only because I'm a Navy man, but because I, and the people of Hawaii, have, I truly believe, a deeper understanding and more profound appreciation of the United States Navy than any other community in the country. We experienced in terror the decimation of our Pacific Fleet on December 7, 1941.*
>
> *...The countries of Southeast Asia, living under the shadow of the Chinese communists, depend upon American sea power to shore them up as they stand with their backs to the sea against the Red Giant. They depend upon our economic assistance. They depend upon our military aid. Most of all, they depend upon our mighty Navy. They depend upon it as a show of retaliatory force indicating the power, the readiness and the willingness of the United States to support them in their efforts to remain free nations.*

His speech was long and full. He spoke of how our big stick had kept the cold war from bursting into flames; he warned, "We must speak softly but with conviction. We must speak with an understanding heart. Something is needed besides mobile military power, economic and military assistance...."

The next day Quinn flew to Pebble Beach, on the picturesque coastline of California, for the Business Advisory Council conference.

The roster of the council read like a "who's who" of the chairmen and presidents of the biggest U.S. business concerns. Officers of the council were: S.D. Bechtel, president of Bechtel Corporation; Roger M. Blough, chairman of U.S. Steel; Ralph J. Cordiner, chairman of General Electric; Frank Stanton, president of Columbia Broadcasting System, and J. Weinberg of Goldman, Sachs and Company.

"So I went and addressed this group," said Quinn. "I was very happy to have the opportunity. I thought I could do good for my state in getting this contact with people as influential as these in the business world." He told the council:

> *I suppose I was asked here tonight because you wanted to take a look at me. I came because I wanted to take a look at you. And this mutual curiosity will give me a chance to thump the barrel for the fabulous people and the fabulous state I represent.*
>
> *Because we are convinced that if we want to attract your attention, to think of locating new industries in Hawaii, government's job is to help provide the best possible business climate—land, roads, homes for your people, schools for your children and a well-informed population sympathetic to your problems and desires.*
>
> *Might I add immodestly that in speaking to Mainland investors, I have coined the phrase "Sun-tanned-gilt-edged" in describing the state and the people I represent. And if you can tell me of any other state in the Union where you could have a profitable business interest you could visit with such personal*

delight, I will eat the hat that I never wear in Honolulu, because we are a people who like to go bola and bareheaded under the sun.

Following the speech and an after-dinner gathering, Quinn went to his hotel room. "I found three or four urgent telephone messages; one or two from newspapers; one from Bob Ellis, my administrative assistant; one from Doc Hill," the state Senate president.

In the closing moments of the Legislature, trouble broke out. "Republican Randy Crossley, who thought he should be governor," Quinn said, had gotten angry with Ellis during the negotiations over the government organization bill. Once again, Crossley got Kinney, "another Republican friend of his who owed him something, and they went to the other side and the bill did not pass."

"They didn't vote it down, but Randy was the one who kept it from being passed before adjournment. I flew right back and I got the leadership together and we finally agreed that we would just have a five-day special session to pass the bill."

Quinn said the dispute was over a small matter. "We settled that in conference and then they just met for about 10 minutes a day for five days at considerable cost, but they passed that bill for the organization of the state government."

The bill cleared the Senate by a 23-2 margin. Voting "no" were Crossley, the proverbial Republican thorn, and Nadao Yoshinaga, a Democrat of Maui.

The bill was personally delivered to the governor by Senate President Hill and House Speaker Cravalho, who, Quinn recalled, summed it up as "mission accomplished."

A week after the second special session was concluded, Quinn's foes criticized:

When Governor Quinn stayed home last week to keep an eye on the Legislature, he was forced—painfully enough—to bypass a gold-plated chance to build national stature for himself.

Behind the smoke screen of criticism for the legislators lay what politicians knew was an unpleasant but inescapable political fact: Quinn should have been there to ride herd on the legislators.

The Honolulu Advertiser

⁓ Chapter Twenty-Three ⁓
Admission Day

*...Justice shall flourish like the palm tree and righteous-
ness shall perpetuate the land."*

WILLIAM F. QUINN

The Honolulu Stadium was located at the foot of Manoa Valley, "valley of the rainbows," a couple of blocks oceanside from the University of Hawaii campus. The stadium was a relic of the 1920s; the only structure of its kind on the island, it was a football-baseball facility enclosed by grandstands with a capacity of nearly 25,000. Most of the old wooden, termite-eaten seats had built-in air-conditioning when the breezes came up through the cracks. Fans used to say, "It's okay...we won't fall through as long as the termites hold hands."

The venerable stadium provided the scene of the historic Statehood Dedication ceremonies on November 29, 1959.

During his remarks, Governor Quinn was enthusiastic in his endorsement of a plan for the East-West Center and he stressed new ways of making the 50th state more useful to the Pacific area and to the world. The ceremonies were filled with pomp and pageantry: an hour-long military band concert, followed by the University of Hawaii chorus, more speeches by state dignitaries and finally the gala 50th State Revue, featuring songs and dances of Hawaii's multiracial peoples: Hawaiians, Chinese, Japanese,

Koreans, Tahitians, Samoans and Filipinos.

For little Mary Quinn, 2-year-old daughter of the governor, the high point of the afternoon was the drill display by the Pacific Fleet Drum and Bugle Corps. Slipping from her chair she gazed upward, mouth open and eyes transfixed; she was awed by a giant uniformed Marine who, towering above her, trumpeted his horn.

After the stadium ceremony, a sparkling fireworks display illuminated Ala Moana Park.

A gala 50th-state dinner was held Saturday night for more than 400 at the Royal Hawaiian Hotel. U.S. senators, congressmen, governors and representatives from Asian countries were seated 50-strong at the longest table ever set up in the Monarch Room. It stretched from the west side, adjacent to Waikiki Beach, across to the dining room's entrance. Quinn had the formidable task of making the introductions.

"The governor did it swiftly and with aplomb and yet had a sentence or more of laudatory remarks for every guest so presented," it was reported.

Popular former Honoluluans, Ambassador and Mrs. You Chan Yang, headed the honoree list. Dr. Yang was the main speaker of the evening. Petite Mrs. Yang was gowned in gold brocade with a white fox cape.

According to the social page of _The Honolulu Advertiser,_ Clare Booth Luce, present with her publisher husband, Henry Luce, was a picture of quiet elegance in her white sheath with blue flower print worn with a black sequined scarf. She wore a necklace, earrings, bracelet and a brooch of diamonds and sapphires. "A gift from my husband," she said, "some 20 years ago."

The ever-glamorous lady was known for her smashing popularity as ambassador to Italy in the '50s; Mrs. Luce was being considered as a possible ambassador to Brazil. She'd been criticized for what she conceded was her use of "very intemperate language" against Presidents Roosevelt and Truman. The New York Herald Tribune on May 2, 1959, had taken her side:

Mrs. Luce's crime lay in the truthfulness of her statement that Franklin Roosevelt "lied us into war in 1941"; and, as a matter of fact, the truth can sound very intemperate indeed.

Mrs. Luce's presence at the Statehood Dinner, as it did just about everywhere, added flair.

Later, she sent the Quinns a postcard from the Magic Kingdom:

> Disneyland is the most fairyland city in the world. I don't think it has a governor...but if it had he couldn't be wiser or smarter or more charming than Hawaii's and there is no princess in Fantasyland lovelier than his lady. This is just a note written on a postal, on the plane, standing off L.A. to tell you both that our visit during the state ceremonies was unforgettable. And that we think you are both terrific.
>
> Happy Holidays—Clare & Harry Luce

Statehood festivities aside, there remained the business of government for Bill Quinn.

Monday at noon the governor flew out to attend the National Governor's Conference in West Virginia. Quinn's journey was cut short. His esteemed cabinet member, Land Commissioner Eric Reppun, only 44, had died of a heart attack. Quinn hastened home for the services.

"I feel a tremendous loss, officially and personally, because Eric was an outstanding member of the cabinet, first as president of the Board of Agriculture and Forestry and more recently as the land commissioner.

"... I relied a great deal on his background knowledge and his counsel. Hawaii has lost a valuable and respected public servant." Quinn had intended Reppun to be commissioner of land and natural resources in the reorganized government.

The political talk in those days across the nation was about the upcoming 1960 presidential election. Quinn was asked about what he'd heard at the Governors' Conference. Quinn predicted that Vice President Richard Nixon would be the Republican Party's 1960 candidate for president. Someone asked Quinn if he had talked about that with Governor Nelson Rockefeller of New York, who was frequently mentioned as a presidential possibility. Quinn said, "We had absolutely no conversation about the presidential race."

Quinn for Vice President "is no joke," wrote Dan Tuttle, professor of government at the University of Hawaii and a political columnist at The Honolulu Advertiser.

"That slogan could intrigue Chicagoans next July at the Republican National Convention. And the people of Chicago are not easily intrigued, least of all by politicians. The Democrats scoff and laugh and the Republicans smile while eyeing the undivided local patronage pie."

Rumors of Quinn's national prominence had come home.

"Quinn is definitely in the running for nomination to be vice president if Nelson Rockefeller, governor of New York, captures top spot on the ticket," Hawaii GOP State Chairman Art Woolaway reported from the Western Republican Conference.

Quinn had received an invitation to speak at the February Lincoln Day dinner from New York City's GOP chairman, Bernard Newman, who was known as a strong force in the Rockefeller camp. Tuttle wrote that Quinn was undecided as to whether or not he would speak at the dinner.

Over coffee cups, in the barber shops and on the streets, there was talk of Quinn's attractive personality, mass appeal and his ability to play his part to the hilt. From the standpoint of political realities, he didn't stand a chance unless he was handpicked by either Rockefeller or Nixon. In that case, he would indeed have a good chance. After all, said political analyst John Ramsey, "He heads the newest state. He's handsome, colorful, forceful. He's made a start at being known nationally."

For Quinn's part, he used his Mainland engagements to promote Hawaii as a land of economic opportunity and a paradise playground for visitors. He spoke at conferences, national meetings, college campuses, medical and science seminars and churches; he spoke on a multitude of subjects—brotherhood, national defense, international peace, law, government administration, labor, land, housing, public safety and education. Thousands heard him orate, thousands more saw him on television and were captured by his charisma. That he was the first elected governor of the new, 50th state helped to place him in the national spotlight.

"I think he wrote most of his speeches," Nancy said. "His press secretaries would do the research, dig out the facts and he'd use that as his springboard. He'd make his notes and then he was ready to speak. His diction was so good and he had a knack of being able to speak appealingly to groups on subjects that he knew little about."

One of his most distinguished invitations was to the National School Board's annual meeting in Chicago on April 25, 1960. Governor Quinn accepted with pleasure. Quinn viewed schools and systems of education as being of great importance to all students, to their communities and to the nation. The invitation was most timely for the governor; he had just come through a trying time over an education issue only the month before with the state Legislature. Quinn was opposed to the Democrats' drive to get quick action on a bill that proposed to have members of the state Board of Education elected instead of appointed.

Star-Bulletin February 28, 1960:

"Governor W.F. Quinn predicted that proposals to have members of the state Board of Education elected instead of appointed would be turned down if the issue were put to a general vote. Quinn said, "We had very able delegates to the Constitutional Convention, which debated this thoroughly. We ought to give it a chance. Therefore, I strongly urge that immediate action be taken to establish the local school advisory councils provided for under the Constitution so that we may proceed with early reorganization of the Department of Education.""

Two months later in Chicago at the National School Board meeting, Quinn opened his speech with reference to Hawaii's educational system and to the transitional problems in setting up the new state Department of Education:

...variety and diversity, stemming from a local autonomy, are a source of strength that should be preserved.

In Hawaii we have a statewide system of education under a single board. Ten years ago we had a convention to draft our Constitution to be effective when we became a state. Great dispute surrounded the question whether the board should be elected or appointed. The ingenious solution was to provide for local advisory councils to be set up by law in various districts that would provide the governor with panels of names from which he must appoint the board. Our Constitution went into effect with statehood almost a decade later.

As you can imagine, becoming a state carries enormous problems with it. Setting up our state Board of Education is one of our major transitional difficulties. This stems from the fact that one group does not accept the constitutional compromise of advisory councils, even though it is proposed these councils be elected.

They want an elected state Board of Education and want to amend the Constitution to provide for it. The other group wants to give the constitutional provision a try before any change is made.

Unfortunately the two groups have become identified with the two political parties. We reached an impasse in the Legislature. Control of our two houses is split. The House of Representatives would not pass the bill setting up the constitutional board unless the amendment proposal was passed also. The Senate refused to pass an amendment proposal until there had been some experience under the Constitution.

As a result, although we have just completed our fourth legislative session since statehood last July, we are still without power to establish a Board of Education. But, I assure you, education will go on. The impasse simply illustrates that we really take our politics seriously in Hawaii.

Whether elected or appointed, the school board member occupies one of the most important posts in public service. And what's more, there is a widening recognition of his importance throughout the land. Controversy swirls around him—controversy concerning some of the basic beliefs and understandings that we all share."

The governor spoke of the many related problems of education facing leaders in the system: fundamental questions of the relative role of home, church and school in raising children; how to educate students for world leadership; the financial burdens accompanying the growth in student population; radio, television and other aids to education; excellence in math and science and fluency in foreign languages. The governor then spoke on the progress of selecting leaders of the 21st Century:

> *Our claim to world leadership lies in the ideals of our revolution—in the assertion then first made for the world to hear and be thrilled by—that all men are created equal—that they are endowed with unalienable rights, rights which even government cannot take away from them.*
>
> *A bright glow of sincerity was cast upon our assertion of the brotherhood of man by the admission of Hawaii as a state. The United States granted equal citizenship to the people of our Pacific islands, 70% of whom are non-Caucasian. The nonwhite peoples of the world were impressed! Such dramatic demonstrations that freedom still rings from the mountaintops are rare.*
>
> *...Above all else, tomorrow's leader of the free world must be passionately devoted to freedom. Whatever else he studies, he must study the great ethical and philosophical traditions which gave rise to our concepts of the dignified nature of man.*
>
> *...Our future leader must know the intimations of immortality which gave rise to the concept of human dignity and the tradition of a spiritual nature in man which is the basis for the claim to freedom. I do not urge religious instruction in our schools, although there has been increasing ingenuity displayed in ways to assure that our young students receive some idea of religious tradition.*
>
> *The separation of church and state should not prevent the study in our schools of the fundamental tenets of American democracy which have their roots and draw their strength from the philosophical and theological wisdom of the past.*
>
> *...The cause of freedom demands articulate champions. Those who founded this land and who fought to give it birth in*

freedom were articulate about freedom and human dignity because they were steeped in the great traditions of the past. Those who will take the grave responsibility to preserve freedom in the world of the future must be as articulate as Tom Paine, as wise as Franklin, Jefferson, Madison and Hamilton.

...History has proved that the creative mind, which can soar beyond the boundaries of existing knowledge, is nurtured in freedom. Both profound insight and common sense lead inevitably to the conclusion that the world of the 21st Century will need creative genius in its leadership.

To distribute food so there is no starvation anywhere in the world; to spread the curing powers of modern medical science to all parts of the world; to devise a system of concord between men and nations that will promote freedom and prevent tyranny, promote amity and neighborliness and prevent enmity and hatred; these objectives will demand creative genius unparalleled in the saga of man. Such leadership must come from the ranks of the free.

Americans will die for freedom. We must also heed the warning of our forefathers that it can be destroyed by slow attrition unless we are eternally vigilant to protect it.

The great task facing those of us who have the responsibility for the next generation and the future of our country— school boards, government, parents and people—is to inject the stuff into our curricula which will breed the love of freedom in the student; to instill a passionate and proud devotion to the American tradition of freedom in our young people; and to install in positions of leadership, present and future, those whose highest aim is the preservation of freedom among mankind. In educating for world leadership, I pray that we accomplish these things above all else."

The local press reported his speaking engagements, some with faint praise. When the state Legislature failed to pass its prime concern, a government reorganization bill, the *Honolulu Star-Bulletin* said: "Quinn was on the mainland making speeches that in effect, if not by intent, added up to political haymaking."

The implication was clear. The criticism that he was "feathering his own political nest" vexed Quinn. One day, for the first time in the memory of the political reporters, he "really got his Irish up." Brian Casey of The *Advertiser* had this to say:

> Irked by newspaper stories about his being invited to address a big Republican affair in New York, Quinn heatedly denied it. He expressed his anger by flinging his glasses on his desk. (No, they didn't break.)
>
> Quinn has shown displeasure at reporters—and their editors—before. But usually all it amounts to is his failure to smile when he talks. No smile and you know he's sore.

In the middle of December, 10 days after the death of Eric Reppun, the governor announced the appointment of Wayne L. Collins, a TV news broadcaster, as president of the Board of Agriculture and Forestry. Reportedly Quinn named Collins over strong opposition from Senate leaders. The appointment came as a complete surprise and stirred an enormous controversy. Collins, however, had a little-known but long record of service to Hawaii. According to *The Advertiser*:

> "He has no administrative or budgetary experience to qualify him for the post. He does, however, have very real and extensive knowledge of Hawaii's forests, ranches, streams and wildlife as well as great enthusiasm for putting them to best use."

Most of Hawaii only knew the young, seemingly modest, deep-voiced news broadcaster on the screen. Few knew of his wide-ranging activities outside the studio or the photographic memory and superior mind.

Reported *The Advertiser*'s Gardiner Jones:

> Eric Reppun had more to do with the appointment than any political considerations. Months ago, when Reppun shifted to the land office, he asked Collins if he wouldn't be interested in the agriculture post.
>
> Reppun also made a strong recommendation that the job go to Collins.
>
> Who can tell how well he'll do? He's young, has enormous enthusiasm, extensive knowledge of his department and what it is supposed to be doing, together with great mental capacity.
>
> Time—and Wayne Collins—will tell.

Before the end of the year, Nelson Rockefeller announced that he would not seek the GOP presidential nomination against Vice President Nixon. This quieted all the "veep" talk revolving around Quinn. Woolaway and the governor said they hoped Rockefeller would run on the Nixon ticket as vice president. "That would be an unbeatable team," said Quinn.

On December 31st an eight-pound, seven-ounce boy, their seventh child and fifth son, was born to Governor and Mrs. Quinn. "Needless to say," *The Advertiser* announced, "there will not be an open house on New Year's Day at Washington Place. The first lady is at Kapiolani Hospital."

The year ended quietly at the executive mansion. The governor was looking ahead to his 500 appointments awaiting the state Senate's approval. He would know soon enough.

Chapter Twenty-Four

Palace Pressures

". . . In the final analysis a governor must choose men
with whom he can work, who he knows will be loyal. . ."
THE HONOLULU ADVERTISER
January 8, 1960

A n *Advertiser* editorial observed: "Picking a cabinet is no easy job, the power is great—but so is the responsibility...it is the governor and the governor alone who must decide because it's the governor alone who stands accountable to the public."

By January 3, Governor Quinn announced his cabinet members. Among them were Larry Nakatsuka as director of the Department of Labor and Bob Ellis as the commissioner of Land and Natural Resources.

The AFL-CIO was angered with Quinn when he appointed his press secretary to head the state Department of Labor. Organized labor raised its powerful voice, claiming the governor failed to live up to a pre-election promise. He didn't discuss Nakatsuka's appointment with union officials before making it public. It was obvious that the Quinn-AFL-CIO honeymoon in Hawaii was over.

In the middle of the fracas, Kapoho volcano on the Big Island erupted.

"The first I heard was that a large triangular segment of land, hundreds of acres, just dropped like four feet in some places," Quinn remembered. He called for Civil Defense to evacuate the area, then flew to Hilo and went out to the area. The volcanologist he met said he didn't think there'd be more action.

"No, Governor, it's just that there's been some movement of lava, but we think it's all over," Quinn recalled him saying.

"So, I went back to Hilo to have dinner and then catch a flight home. I hadn't even been served when the word came to me that the volcano was erupting!"

It was a grim race to save the little town of Kapoho. As 300 Big Island residents moved out, massive bulldozers moved in. Policemen, dike builders and machinery remained, working frantically in the eerie light of Madam Pele's fire. Lava continually pooled up behind the town; every second counted. Cinder blanketed the earth and choking smoke engulfed the entire area; tongues of red molten lava flowed southward toward the sea.

The fiery river cascaded into the orchid-lined pool of Warm Springs and buried the lush resort under 20 feet of smoking *a'a* lava. Half a dozen fountains pumped furiously from the volcano, spilling intensely hot streams, setting fire to the lush jungle foliage and turning telephone poles and large trees into deadly torches.

Advertiser January 19, 1960:

Governor Quinn declared Puna a "major disaster area" and fired off a telegram to President Eisenhower asking him for federal emergency funds.

While Quinn was returning to Oahu late yesterday afternoon, he radioed ahead for the state attorney general to prepare the proclamation to be sent to the president. He went directly from the airport to his office and signed the document.

With the governor on the trip were General Fred A. Makinney, adjutant for the Hawaii National Guard; Wayne Collins, newly appointed state agriculture chief; Tim Ho, state highway director; Sam Hirota, state Bureau of Public

Works; Frank Palmer, U.S. Corps of Engineers, and Frank Carlson, U.S. Bureau of Public Roads.

The next day Quinn attended oath-of-office ceremonies for some appointees. First to be sworn in was Raymond Y.C. Ho as director of the Department of Budget and Review; Ho had served as territorial treasurer before the reorganization. Charles Silva, who had been director of institutions, became director of the Department of Treasury and Regulation. Mary Noonan took the oath as director of the Department of Social Services in charge of both the state's welfare program and its prison system.

"When we joined the departments of Social Services and Institutions together, I put Joe Harper, who had been the warden of the prisons, under Mary Noonan, a long-time Republican," Quinn said. "But Joe remained bitter and angry. He wanted to be his own boss."

George Mason had already taken his oath as head of the new Department of Economic Development. Mason had been director of the Economic Planning and Co-ordination Authority before that agency was merged into the new department.

Quinn named John Henry Felix as executive assistant to the governor, replacing Ed Johnston, who had left to return to his insurance business.

"When I was asked to take the position," said Felix, "I was executive vice president in Roy Kelley's hotel chain, but the job with the governor of our new state was an exciting challenge and an offer that I could not refuse.

"It took a lot of energy. My office was right next to his in one of those appendages of Iolani Palace...I had to go through a window to reach him," Felix said.

At the end of January, the governor called a special session of the state Senate. His cabinet was not yet fixed; he needed Senate confirmation on more appointments. They needed time to act before the entire Legislature convened in mid-February.

"In those early days of '60 it didn't seem as though I could get any help from anybody," said Quinn.

There was a majority of Republicans in the Senate, 14 to 11. Yet Quinn was having major trouble.

"When they got into my cabinet appointees, it was day after day the Senate was meeting and not a single thing was done. And they still had 500 appointments to process."

The newspapers were full of talk about the chances of Nakatsuka and Ellis. Headlines read: "Quinn's Boys Face Battle," "Perils in Paradise," "Knives in the Dark," which referred to the lack of reasonable documentation to prove unfitness of either Nakatsuka or Ellis. "It's been a case of knife-throwing in the dark," said one source, "and even the identities of all the opposing senators are not definitely known."

Senate President William "Doc" Hill remarked that "the situation is one of those hot potatoes that are dropped in the Senate's lap once in a while. We'd like to get rid of it soonest, but we don't quite know how."

Why was the governor having appointment troubles with the Republican-controlled Senate, a reporter asked Hill.

"He just is, that's all. It's a matter of personalities. Some senators have questioned the appointees' abilities and the ILWU is in the picture and they have their influence," the Senate president said.

Hawaii Hochi February 2, 1960

One thing is certain. The controversy could not be over the qualifications of the Quinn appointees. Both Ellis and Nakatsuka are known to be men of integrity and ability...to reject either nomination would admit to rejecting confidence in the governor.

The newspaper talk about whether Nakatsuka and Ellis would make it went on day after day; the senators remained deadlocked.

"It was such a massive job," Quinn said, "and there they were hung up on those two."

On February 17, 1960, the Senate rejected Nakatsuka, Ellis and the entire seven appointees to the Board of Agriculture and Conservation. It was undoubtedly the biggest setback for Quinn since he took office as territorial governor in 1957.

Quinn saw it as a major loss for his party.

"The Republican Party, right there in 1959 and 1960, lost the opportunity to come back after that great defeat of '54 and again in '56," Quinn said.

The Republican senators who voted against the nominations "contributed to the failure of re-establishing the Republicans as an equal party, able to do battle.

"They lost it because these men—some of them had been in the Legislature prior to '54 like Heb Porteus and Doc Hill— were interested in having their own way. They were used to circumventing the governor, going their way in their little empires and didn't give us a chance at all."

Senator Ward Russell, a staunch Republican with a long record of public service who voted for the confirmations, said, "I could never understand why Randy Crossley went after Quinn's administrative assistant, Bob Ellis. When he voted against Ellis's nomination, he was being petty...Randy wanted to establish himself as a power in the Republican Party.

"It was unfortunate for everybody that the group Bill had in the Senate, Fukushima, Porteus, Crossley, Yates, etc., were such a bunch of prima donnas. They wanted to get their names in the press...they wanted publicity."

For Quinn, the episode is a shocking memory:

"Can you imagine people in the Congress of the United States saying, 'This is a Republican appointee so all the

Democrats are going to vote against him'? It's a terrible thing they did when you reflect on it. And it was terrible for a new state to try to get started under those circumstances.

"I sent down to the first state Legislature a package of about 20 bills and they were really good, solid legislative programs." Quinn said. "Bills one through 20...I had talked to the Senate about them. I thought I had concurrence. It was an integrated legislative program. The Republican convention and their legislative committee said, 'Yes, this is what we want to do.' The party could ride high in this well-identified legislative program."

Among the 20 bills was a capital improvements plan with a chief aim to develop tourism on the Neighbor Islands. Kona was high on the list; Kaanapali on Maui was to receive some public improvements. The Legislature ended up approving the Kaanapali improvements but the Senate Republicans didn't support the Kona improvements.

"They thought it called for too much money in one district," Quinn said.

"In fact," he continued, "the whole legislative program, bills one through 20, was broken up and destroyed. Bill No. 1 was introduced as Bill 45, and a few days later Bill No. 6 was introduced as Bill 80. The program lost its identity, its shape as a program, and failed. The Republicans could claim nothing as a result of it.

"Absolutely nothing!

"The end result was that the Kona plan was shelved and they broke up that money into bits and pieces and threw it into every part of the state. It was a tragic thing."

Lamentable as that was for Quinn, he found the chief disappointment of his entire term was the inability to get the Republicans to accept high priorities and stick with them.

"We were able to obtain approval of a few things like the road opening up Mauna Kea. But the integrated Kona plan failed to get approval. Most of it was done a quarter of a century later."

In a hearing for the budgets of the governor and lieutenant governor, the House Finance Committee laid down the proverbial red carpet for Jimmy Kealoha—then rolled it back up when Governor Quinn's aides entered. Everything was questioned, ridiculed, including the necessity for two maids and a nurse in Washington Place, and the governor's request for a new car. He wanted to replace the 12-year-old Cadillac that was costly to maintain.

The governor had asked also for extra office help, which was denied. The committee ignored the authority and dignity of the governor's office. The legislative action was nothing but harassment.

The Honolulu Advertiser:

> Twice within the past few days witnesses before the state House of Representatives have been subject to hostile, intemperate treatment. Both times the officials of the Republican administration were browbeaten or ridiculed by Democratic House members.
>
> Partisanship has its place—and so do decorum and courtesy.
>
> The jibes and sneers heaped on an employee of the governor's office by a finance Committee member were boorish and uncouth. The majority of the Legislature treat witnesses decently. But those few who use their positions to work out their personal peeves and prejudices strip legislative proceedings of dignity. And their behavior does not advance the work of the sessions.

Before the week was out, the state House of Representatives and a GOP lawmaker who had volunteered his expertise as an auto mechanic would be proven fools.

Representative Richard M. Kennedy of Kailua had assured the people of Hawaii that the governor's 1947 Cadillac was nothing to be ashamed of and was good for at least another year. On Tuesday, March 23, 1960, German Chancellor Konrad Adenauer, 84 years old, arrived in Hawaii for a two-day visit. Governor Quinn greeted him; Adenauer received a yellow carnation lei and a military band played national anthems of both countries. Military brass decked out in swords and medals gave their welcome accompanied by canon salutes. Four hundred spectators gathered for a look at the man most clearly identified with Germany's amazing post-World War II recovery.

After a stag luncheon hosted by Quinn at Iolani Palace, the governor's chauffeur, Daniel Kaulahao, drove Adenauer on a sight-seeing trip to the Pali Lookout. On the Pali Highway, the '47 Cadillac broke down. Oil leaked from the engine and dripped on the muffler, creating a thick, black smoke that enveloped the limousine. The chauffeur opened all the doors to clear the smoke-filled interior. The West German chancellor had to be transferred to another car in the caravan.

On April 17 *The Advertiser* carried the announcement that Governor Quinn would get his new car but that there had been a compromise:

> Governor Quinn is going to get a new Cadillac, but he will have to wait until fall to buy a 1961 model. It was reported that the joint Senate-House committee allocated $11,000 but specified it would be of 1961 design.
>
> "You must be kidding," Quinn was said to have commented when a member of his staff told him about it.
>
> The compromise consisted of forcing the governor to use the '47 model for four or five months longer than he would have had to if permitted to buy a 1960 Cadillac in July.
>
> Only Thursday it developed a flat tire while the Quinns were en route to Fort Shafter to a luncheon. A policeman

happened to pass by while Governor Quinn was helping his driver change the tire, and gave the family a ride to their appointment.

House representatives had refused to allocate any money for a new Cadillac and the Senate had approved it. The matter will be hashed out by the conference committee in an attempt to reconcile the two different versions of the operating budget.

Senate President Hill predicted, "The dignity of the office demands it. I think he'll get his car."

Years later, Quinn reflected on that lunch with Adenauer.

"The luncheon was a success," said Quinn. "We had gotten word that the chancellor preferred a sit-down, European-style lunch with wine. So I asked John Henry Felix, my protocol aide, to take over. Adenauer sat on my right and the interpreter was in-between the two of us. He was the best I've ever encountered in all my life. There were no pauses...as I said something he was already saying it in simple language and in the same way for Adenauer. If I told a joke, the chancellor would be laughing right along with myself. It was remarkable. He was speaking in German and I in English.

"When the wine was served, I died," Quinn said.

It was a sparkling red wine and Quinn assumed it must be cheap and artificial.

"I was furious and at the first opportunity I called John Henry in and read him the riot act. When I finally calmed down, John showed me the label and pointed out that it was a rare sparkling European red wine."

Felix remembered the day, too.

"The luncheon was set up on the second-floor balcony of Iolani Palace. It was memorable, all right. I ordered a Grenache

Rosé wine and the governor had a fit but I was right. It was the correct wine to serve. The governor felt very bad when he discovered that I was absolutely right."

Of medium height with dark hair in those days, John Henry Felix had large Latin eyes with high-arched black eyebrows. He was brisk, quick and always in the thick of things. Felix was aide to the governor in myriad ways that were not always routine.

"Bill was an absolute perfectionist. He always wanted to know how the table was going to set up and exactly what was on the menu. In those days I had to be a jack of all trades: executive assistant, protocol, caterer, travel arranger, speech writer, speech giver, social letter writer; but it was all a great experience...do everything and anything and never question.

"Bill Quinn was the first governor to take his cabinet to the Neighbor Islands....We even went to Niihau.

"The governor was very innovative and he was never on the negative side....If something appeared impossible to do, he would say find out how it can be done."

Invariably much of the business of any Legislature is passed with little scrutiny by the public. A lot is routine, or embodies financial provisions too long and complex for most people to follow. But by April 10, 1960, in the final days of the budget session, Senate Bill 232, labeled the "Frank Silva Bill," passed the Senate 19 to 6 and the House by 36 to 15. When it was announced that the bill was awaiting the governor's signature, frenzied citizens protested.

The bill would limit inquiries into the personal history of applicants to government service to eight years. In 1950, Frank G. Silva, an ex-ILWU official, was ousted from the territorial Constitutional Convention for refusing to respond to the question, posed the year before by the House un-American Activities Committee: "Are you now or have you ever been a communist?"

Silva reportedly was prepared to say that he hadn't been a

communist for the last eight years, a period of time that coincided with the date the Communist Party in Hawaii went underground.

Governor Quinn realized immediately the implications and danger of Bill 232 and sent out the message that he would veto the "Frank Silva Bill."

The announcement was short and sharp:

> *I am astonished that the measure should have received more than two-thirds of the members of both houses of the state Legislature. That it had such strong legislative support makes the exercise of the veto power all the more difficult.*
>
> *Communism is the greatest threat to the continued existence of our cherished American freedoms. One of the highest aims of government is the protection of those freedoms.*
>
> *Government employees should be screened to determine their devotion to the American ideal. If they have erred in the past and disclose the error, they will not be hounded or made objects of discrimination.*
>
> *It is arbitrary and unwise to limit the period in a man's life which can be scrutinized to determine his worthiness for public employment.*

On May 20, 1960, *The Advertiser* reported that the GOP senators killed the "Frank Silva Bill" by deciding not to reconvene and try to override Governor Quinn's veto.

≈Chapter Twenty-Five≈
Tsunami

"When a shock wave is going through water, it travels at a constant rate of speed like electricity through a wire ..."

GOV. WILLIAM F. QUINN
Journal May 23, 1960

President Sukarno of Indonesia came to visit Hawaii on May 22, 1960. The next day he would fly to Tokyo en route home after his stopover in Honolulu. Indonesia is the island chain that straddles the equator northwest of Australia, covers a vast area in the South Pacific, from the Island of Java west to the magic island of Bali. Sukarno's people were mostly Muslim, underlain with ancient Hindu Javanese features.

"He was an interesting man, colorful," said Quinn. "He was highly regarded as father of his country, even though (later) he was kicked out for being too friendly with the communist nations."

On one of his visits through Hawaii, Sukarno was given a lei and a kiss on the cheek by a Pan American stewardess.

"Of course," Quinn said, "this is a violation of every Muslim tradition known." Sukarno, however, was able to get away with it.

"He immediately decided he was going to have this woman, and he pursued her," Quinn remembered.

Before the official luncheon at Washington Place, Sukarno

called at the home of the pretty stewardess, dark-haired, dark-eyed Carol Ah You. After Sukarno and Carol left for luncheon at the governor's mansion, someone asked Mrs. Ah You how she reacted to Sukarno's interest in her daughter. She replied, "I don't know quite what to make of it."

On a subsequent weekend visit, Sukarno asked if there were a jewelry store open. Stores, markets, bars and the like remained closed on Sundays during those years. The governor called John Henry Felix and Felix called somebody and somebody opened up his jewelry store.

"The president went in and bought a very expensive gold and diamond wristwatch, then we drove him out to see the girl. In time President Sukarno really sought her to be a wife," said Quinn, "but then she'd have been wife number four."

Memories of Sukarno's May 1960 visit are intertwined with other, more dramatic recollections. Sixteen years later, Quinn reflected in his journal writings on the events which unfolded May 23, 1960.

> *We were seated at luncheon for President Sukarno when I received a call from the Coast Guard reporting to me that there had been a major earthquake in Chile. He said, "We don't know whether or not it has generated a tsunami, but if it has, it will hit Hawaii around midnight."*
>
> *I don't know whether I questioned him then or learned afterwards, but when a tsunami, a shock wave, is going through water, it travels at a constant rate of speed like electricity through a wire, so they could almost say to the minute when it would hit.*
>
> *I went back, resumed lunch, got the president off, called a group of people together and said, "We've got to find out first whether there's a tidal wave generated." Several calls later and we quickly learned that there were no stations between Chile*

and the state of Hawaii that could tell us scientifically whether a tsunami had been generated or not.

...If the wave was coming from Chile, it would pass by Tahiti at about 4 o'clock in the afternoon. So we found a ham operator who had contact with a ham operator in Papeete. We got the message to him to go to the harbor at Papeete...report to us anything unusual.

...He called back by radio and said, "Around 4 o'clock it seemed as though the water just rose maybe five or six inches, stayed there for a while and then went back down." I knew then that Hawaii most likely would be hit by a wave and made the call to my administrative director telling him to meet me at our Civil Defense headquarters, Burkheimer Tunnel at Diamond Head. What had begun as disturbing information on that peaceful Sunday afternoon developed into a hectic, frustrating series of speculations, information and misinformation regarding the wave and its probable impact on our state of Hawaii.

It was about 8 in the evening when I was being driven from downtown to Diamond Head that we went by the Ala Wai Yacht Harbor. I saw all these boats tied up and found only one watchman there. "Haven't you heard about the impending tidal wave?" I asked. No, he hadn't. So I told him to call the owners to get the boats out to sea before they were destroyed...I learned later that he did call and most of the boats were taken out but the few remaining were totaled.

Then we drove into Waikiki and I stopped at the Royal Hawaiian Hotel...."I suggest that you get people off the first floor because it can always come in. It hasn't, historically, but it can roll into Waikiki Beach. Get the people up and away from there." I asked him (the assistant manager), too, to get word out to the industry to evacuate their first floors and they did.

The hours spent at Civil Defense headquarters were agonizing. Accurate reports were not readily available and as in most situations of this sort, there were people who nervously wanted something done and there were others who said there's nothing to worry about—relax.

The Tahiti wave information was broadcast widely throughout the state....At about 9 p.m. sirens were sounded and warnings went out...to leave the low-lying areas. However, the radio reports of small-wave action gave people a very false sense of security, plus we already had had a history of false alarms....

We had one person who was a radio voice in Hilo and we asked him to observe what happened and keep us advised. We couldn't fly over there. There were no lights. So we sat and listened. At midnight our radio man in Hilo started to say:

"...The water is receding, It's going out further than it usually does." We waited. He came back on about 12:30....

"The water is coming in. It's coming up the river. It's rising higher than it usually does." Then he started describing it going back out and that took about a half hour.

"This one," he said, "has gone out quite far. The reef is partially exposed out there. We don't see that very often."

It came back in and it rose higher. He described what was happening. What he didn't say and what we didn't know was that there were a lot of people hanging on the bridge watching right down there at the waterfront, including a couple of policemen. Then the water went out again. He was still talking and he was describing this third wave.

"It's gone out and my God, it's way out. The reef is totally exposed. Now it's beginning to come in." His voice got more and more excited. "My God, I've never seen anything like it...and listen to that roar....My God, It's 50 or 60 feet high!"

And he was off the air.

We flew by National Guard plane to Hilo at dawn. What we were to see and hear in the hours that followed our arrival became indelibly etched in our minds. At least four waves of varying sizes hit the Hilo area during a two-hour period. The initial shocking news was that 26 people were dead, 26 people were reported to be missing and 53 were said to be injured and the residential and business districts of Hilo's waterfront town were gone.

We debarked to an appalling sight. Thick slimy mud covered the streets of Hilo. Fish abandoned by the water that had carried them over the sea wall were strewn about. The third wave had recaptured Hilo's sewage from the bay and carried it into the face of the city, filling the air with a noxious stench. North of Haili Street, stores had been gutted and their contents strewn in the streets. Broken power poles, tangled wires, yardage goods and muck clogged the street. Along Kamehameha Avenue all the strong parking meter poles had been laid flat. Mamo Street, stores and residences, was a shambles. Beyond Mamo, the row of stores that had walled the west side of Kamehameha Avenue was gone.

Occasional building skeletons could be identified.

When we reached this scene of unspeakable wreckage in the gray light of dawn, we saw the tragic figures of a few men and women, mostly old, picking through the wreckage in search of valuables, and in some cases, loved ones.

Indelibly printed in my mind is the picture of three young boys, one strumming an ukulele, wandering around the ruins, picking up whatever struck their fancies.

Reviewing the chain of events and activities, I remember that Waiakea Bridge was crowded with spectators when the largest wave hit. Apparently spellbound at the time of the large wave's arrival, people on the bridge were tragically swept off and many drowned. It was estimated that the wave was about 35 feet high at impact.

I toured all districts by riding and walking through the dev-

astated areas. The scene, the discussions with people and the frantic searching for bodies revealed the full extent of the tragedy that was visited upon Hilo. Then began the inevitable chores of doing what had to be done—to assist the people of Hilo and to begin the terrible job of cleaning up.

I recall doing many things that morning of May 23, 1960: I held a meeting in the office of the chairman of the Board of Supervisors at 10:00 a.m.; Chairman Thomas Cook called his department heads and I had all mine; I officially declared a state of emergency and urged all people to boil drinking water because of possible contamination.

It became difficult to find bodies in the deep rubble. Digging into the mounds of debris had to be painstakingly done. The sadness of this terrible event became truly established when the dead were buried in the following days. So bad was the devastation in some districts that the locating of the dead was aided only by the stench of decomposing bodies beneath the piles of dirt and broken buildings.

Felix flew with Quinn to Hilo.

"It was like an atom bomb had hit it," Felix said. "The devastation was ghastly, but the thing that will always remain in my mind is the Hilo Hospital emergency morgue. There were lines of bodies stretched out, 50-plus bodies with newspaper covering them. It was a large holding area but there were so many dead, it was the only way they could handle the situation.

"Bill's leadership ability took over," said Felix, "he got accurate dollar cost estimates of the damage, which were necessary to prepare the request for federal funds; he ordered 70 National Guardsmen to be on the scene to prevent looting and to maintain order, and with the governor's help the national Red Cross set up quickly to provide food, shelter and clothing to the victims.

"I can only praise Governor Quinn's leadership, his responsiveness, his taking charge without taking away any authority's jurisdiction. He was a great believer in home rule. You always knew who was in charge; he was loving, compassionate and a renaissance man...a man for all seasons. He was a statesman, not a politician. That is not a criticism but an observation of what was fact."

Leo Pritchard, Quinn's administrative director, had been up to his ears in the job of guiding the reorganization of the state's 18 consolidated departments. As The Advertiser reported a month before the tsunami, Pritchard "has a big job." The paper said his primary purpose "is to provide competent people to perform necessary jobs in the public interest."

After May 23, however, Pritchard's work was diverted to Hilo, as Quinn noted as his journal continued:

> *My administrative director, Leo Pritchard, remained in Hilo to direct the state's efforts in what had to be done to begin the rehabilitation of Hilo. So extensive was this, he stayed for two weeks.*
>
> *The reports of damage included the Hilo Gas Company being completely wiped out and 2,000 gas consumers without gas. The Hilo Electric Light Company main power plant at Waiakea was damaged to the extent of about a quarter of a million dollars with the likelihood that restoring the plant to service would take about seven to 10 days. There were varying estimates of the damage costs—up to $50 million.*
>
> *I arranged for a military transport tanker to leave Pearl Harbor for Kawaihae to put the generators to work providing electricity for the crippled Big Island power system.*
>
> *Damages to public facilities were extensive—schools, bridges, roads, water mains, public buildings and public parks. About 1,000 of Hilo's work force of 8,000 workers were without jobs as a result of the disaster. About 600 residences were dam-*

aged, many destroyed.

So, it can be recalled that some fast action was taken imme-diately; and, by the second or third day after the wave, resources for rehabilitation had been determined and put in place. There were relocations of victims to be acted on. I selected three state land parcels for possible site developments and determined that $700,000 could be made available for this.

On May 27th, newspapers reported that the disaster may become a political issue. A joint legislative-county committee had been formed, with Senator Nelson K. Doi as chairman, who prepared an agenda for a meeting with me and my executive staff. However, I chaired the meeting and used my own agenda. An argument between Doi and myself developed over which item would be discussed first: zoning or land for relocation. We discussed relocation as I wanted and I charged Representative Hara with trying to document a case for a special legislative ses-sion. I insisted the $400,000 to pay for a special session would be better used to assist Hilo. However, I did believe a special session would be necessary. The final death toll figures were announced on May 31, 1960: the count was 57.

From the beginning, Republican Chairman Cook in Hilo was accused of moving too slowly or moving too quickly by the Democrats. John A. Burns declared that the disaster warning system would be an issue in the next campaign. I was criticized by him for not declaring a state emergency before the wave hit the Islands. However, an officer of the Coast and Geodetic Survey Station at Barbers Point said, "There's no way to predict whether a wave will be deadly or harmless when it hits the Islands. If such a predictive toll existed, we would use it."

On June 8, 1960 a committee of scientists submitted a 14-page report to the state Civil Defense director. It emphasized that the deaths in Hilo were technically preventable. The story about this received much front-page treatment in the Star

Bulletin. The following day I heavily criticized two key reporters as being entirely in error on their point that scientists are capable of predicting the severity of a tidal wave before it strikes land.

I stated that the two reporters lacked scholarship in evaluating the warning system. My major emphasis during all subsequent critiques was that the warning system did not fail. What was to be improved was increased public education, more authority to force evacuation and improvement in the use of information by the broadcasting media.

I suppose that some of the controversies that arose during that period still persist. There were reports that I responded to the disaster quickly and decisively. There were other reports to the contrary. I know that I and others with me gave of ourselves unstintingly in those hours of turmoil and in the days and weeks that followed. I was saddened and burdened by the deaths and other casualties. Yet I still am proud of the way we responded to people's needs.

The present-day method of broadcasting of alerts and testing of the alert system stemmed from my most important action of meeting with newsmen and broadcasters. I formed a vital Broadcasting Coordinating Committee and charged it with the responsibility and task of developing the linkage of all broadcast stations in order to carry disaster information in a coordinated manner. Each station was to carry only official Civil Defense information.

It is interesting that following the 1960 "tidal wave" the identity of such an occurrence began to be understood properly as tsunami, as we know it today.

All in all, the May 23, 1960 disaster was a most devastating one that still burns in my memory. But as always, such events bring out the best in most and not the best in others. Criticisms are made prematurely and they grow out of not enough information and, unfortunately, from political opportunism.

It is on occasions such as the 1960 tsunami that well-intentioned men who dedicate themselves to their responsibilities will act courageously. There will be barriers placed in their paths. But when they have courage of convictions and belief in their actions and if they have honesty of purpose and plan, the results will be positive and supportable.

Beginning on June 15, 1960, the Hilo newspaper treatment of me began to improve markedly in editorial tone. The press there began to praise my approach and my actions. I was happy with this turn of events because prior to this time my charge that news reporters lacked scholarship dominated the front page of all papers, it seemed. Strangely, that new controversy began to nudge the gruesome details of death and destruction onto pages two and three.

Later in the year, 1960, I had occasion to do some work in my office on a Sunday afternoon. Also there was my administrative director. We were chatting informally in a manner not always available to us in the heat of getting a very large job done. He asked me about my approach to the political job I was in and how I viewed unfair political motives and attacks. He wanted to know how a man of high integrity, a religious man, deals with political dishonesty and how he can live within such a setting. He recalled the false charges, the unfair criticism during May and June and attempts to turn the Hilo disaster into a political issue in future campaigns.

I suppose the majority of politicians ask themselves the same kinds of questions he asked me that Sunday afternoon. And, I suppose, most politicians do everything in their power to work forthrightly and diligently to cause their vocations to be of top integrity and viewed as that by God and country.

I look upon the Hilo experience as a great test of my belief

> *that solid, honest actions will eventually be viewed as being supe-*
> *rior to unfair political criticism. I have been strengthened by*
> *weathering that disaster and the storm that followed. I am*
> *grateful that I was in the position of leadership at that time....*
>
> WILLIAM F. QUINN, 1976.

A special session of the Legislature opened on June 13, 1960. It lasted 17 days and produced 12 bills dealing with the tsunami disaster.

"I signed them all. I had asked for a completely bipartisan approach and the legislators had agreed," Quinn said.

"The special session's sole business was relief for the Hilo disaster victims. It gave me an opportunity to show that the Second *Mahele* wasn't just a lot of hot air. You know, the Second *Mahele* that I had given the wrong name to, and I've kicked myself from then until now about that," said Quinn.

"But it did give me the chance to show that you could take state land and use it for social purposes for the betterment of the people of Hawaii, and that the main thing is you don't put it up for auction so people come in that don't deserve to have it.

"You select the class of people you want to have it—in this case, the people who were damaged and destroyed by that tidal wave—and let them draw by lot. The lucky ones get the prime pieces, but they all get something. That's exactly what happened and it worked.

"You can see it over there in Hilo, you can see it in the prosperous business community and the residences up higher...a nice waterfront park and the knowledge that the terrible damage will never happen in Hilo again."

≈Chapter Twenty-Six≈
A Royal Welcome

"Hawaii is the pathway between two parts of the world which are different..."

KING BHUMIBOL ADULYADEJ OF THAILAND
June 16, 1960

Two rows of uniformed airmen jogged up to lay a red carpet and place stands with ropes on either side. Alexis Johnson, U.S. ambassador to Thailand, mounted the steps to the plane, homburg in hand. *The Advertiser* reported: "As he disappeared into the plane, the two lines of airmen standing almost shoulder-to-shoulder inched forward so that their toes were over the edge of the carpet to keep the stiff breeze from whisking it away. A few minutes later, the 33-year-old King Bhumibol Adulyadej and his lovely Queen Sirikit stepped from the plane and walked down the ramp followed by Ambassador Johnson."

The slender king and doll-like queen of Thailand arrived in Hawaii for four days, their first visit to the United States. King Bhumibol, as commander-in-chief of Thailand's armed forces, wore the white, gold-braided uniform of an admiral and the petite queen was wearing a pink Thai dress with a white hat, gloves, shoes and accessories.

Governor and Mrs. Quinn waited at the end of the red carpet with other members of the welcoming party. As they moved along the receiving line, the queen kept one hand on her wide-brimmed hat, which the wind threatened to remove.

The official greeting included a military band, which played the Thailand national anthem and then the "Star Spangled Banner." Following a 21-gun salute and inspection of the honor guards of the Army, Air Police, Marine and Navy units, the Quinns escorted the Thai king and queen to the Royal Hawaiian Hotel.

"The king was with me in my car, and Queen Sirikit and Her Serene Highness Princess Vibhavadi Rangsit, lady-in-waiting, were with Nancy in a second car," Quinn said.

Quinn planned the program for the royal visit. He'd been informed they were coming to Hawaii, "but the State Department took no responsibility until they got to Washington. So, they were my guests," said Quinn, "and my responsibility."

The king told Quinn his wife had never left Thailand before.

"It was also the first time that she had ever worn a hat and she asked Nancy, 'How does this go?' and Nancy gave her a little advice," Quinn said.

"She was such a lovely person," said Nancy. "She spoke softly...innately shy, I'm sure...just the way Thai people are." Thailand, known as The Land of Temples, with splendid religious buildings, its Buddhist celebrations with candles, incense and flowers, is also the "land of smiles," a country filled with warmth and hospitality.

"We did things together. We went to the Art Academy, where there was a special exhibit of Oriental art," said Quinn.

"The king at one time had donned his yellow robe and taken his rice bowl and gone among his people, so he was a very devout Buddhist. It was so interesting because he explained much of the symbolism in the various paintings to me. We just had a great time."

The Quinns went with the Thai royal couple to the Big Island and stopped at the Volcano House for lunch.

"Afterwards," Nancy said, "on our way to the cars, the king and queen were walking ahead of us when she slipped her hand into his and they held tightly. She probably was wondering if they would ever be alone."

"We had a public reception," said Quinn. "The culmination was going to be a formal dinner party, but the big question was, how do we work out the guest list? We conferred with Ambassador Johnson and included all the consuls and spouses and eventually had a guest list of 50 people for a sit-down state dinner."

Honolulu Star-Bulletin June 16, 1960:

Governor Quinn proposed the toast to the king and queen and the king responded first with a toast to the president and the people of the United States and then to the Quinns.

Next, Mr. Kitayakara, private secretary to the king, appeared with a gold stand bearing gifts: The king presented the decoration of the Most Exalted Order of the White Elephant to Governor Quinn. This consists of two pendants—one worn on the left pocket and the other on a red and green riband.

Next, the monarch gave Governor Quinn a cigar box inscribed: "To Governor William F. Quinn, in deep appreciation of the kind welcome accorded by the state which though heterogeneous in race is homogeneous in spirit."

Queen Sirikit's gift to Mrs. Quinn was beige Thai silk interwoven with gold pattern.

After dinner, guests were entertained by Iolani Lauhine dancing ancient hulas and then Ken Alford and his Dixiecats playing a potpourri of songs of the Southland.

Quinn enjoyed telling the story that the star of the evening was no other than the king himself.

"I had learned that the king loved to play the clarinet and that he was very good. In fact, the advance guard had even brought a couple of records that he had made. We engaged Kenny Alford and His Dixiecats to be the entertainment that night and told them to get a silver mouthpiece. After dinner we all sat down out on the patio. The Dixieland band played a couple of numbers. I turned to the king and said, 'Your Majesty, I understand that you play a mean clarinet. I wonder If you would join the band? He turned to her majesty and said, 'What do you think?' She said, 'If the governor will sing, then it's all right.' So I sang a number or so and then he got up. He stood with the band for about an hour playing music."

With a borrowed clarinet, King Bhumibol had a ball. Joining the band in a jam session, he swung into Dixieland jazz, and "Blues in B Flat" and "Back Home in Indiana." He received a standing ovation.

The next morning began with a fast tour by the royal couple of downtown, Chinatown and Bishop Street. Then, as tourists in shorts and muumuus milled around Iolani Palace hoping to catch a glimpse of the young rulers, King Bhumibol addressed the joint session of the Legislature in the Senate chambers:

> *...You are gathered here because of a tragedy that has overtaken many of your people, a disastrous tidal wave that has brought calamity and death and suffering. Let me express to you our deepest sympathy.*
>
> *I greatly appreciate the honor you do me—by pausing in these grave deliberations—to invite me to be among the first visitors to address this high institution of the state of Hawaii.*
>
> *...Hawaii may be the youngest state of the union, but its vigorous and progressive development is already well known. By combining the best qualities of many races, Hawaii has suc-*

ceeded in forging a new community, which is universal in character, harmonious in spirit and forward-looking in outlook.

He spoke of the importance of Hawaii's role in the Pacific as a vital link between the peoples of the United States and the peoples of Thailand and Southeast Asia. The exchange of education, he said, would be a means for lasting peace.

The royal couple received thunderous applause as they walked to the waiting limos.

"Before the king and queen left here to go to the Mainland, Nancy and I went to see them off. We had leis for them, and surprisingly his majesty had a Thai lei for me. We had gotten quite close," said Quinn.

"When I was saying goodbye to the young monarch and knowing what he had in store for him for the rest of his life, I had a tear in my eye and he did, too. Alex Johnson said to me, after they departed, 'You know, Governor, you're the first friend this king has ever had. In Thailand they still approach the king on their knees and there's nobody that he has any closeness with except possibly a relative or two.' He said, 'You're the best friend he's ever had.'"

That afternoon, adjacent to the *Star-Bulletin*'s article covering the king's speech, was this headline: State Dinner? Not Invited, Kealoha Says.

"That's true," Quinn conceded. "The lieutenant governor was not invited to the dinner. However, he and Mrs. Kealoha were at the reception and in the receiving line. The news emphasized how I was slighting my lieutenant governor" says Quinn, "how I once again was refusing to let him be part of the government."

Quinn said the issue of the lieutenant governor and his role in the administration started two weeks after the 1959 election and continued through to 1962.

"Every time there was a chance for a reporter to play that theme, he'd do it. If there's one, there's five dozen stories over that limited period of time on that subject. It was just awful," Quinn said.

Hail to the Chief

The Thai royal party departed on June 17 and on Monday, June 20, President Eisenhower was to arrive in the Islands. He was scheduled to travel to the Far East, but suddenly that goodwill tour was canceled. Therefore, he was to have a five-day stay for rest and relaxation. He would reside at the Kaneohe Marine Corps Air Station in the same quarters he occupied in 1952. As the president was expected to make liberal use of the Kaneohe Klipper Golf Course, only two official events were planned. He was to receive an honorary degree from the University of Hawaii, and he was to be the guest of honor at the governor's reception on the Marine Air base on Friday.

"We wanted to hold a reception at Washington Place, but the president said 'no.' He did suggest inviting 50 people or so, and having it right at the Marine base," said Nancy. "We laughed at the number, saying that that was impossible, so we finally agreed to invite 250 guests and, I believe, we had 350."

Quinn proclaimed Monday, June 20, a half-day holiday in order to encourage a large turnout at the airport to greet the president: "I think it is vital that as many of us as possible come out to give the president a rousing welcome when he makes his first appearance here in our newest state."

Thousands responded—200,000 was the estimate.

Not even the end of World War II brought out such crowds in Hawaii. A solid mass of humanity pushed against the steel fence fronting the airport terminal minutes before the Boeing 707 whined in for a 12:14 touchdown. At the south end of the ramp, a squadron of olive-drab Marine helicopters squatted toadlike on the hot asphalt.

Following the president down the ramp were his Navy aide, Captain Evan P. Aurand, and Lieutenant John and Barbara Eisenhower, son and daughter-in-law of the president.

Six Hawaii schoolchildren welcomed the president on behalf of "Pennies for Peace." Nine-year-old Annette Tokujo, and a fifth-grader, delivered their message:

> *"Welcome to Hawaii. There are 141,000 public-schoolchildren in our state, and the six of us here today are speaking for them. When we read that you were coming to visit us, we wanted you to know how proud we are of you and of our country.*
>
> *"So all 141,000 of us gave a penny each to help the East-West Center because we believe that all children and grown-up people, too, want to live in peace.*
>
> *"We would like you to have this little bag with a few of the 141,000 'Pennies for Peace.' And when the center is ready, we hope you will come back and see it."*

There was no doubt that the children had touched President Eisenhower. Beaming his famous smile, the President accepted the small white cloth bag.

The Honolulu Advertiser, June 21, 1960

By Jack Teehan

They jammed Honolulu National Airport and the streets and byways. They waved little flags and crude, homemade "Aloha Ike" signs.

Because they were Americans, they didn't dress up for the president.

It was hot—so they wore shorts, bathing suits, muumuus, aloha shirts.

Husky construction workers, stripped to the waist and wearing hard hats, waved as the cavalcade drove by.

All Hawaii passed in review.

The 50th state was right there on King St. to Beretania-Nuuanu and N. Kalaheo.

They jam-packed the sidewalks. They teetered precariously from office windows. They perched on stepladders. They hunkered on curbs. They squatted on folding chairs.

They came on crutches and on wheelchairs.

They cheered from gasoline storage tanks,

roof tops and car tops.

Hawaii poured its heart out for a man—

Hawaii poured its heart out to the

president of the United States.

For Bill Quinn, however, political jabs flew before the president's sliver-and-orange Military Air Transport Service plane could touch its wheels down onto Honolulu Airport's long runway. There were accusations by House Speaker Elmer Cravalho that Governor Quinn was guilty of "narrow partisanship" in issuing invitations to Eisenhower's reception. Cravalho, in a much-publicized letter filled with innuendo, wrote that failure to invite more Democrats was an "insult to the people of Hawaii." He charged that he was the only member of the majority party of the House invited to honor the president while the entire membership of the minority party of the House Republicans received individual invitations.

"The president did not want to travel anywhere," Quinn pointed out later. "So the honorary degree was bestowed right at the base and my reception was held at the Officers Club. I invited the leadership of the House and the Senate, and Tom Gill comes out with, 'What do you mean? If you're not going to invite every member of this House, you're not going to get me to go.' Elmer Cravalho said, 'That's right. We are the people; we are the government; we are the ones who should meet the president.' This went on and on. They said, 'We aren't going to go.' and they didn't. I couldn't believe It. It was just so bad.'"

Five days later, a beaming, sun-burned, relaxed and smiling president bid aloha, along with prayers for success of the proposed East-West Center. He termed the center a prospective mechanism for bringing the friendly nations rimming the Pacific together.

In Quinn's farewell to the president, the governor declared that Ike's visit had been "one of the happiest days in the history of Hawaii."

The bashing of the governor continued.

Within hours of Ike's departure, state Representative Frank W.C. Loo delivered on the floor of the House one of the bitterest attacks ever launched against Quinn. He lashed at the governor for allegedly using public funds, public buildings and public functions for his own personal purposes, and characterized Quinn as a "money-changer who occupies the temple."

The House Republican leaders, Joe Garcia Jr. and Webley Edwards, repeatedly tried to shut off Loo's speech from the floor, claiming it had nothing to do with legislation to relieve the Hilo tsunami disaster victims. But Cravalho ruled that Loo had a right to speak as a matter of privilege.

The Honolulu Advertiser, June 27, 1960:

> Loo also pointed out that Cravalho was not invited to the reception for King Bhumibol and Lieutenant Governor James Kealoha didn't receive an invitation to the presidential reception.
>
> Garcia protested: "Mr. Speaker, this is going too far. What about Loo going to the press and asking that legislators of Hawaiian descent be allowed to accompany the president on his Far East tour?"

When Representative Tom Gill moved to close Saturday's House session, Edwards said, "I second the motion, bringing this tempest in a teapot to a close."

The media liaison for the governor during this hot period was the newest appointee on the staff, Press Secretary Roger Coryell. Coryell had been a big voice in the tsunami story. As news editor at KGMB-TV, he tracked down, without permission from his superior, rumors and untruths being spread by other radio stations. "Perhaps," said Coryell later, "I was heard by the governor, who was doing a gigantic job himself, physically as well as officially."

Coryell was 34, slender, medium height, with attentive blue eyes. He was in awe of Quinn. However, he learned his job fast. "Where there were only two or three of us at the station, here I was surrounded by squads of people carrying on," said Coryell. "I was kidded a lot and the first time I went into the press room, the hard-core *kamaaina* newsmen yelled, 'Hey, Roger, the governor's getting ready to fire you. Is there any truth in that?'

"I was green. I let them teach me and they were tough on me. They'd just as soon chew me up and spit me out if they could. Bit by bit they taught me how to be a press secretary. Before I even reported to my new office, I was told to write a speech for the governor that was to be delivered the next day, the 4th of July, when the 49-star flag was replaced with the 50-star flag. I remember how proud I was to be asked to fill the position."

≈Chapter Twenty-Seven≈
Hawaii on the Map

"We believe that Hawaii's star can be made to shine like the Star of Bethlehem, leading all men in the cause of peace..."

GOV. WILLIAM F. QUINN
July 4, 1960

A Fourth of July crowd of 10,000 saw the new 50-star banner go up the staff atop Iolani Palace. The National Anthem chorused by the 40-strong voices of the Kamehameha Alumni Glee Club opened the ceremony; the entire throng pledged allegiance to the flag of the United States.

Stirring and inspiring was Governor Quinn's patriotic address:

"This day is a great day for free people...this flag we have raised above Iolani Palace today is our symbol of patriotism. With it we declare that we love our country....It stands for a state where peoples of every nationality and culture have learned to live in harmony with each other. We are proud that we have not found this difficult to do....We believe that Hawaii's star can be made to shine like the Star of Bethlehem, leading all men in the cause of peace...."

Following Quinn's speech, six 105-millimeter howitzers of the 25th Division boomed a 50-gun salute in staccato rotation from the Diamond Head corner of the grounds. Bishop Harry S. Kennedy and Father Charles A. Kekumano pronounced benedictions and the audience joined the Kamehameha Choir to sing "Hawaii Ponoi."

Commemorative events popped like the mammoth fireworks display in the harbor that evening. U.S. Senator Hiram Fong arrived home from Washington with the 50-star U.S. flag that flew in Hawaii's honor at Philadelphia's Independence Square celebration. The governor signed a petition that Monday: July 4 would be Soap Box Derby Day and four little contestants wearing T-shirts and hard hats had their pictures taken with him. Two 11-year-old boys from New York City on a "Young Citizens Exchange" program called on the governor to learn the history of the Hawaii flag. The governor bought tickets and posed with police officers in front of the 50-star flag to support the Honolulu Police Choral Group "Stars-A-Poppin'" luau to be held in Kapiolani Park on Sunday. Saysana, a young Laotian student, called on the governor to thank the people of Hawaii for contributing 50,000 textbooks for Laos. He brought a hand-worked dagger whip to Quinn and expressed his wish to study at the East-West Center. "Perhaps," he said, "I will be able to return and study there when it is completed."

The governor maintained an open-door policy one day or part of a day each week. "During these periods, and for as much time as was available," said Quinn, "I instructed my staff to allow appointments to those who wanted them at about 15-minute intervals. There was a great deal of waste-of-time, but there were also some valuable matters learned from people who took the trouble to come in to see me personally.

"In addition to the open-door policy, I had weekly news conferences on television as well as news conferences when any special matters would arise," Quinn said.

Each week in the televised conference, a panel of leading

political reporters would fire questions at Quinn "without any advance knowledge on my part. After 15 or 20 minutes of the press conference, members of the viewing audience were invited to call. This worked very well. It kept me abreast of the concerns of the press and the people, and also allowed regular communication between the media, the people and the administration."

On July 7, 1960, the special session on Hilo relief ended; 12 bills were sent to the governor for signature. He signed with pleasure.

"This is a good one. Bill I (Act 4) to provide public lands for the relocation of businesses wiped out by the tidal wave was the basic reason for my calling this special session," Quinn said.

The other bills authorized direct grants for emergency relief, loans to businesses, reconstruction of Waiakea school and money to beef up the warning system.

"Generally speaking, in those days Hawaii was prosperous," said Quinn. "I used to describe the economy as sturdily supported by four legs: federal spending, sugar, pineapple and tourism."

Quinn recognized, however, that the prosperity was deceiving.

"The prosperity was only on Oahu. The Neighbor Islands were greatly depressed," he said.

The sugar industry had mechanized, reducing the number of jobs in the industry and impacting the shops and services that catered to the plantations and their employees. Tourism was growing, but there were few tourist facilities on the Neighbor Islands.

"The solution seemed to be to find other places besides Waikiki where tourists could be attracted....If we could encourage the development of the Neighbor Island tourist facilities, we might be able to stem the plunge of outer islands' economies," Quinn said.

251

Earlier, he had put together a team to identify places on the Neighbor Islands that could serve as tourist destination areas.

"A team consisting of planners, architects, contractors, developers, accountants and financial people...identified about 20 prime locations—Kaanapali, Poipu, Wailea, Kaunaoa Bay on the Big Island where Mauna Kea Beach now is, and many more.

"...I used the plan to develop our capital budget, giving preference to roads, water, airports, parks and other facilities necessary to open up these destinations and make them attractive to developers and hotel operators. At Kaanapali, Amfac had already started planning to convert the beach lands of Pioneer Mill to a resort center."

Just after the statehood election, Bill and Nancy Quinn had stayed at Laurance Rockefeller's lavish Dorado Beach hotel during a governors' conference in Puerto Rico. The place impressed Quinn so much, he wrote to Rockefeller and invited him to create the same kind of resort in Hawaii.

"He replied courteously, informing me that his interest was in the Caribbean, not the Pacific. But, he added, as chairman of President Eisenhower's Recreational Areas Committee, he would be in Alaska shortly and he'd be happy to visit Hawaii to see if he could be of any assistance to our new state in recreational area planning. That was all we needed."

Laurance Rockefeller, New York Governor Nelson Rockefeller's younger brother, was tall, standing shoulder to shoulder to 6-foot,one-inch Quinn, was regarded generally as the most business-minded of the oil billionaire's five grandsons.

TIME magazine in a special article tagged him as a "space age risk capitalist," and said he favored investments for the long pull, expecting his ventures to take 10, even 20, years to pay off.

"As soon as we knew that he was coming, I assigned George Mason, director of economic development, and Frank Lombardi, director of planning, to make out an island-wide itinerary that took him to just about every potential tourist destination area described in the study," said Quinn. Rockefeller came in mid-July 1960.

"Before he left, he had fallen in love with the site of Mauna Kea Beach on the Big Island and had committed for its purchase and lease from Parker Ranch."

Quinn viewed Frank Lombardi as a key player in the state's planning for the future. But he continued to be dogged by problems with Lombardi's appointment.

"Frank Lombardi, as state planner, was a department head and had to be a three-year resident. I had gotten special dispensation in the first legislative session for Frank, but the problem remained. A lot of the senators did not like Frank Lombardi because, as my instrument, he came up with the tourist destinations area study. That study was one of our major efforts for several years, Mauna Kea and Kaanapali being the first two. These capital improvement programs did not include the senators' pet projects like the cafetoria, the natatoria, the auditoria and instead included roads, airports, harbors, parks and water systems." Quinn said the senators whose districts weren't to see some of those improvements "were out to get" Lombardi.

"He was very effective, but he was not a political person at all." Finally, with some political savvy, Quinn was able to keep Lombardi in place. The state planner's three-year residence requirement was passed over and Lombardi remained on the governor's staff as long as Quinn was in office.

In Chicago, on July 26, 1960, the Republican National Convention put out the welcome mat for the Hawaii delegation. A special "Hawaii Night" salute with performers, flowers and music and, as reported by Frank Hewlett of the Star-Bulletin convention bureau, "Never was the coveted 50th star so radiant. Governor Quinn packed so much into his three-minute speech that he was applauded six times by 12,000 people who filled the

International Amphitheater. From his greeting—ALOHA—to his conclusion—MAHALO—they cheered."

The next day, he did it again. At the *hukilau* luncheon held in the elegant Palmer House, Governor Quinn was a hit with his political speeches and then he turned to the musicians and said, "Give me 'Blue Hawaii' in the key of B flat." He charmed all 2,400 at the women-only affair. They demanded another song, so he followed with Harry Owens' nostalgic "Sweet Leilani."

Back home, reports of Quinn's reception and popularity in Chicago galled his critics. Even Dan Inouye, home from Washington, D.C., to open his campaign for re-election, was critical of the governor's reception for King Bhumibol and Queen Sirikit of Thailand and the presidential visit.

He tartly rebuked President Eisenhower for refusing to step outside the gates of Kaneohe Marine Air Station during his recent visit. He said that he "nearly flipped" when he read that the University of Hawaii degree ceremony took place at the Marine Air Station. He also took a few swipes at Governor Quinn's handling of his reception for the president: "Governor Quinn's guest list was lopsided, to say the least."

Inouye had nothing to say about the Hilo relief bills that had been passed and signed, but he did say that in his swing through the Islands he planned to concentrate on "major issues." "It would be unjust to the people of Hawaii if I just discuss local problems." Inouye didn't fail to plug and staunchly defend Lyndon B. Johnson, the Democrats' vice president nominee, as a champion of civil rights.

Also while Quinn was away, the family dog was lost. Two days after the governor left for Chicago, there was a report that first-floor employees in The Advertiser building spent an hour chasing a friendly, brown and white, tail-wagging dog out of the building. The Humane Society knew immediately that it was Governor Quinn's "Danny Boy." Nancy was quoted as saying,

"Danny Boy has the habit of leaving home every time the governor leaves town."

No sooner had the governor (and Danny Boy) returned home, Republican Vice President Richard Nixon arrived in Hawaii to open his campaign for president. Accompanying him on his two-day tour of the Islands was his wife, Pat, U.S. Senator Hiram L. Fong, Secretary of the Interior Fred Seaton and campaign aides. August 3, 1960, was balmy and sunny. Nixon was greeted by Governor Quinn, Mayor Neal Blaisdell and other GOP leaders, including Republican Party Chairman Arthur Woolaway, Oahu County Chairman Ben F. Dillingham, state Senators J. Ward Russell and Randolph Crossley, Mrs. Joseph R. Farrington and Sheriff Duke P. Kahanamoku.

It was a whirlwind trip that included Oahu, Maui, Kauai and Hawaii. People swarmed the Nixons wherever they stopped, in Chinatown, at Iolani Palace, on King Street fronting Kamehameha's statue, along Kalakaua Avenue into Waikiki and the Royal Hawaiian Hotel. *Keiki* danced and sang, lei and brilliant red *kahili* decorated the entrance stairs. Pat and Dick loved it all.

"I can only hope that we can carry the music of Hawaii in our hearts as we travel through the United States and through the world. The warm affection and friendship for those who come among you is something the world needs, and we thank you from our hearts," Nixon said.

On the heels of the Nixon visit, Leonard Bernstein, noted conductor, performed with the New York Philharmonic Orchestra at the Waikiki Shell. After the conclusion of Friday's starlight performance, 120 members of the orchestra were bused to Washington Place for the governor's reception. They and their maestro were guests of honor, and they met 400 of the community's avid symphony patrons.

Celebrities continued to arrive. Hawaii was on the map. The

50th state was a shining star welcoming the rich and the famous, but more importantly, the state was the bridge linking the Pacific Islands and ancient world of Asia with America.

In mid-August the governor's office received word that Prince and Princess Takamatsu of Japan would visit. The prince was the younger brother of Emperor Hirohito. Their imperial highnesses were to celebrate the 75th anniversary of the first Japanese contract immigrants to arrive in Hawaii. The Quinns were to host a reception at Washington Place for the royal couple.

Again the guest list raised questions. As The Advertiser commented, "Governor Quinn is having invitation problems again." The ILWU's secretary-treasurer, Newton Miyagi, was invited and then the invitation was withdrawn by the governor on the grounds that Miyagi's outspoken views on international politics might be offensive to the royal couple.

"Miyagi's views on world politics are repugnant to me," the governor was quoted as saying.

"I have associated with Mr. Miyagi in the past for political or business reasons, but I don't care to associate with him on a social level. The mailed invitation to him was a clerical error."

Miyagi had recently returned from a Caribbean tour; he sang the praises of Castro's Cuba and said that he believed that the U.S. press had presented an unfair and false picture of the Castro regime in Cuba.

Jack Hall, ILWU chief, revealed to the press that the governor had asked him to recommend somebody to represent the union at a reception. When Hall named Miyagi, the governor asked for someone else, saying that Newton was "too controversial." Hall told the governor that no one else could possibly represent the union and that he refused to name anyone else.

"Nobody is going to tell us who is going to represent our union at any place. It's a matter of principle," Hall was quoted as saying.

According to Hall's published account, Quinn said, "Well, nobody's going to tell me how to run my reception, either."

A Quinn spokesman responded, "Two union officials, Robert Hasegawa, executive secretary of the Central Labor Council, and James Takano, secretary-treasurer of the Teamsters Union, are invited to the reception, and all segments of the community, including the leadership of both houses of the Legislature, the governor's cabinet, Japanese chambers and societies, have been invited."

Just four weeks later, Hawaii again honored Japanese Crown Prince Akihito and Princess Michiko. Fifty thousand people joined in the dazzling welcome. Following airport formalities, the royal couple paid their respects to the American dead at the National Cemetery of the Pacific and the 1,102 men entombed in the USS Arizona.

The crowning event of the day was the formal reception and dinner at Washington Place. Before 500 black-tie gentlemen and long-gowned ladies, Governor Quinn offered a toast first to the emperor and then the royal couple. Prince Akihito responded with a toast to the president of the United States and second to Governor Quinn and First Lady Nancy.

Two days later, in his weekly television broadcast, the governor answered a criticism on the subject of entertaining guests. "The state of Hawaii has no other choice but to entertain foreign dignitaries at state expense, although the burden to the state budget may be heavy.

"The alternative would be to ignore the visits of such persons as the king and queen of Thailand and of Prince Akihito and Princess Michiko. And this is unthinkable."

The next day, September 28, 1960, the *Honolulu Star-Bulletin* defended the governor:

Governor William F. Quinn has a real point in his asser-
tion that the state of Hawaii has no choice but to entertain
foreign dignitaries whether or not the federal government
helps pay the bill.

The governor is 100 percent right.

Hawaii and its governor are in a position occupied by no
other state and no other governor. Hawaii is the first port of
call for kings, princes, prime ministers and other representatives of Asiatic nations whose importance to us in the ideo-
logical struggle is incalculable. Slights, insults, breaches of
protocol mean more to Asians, more than to almost anyone
else. Our governor is in a position in which he must extend
full courtesies to these Asian leaders, whether federal financial assistance is available or not.

Before Quinn could savor any satisfaction, the *Star-Bulletin*
was right back batting him for his "GOPoliticking" (a 1960
TIME euphemism):

Star-Bulletin October 5, 1960:
THE HOME FIRES NEED TENDING

Don't look now, Governor, but while you were off campaigning for Vice President Nixon last week in California and
Washington (after casting your absentee ballot) your boy
Fred Titcomb got pretty badly mauled in the primary. For
every vote he got, Congressman Dan Inouye got three.

...We haven't been hearing any convincing voices getting
across the Republican message. Senator Hiram Fong has
been busy telling the Nixon forces how to win on the
Mainland. And you have made three trips to the Mainland
since the Chicago convention to kindle fires for the Nixon
campaign.

Meanwhile your home fires have been burning pretty low. They can do with a lot of top-level fanning. Your eloquent charm, so much in demand overseas, is about the best fan we have around.

The first rule in politics is to never let the home fires go out.

While Quinn had been attending the Republican convention in August, a riot broke out at Oahu Prison. Quinn was not notified of the incident because it was quickly brought under control, and it did not need his immediate attention. Democratic leaders blamed Quinn's absenteeism for the prison row. The bitter fight between Warden Joe Harper and Social Services Director Mary Noonan simmered. For many years Harper had had almost autonomous control over the prison when it was under the Department of Institutions. He resisted accepting direction from Noonan. For her part, she came into the position knowing little about prison administration.

On October 5 in the *Star-Bulletin*, House Majority Leader Thomas P. Gill was quoted: "The Noonan-Harper squabble is symptomatic of the general laxness of the Quinn administration. His absenteeism is one of the reasons why the reorganization of the state government has not been accomplished as smoothly as hoped for."

On the same date *The Advertiser* blasted the governor's frequent trips and pointed to eight trips in nine months and filing an absentee ballot for the primary because of "political travels." The newspaper accused him of being "somewhat out of touch with local affairs." The editorial was accompanied by one of Harry Lyons' political cartoons, Quinn as Aladdin riding a flying carpet with luggage labeled San Francisco, New York, Apple Blossom Festival, Chicago. The cartoon was entitled: Stow That Flying Carpet.

Governor Quinn says one reason why he stepped into the Harper-Noonan fracas was because the newspapers were "crucifying" them. Well now, Governor, we would take umbrage at that remark if we didn't know that because of your recent political travels, you've been somewhat out of touch with local affairs.

They haven't been able to get along very well, and things have been building up for some time. Anyhow, while you were traveling they had a real blow-off. If there was any crucifying going on, it was within your administration and you got back just in time to stop it.

...Now we read you've been invited to Japan. As we said, there are legitimate reasons for travel and this is one because it honors our state. We think you ought to go. Besides, it will be a welcome respite from your heavy responsibilities as a national campaigner.

Meantime, watch out for Jimmy Kealoha.

The governor met with Noonan and Harper in an hour-long conference. "I believe that an agreement has been reached and the two will work together," Quinn reported after the meeting.

When asked, Harper responded, "The whole tenor of the meeting was finding ways of resolving differences and to get on with the business of reorganization. I have confidence things will work out."

Quinn knew that it was up to Noonan and Harper. He believed that each had the strength to make things right and that each was capable of managing his and her position. He also knew that the fracas had caused doubts in some people's mind about the efficiency of his administration and his office.

Many years later, Ward Russell, good Republican friend of Quinn's, said he thought the governor was wrong.

"Speaking of the problems with Joe Harper, I think that Bill

was way out of line. I look at it from the outside, as a businessman, because I was not involved in it. I wouldn't have tolerated
some of those things. Either you shape up or get out would be
my attitude."

Russell pointed out that the consolidation of the two departments had the support of the Legislature.

"For such a rebellion to occur...was unallowable. These problems along with the weakness of the Republican Party had a negative impact on the voter."

⇜Chapter Twenty-Eight⇝
Amity, Diplomacy and Tourism

"We are living in what might be termed the last frontier of world travel..."

GOVERNOR WILLIAM F. QUINN
January 6, 1961

The numerous official visits in the 50th state during the governor's first year of elected office helped establish Hawaii as the "pathway between two parts of the world." The Islands charmed distinguished visitors and furthered America's goodwill in Asia.

The invitation to Governor Quinn, from Japan's foreign minister, to the final ceremonies in the centennial celebration of the U.S. Treaty of Trade and Amity was a crowning honor for Hawaii.

Hawaii's official party on the 25-day tour of the Far East would include the governor and first lady, Senate President William B. Hill, Attorney General Shiro Kashiwa, Deputy Social Services Director Lawrence Nakatsuka and their wives. Quinn was believed to be the first American governor invited for an official visit by the Japanese government. While in Japan, Governor and Mrs. Quinn would be guests of the government.

"I see in the news that some 34 governors are on their way to visit Argentina and Brazil, which makes me feel it's no less important for me to make a trip in this direction (to Japan) where Hawaii and I have many friends," Quinn said as the group left.

Quinn and his party were to have an audience with Emperor Hirohito and Empress Nagato and be feted by Prince and Princess Takamatsu. Because of other invitations, Quinn would also visit Okinawa, Taiwan, Hong Kong, Thailand and the Philippines. The governor would meet with Generalissimo and Madame Chiang Kai-shek and Philippines President Carlos Garcia.

Quinn said later he'd never seen such hospitality as he did in Japan. The group did a lot of sightseeing, "and I made a lot of speeches," he said. The governor spoke of meeting the emperor:

"We went into the palace, where we were met by the aides-de-camp, who were dressed in morning coats, tails and striped pants. We were conducted into the presence...the emperor and empress entered.

"The emperor and I had quite a long talk about his collection of tropical fish and about Hawaii...very cordial but very impressive and a rare moment for anybody."

Later that day, Quinn reported, they had lunch at Prince Takamatsu's home on the palace grounds.

"They had a beautiful lunch set up for us with one person, liveried, standing behind each chair. They had some dishes served with silver chopsticks and some served with knife and fork. It was just lovely, but we had to leave early because Ouida was ill," Quinn said. Ouida Hill, wife of the Senate president, was the first one to get sick from the fish eaten the day before.

"...That night the foreign minister had a dinner party for us. He had just concluded a successful election....At any rate, the foreign minister was just elated and in his element. He gave this beautiful teahouse party.

"I was prepared. I had learned to sing 'Kuroda Bushi.'...The foreign minister wrapped a silk shawl around his head, got up and did a dance. I got up and sang 'Kuroda Bushi' but all of a sudden in the latter part—I made it—but I was the last one to get sick from that fish. Right there at that party. I'm sure I turned green.

"Then we went to Taiwan. We were met by the foreign minister, who informed us that Generalissimo and Madame Chiang were at Sun Moon Lake and wondered if we could join them for lunch...just Nancy and me. We were flown to his country estate up on a mountain overlooking Sun Moon Lake. Before lunch we exchanged gifts and, as I remember, I gave him an oil painting.

"After lunch the generalissimo and I stepped out onto a balcony overlooking the magnificent lake with the mountain in the distance. He was a frail man with absolutely smooth skin drawn tightly, like parchment. He had bony fingers, was terribly thin and in his 80s. We talked a little bit about how he had left mainland China. He crooked a finger and pointed to the mainland and looked me right in the eye. He said, 'We will go back.'"

The group went to the Philippines after Taiwan. President Carlos Garcia was hosting an international conference with participants from many nations.

"There was a large reception held at Malacanang Palace and on the advice of Vargas (the Philippines foreign secretary) I wore my new barong. When we got there, the president had not arrived but hundreds of people had and they were all in tuxedos or white coat and black tie and there I was in a barong.

"Next, in came the president with Madame Garcia and the foreign secretary, all in black tie. I went through the receiving line, got to the secretary and I said, 'Boy, you sure misled me.' He said, 'This was the president's decision at 3 o'clock this afternoon.' Well, I wasn't out of place particularly, but I sure felt it."

While the official party was still on tour, coverage of their journey in Japan arrived at Quinn's office. Among the papers was *The American-Japan Society Bulletin*, which published a detailed account of a "welcome luncheon in honor of Honorable William F. Quinn, governor of Hawaii, and the members of his party and their ladies." It printed the entire text of Quinn's address and reported that Douglas MacArthur II, son of the famous World War II general, delivered the introductory remarks for the governor.

Quinn first spoke about a rare moment in history. He told the 200 guests about a happening of long ago. He chose the anecdote as an example of the strong ties that bind Japan and the United States:

> *Perhaps more than any other American state, Hawaii has a vital interest in the progress of Japanese-American relations. That concern is rooted firmly in the history of the Hawaiian Islands, dating back to the days of the Hawaiian monarchy. As an interesting sidelight, the first official relationship between the Kingdom of Hawaii and the Empire of Japan occurred in the year 1860, and involved the special embassy that had been dispatched by Japan to exchange ratification of the Treaty of Amity and Commerce between the United States and Japan.*
>
> *Because of strong headwinds and a shortage of coal while en route to San Francisco, the American freighter Powhatan carrying the Japanese embassy was forced to detour to Honolulu. For 14 days the visitors found rest and change in a strange Polynesian setting. They were greeted by King Kamehameha IV and also the American and French ministers stationed there. This was the first time any representatives of the Japanese government had set foot on Hawaiian soil.*

He spoke of eight years later, 1868, when the very first group of 148 Japanese immigrants arrived in Hawaii to work in the sugar cane fields:

> *The pioneers endured a hard life. They labored in the sugar fields and in the mills from dawn to dusk. Their wages were low, their tasks back-breaking. They lived in crude shacks and all in all fared frugally....In time, the nisei children made life easier*

265

for their issei parents and for themselves....

Economically, socially and culturally, the American-born children of immigrant Japanese steadily moved up the ladder of success...

In my official family, three nisei serve as cabinet officers, and many more in other positions in the state government. It was my privilege last year to appoint a nisei as the first chief justice of the new state of Hawaii...

He closed his speech by speaking of Hawaii's year-long celebration of statehood and how fitting it was to have so many distinguished visitors from Japan.

The outstanding event, of course, was the visit of Their Imperial Highnesses Crown Prince Akihito and Princess Michiko last September.

By coincidence in this centennial year, Hawaii is bringing into reality a dream it has nurtured for a long time. I am speaking of our East-West Center for cultural and technical interchange at the University of Hawaii. The Center will be the major massive effort of Hawaii's people to serve as the bridge between the East and West. We see this project as our best contribution to the second century of Japanese-American relations and a new Pacific era.

Christmas was only one week away when the group got home; the Quinns had little time to reflect upon their exotic Far East travels. At the airport they were met by reporters, dozens of questions and their children. Six-year-old Cecily had a surprise— she had lost her two front teeth.

The governor said that he found the people in the Orient interested in the East-West Center and in development of tourism in the Pacific. He said that the East-West Center was one of the topics brought up by Emperor Hirohito of Japan and

President Chang Kai-shek of Nationalist China. Quinn said both hope that their countries would have some advisory voice in the direction the center might take.

The governor's travel schedule came up in the reporters' questions. Asked if he would attend the mid-January inauguration of President Kennedy, Quinn said he probably would. He announced that he would serve as the grand marshal in the Tournament of Roses Parade in Pasadena, California, on January 1. Questioned how he could be away so long, Quinn answered that he would be in Washington, D.C., "the shortest possible time" and that the Rose Parade would be just over the New Year's holiday.

Nineteen sixty had been quite a year in Hawaii, what with the honors bestowed on the 50th state, royal and celebrity visitors, the disastrous tsunami, the crisis problems at the prison and the spectacular tourist boom, "greater than any other part of the world," as reported at the weeklong American Society of Travel Agents convention held in Waikiki. Two thousand agents attended—very important to the future of Hawaii's fastest-growing industry of tourism.

On January 1, 1961, the 72nd Tournament of Roses honored the famous flowers of Hawaii with its theme, "Ballads in Blossoms," and Quinn was grand marshall. Bill Henry of the *Los Angeles Times* described Hawaii's governor as "Hawaiian by adoption":

> Our pals over in Pasadena, with their penchant of timely choices for grand marshalls for the Tournament of Roses, have chosen a mighty interesting individual. This time in the person of William Francis Quinn. Mr. Quinn is not chosen because he is Mr. Quinn, but because he is the first governor

of the 50th state.

He is a tall fellow with curly hair, enormous enthusiasm and a resonant tenor voice. In addition he has half a dozen children and a very good-looking and sprightly wife. Quinn is a typical Hawaiian, meaning that he comes from someplace else. Left to themselves, the Hawaiians might never have made anything of their islands. But guys like Harry Owens, who came from someplace else, started immortalizing Hawaii's music; Webb Edwards, also from someplace else, keeps it going with his world-renowned "Hawaii Calls" radio program; Bing Crosby, likewise from some-place else, first gave coast-to-coast hearing to the Islands' plaintive songs, then completely immortalizes one of them by naming a race-horse "Sweet Leilani" and having it come off a winner at Santa Anita at a payoff of some $600 for a two-dollar ticket. So Governor Quinn is that kind of a Hawaiian too.

After the quick trip to Pasadena, the governor found the long-awaited new official car, a gleaming 1961 Cadillac limousine, waiting for him. Quinn's smile was just as shining and bright as the "Granada green" automobile parked at the foot of the Iolani Palace steps. The car carried two flags in front: an American one on the right and a red, white and blue one with a circle of eight white stars (for the eight islands) on the left. Inside the eight-passenger auto were two telephones, a police radio receiver and transmitter, an air-conditioning unit and an electric shaver. The new vehicle cost the state $5,876.10 ($9,351.10 less $3,475 for trade-in of the old one).

Pacific Area Travel Association, PATA, 150 delegates from 22 areas of the Pacific, held their 10th-annual conference in Waikiki. The weeklong meeting, which began on January 6, 1961 scheduled top speakers in the industry. Quinn delivered the opening address. F. Marvin Plake, PATA executive director, introduced

Quinn:

"Governor Quinn has led the way in maintaining Hawaii's place as the fastest-growing tourist destination in the Pacific."

Quinn acknowledged that PATA's message in the decade just ended had been "Discover the Pacific" and suggested that the new theme for the next 10 years be, "The Pacific's Decade of Opportunity."

"PATA was founded here 10 years ago to help in the discovery...but the fact is, ladies and gentlemen, that in terms of the travel market and the potential, the Pacific still remains to be discovered...."

Thurston Twigg-Smith, who in 1961 had just become publisher of *The Honolulu Advertiser*, served on the board of PATA at the time. He said Plake, who was based in San Francisco, "was telling me how one day Quinn came into the city to speak at a meeting. Plake picked him up at the airport and had a speech ready for him. It was a long speech on travel and what PATA could mean to the other states and to the world and all that. As they rode in from the airport, Quinn went through the speech, turning the pages fairly rapidly.

"Plake himself was a terrific speaker and also wrote good speeches. Bill turned it back to him and said, 'There's a lot of fine stuff in there' and Plake said, 'Don't you want it? It's for you.' Quinn answered, 'I've got it.' According to Plake, Quinn got to the platform and gave the speech almost word for word... concept after concept...the whole thing. Quinn's mind was like a steel trap. He had picked that speech up by just reading through it and he was impressive. A tremendous intellect."

In February, the governor gave his message to the First State Legislature General Session of 1961. He spoke of the critical importance of proper planning and development of statewide resources in tourist destination areas:

"The failure to do so is already glaringly evident in what has happened and is happening to Waikiki. We must remember that we are competing for tourist business with many other areas in the world that enjoy certain advantages over us, such as Mexico, Puerto Rico, the Bahamas, Bermuda, the West Indies and others. The only way we can compete is to maintain the unique Hawaiian beauty and character of our tourist destination areas.

"This cannot be done if we permit a series of small-scale Miami Beaches to spring up all over our Islands. It can only be done if we control our development so as to preserve the natural beauty and charm of Hawaii.

"Such control is not easily accomplished, however. The forces of speculative gain and immediate profit-making are formidable and their tactics are persuasive, insidious and too often overwhelming. For this reason, the state must bolster and supplement the zoning powers of the counties.

"As we look at Waikiki today, there is only one term that is appropriate, 'Paradise Lost.' Can this paradise be regained? Yes, but only if we act forthrightly, courageously and immediately. He who spoils and defaces Waikiki or Kona or any other spot in our state not only ruins these specific areas, but he also weakens and undermines the whole state of Hawaii as a tourist attraction. The state has a vital interest in this matter and must act to preserve and protect this interest. However, it is going to take bold action if we are to succeed in preserving Waikiki as one of the world's great playgrounds."

PART FIVE

≈Chapter Twenty-Nine≈

Omnibus or Bust

"... All in all it was a good message, thoughtful and realistic. The lawmakers should respond in like spirit."
THE HONOLULU ADVERTISER
February 17, 1961

The Quinn administration had major preparations for the 1961 legislative general session. There were significant problems caused by statehood that needed to be solved. Many federal laws applied only to the territory of Hawaii. For instance, up until statehood the federal antitrust laws regulated territorial commerce; with statehood, the federal laws no longer applied.

The statehood bill said, "All such laws shall remain in existence for two years, after which they shall expire." Hawaii lawmakers had to study what would expire and what the Legislature needed to pass.

"I had a new Land Use Commission that I was proposing and that was very unique throughout the nation. My motivation for it was that in those days Honolulu was not organized and did not have decent planning or zoning, and people were going hog-wild. They were trying to build business and residential structures wherever they could without coordination and planning," said Quinn.

Quinn believed it urgent to get a system of state planning that would bring pattern and control into the rushing development.

The governor and his aides spent hours drafting a code that would be presented to the Legislature. He called for sweeping changes on land legislation. Republicans hailed the program as "terrific" and the Democrats claimed that Quinn was really agreeing in principle with their own proposals.

> *Honolulu Star-Bulletin* January 29, 1961:
>
> GOVERNOR OUTLINES LAND POLICY VIEWS
>
> Most of the existing land laws expire next August, two years after statehood," said Quinn. "A realistic and effective land policy for the state of Hawaii must recognize and be founded on two basic policies: widespread ownership and development and the second, conservation.
>
> A little more than a century ago, all land in Hawaii was owned by the king. However, the growth of democratic institutions brought wider ownership of the land. Kamehameha III carried out the Great Mahele, expanding the ownership of the land and setting the pattern for the land system as it exists today. At the time of the Great Mahele one-third was made public, one-third was given to the government and one-third became lands of the monarch. Of the latter, one half of that land became public and the other half private.
>
> Actually, the Great Mahele failed, the wrong people grabbed the lands and the people were left without.

"One of the major effects of our transition from territorial status to statehood," Quinn explained, "was the fact that after annexation when the Islands first became a republic, then a territory, all of the public lands once owned by the kingdom became federal lands.

"The federal government became the owner of all those public lands, which included the acreages of Fort DeRussy, Ruger,

Pearl Harbor, Waimanalo and others; tremendous land resources and a Defense Department that was going to try to hold on to everything that it had.

"Also, Hawaii state suddenly had more land than any other state government. We also had the Hawaiian Homes Commission with 200,000 acres of secondary lands. Meant for the Hawaiian people, these properties had been developed in a program introduced by Delegate Prince Jonah Kuhio Kalanianaole in an act passed by Congress in 1920.

"When I first came in as territorial governor, I discovered that if the territory wanted a piece of land and it happened to be Hawaiian Homes land, they'd just take it and use it. I put a stop to that practice and used a system of land trade, instead. For example, when we needed Hawaiian Home lands on a Neighbor Island for a public project, we traded government lands in Waimanalo, which developed into a fine Hawaiian Homes project.

"Another problem was that many Hawaiians lived in Honolulu and there was no land available for them under the Hawaiian Homes Commission. I wanted to contribute Oahu public lands to the commissions and make available homelands to Oahu urban workers. This required a change in the Hawaiian Homes Act. But the Hawaiians themselves rose up in arms against any amendment at all. 'Don't even change a comma,' they cried. They viewed the Homes Commission Act as a gift to them from Prince Kuhio and didn't want the state to meddle with it at all even though under the program many more Hawaiians would be benefited. Now more than three decades later the Hawaiians are fighting for what we tried to give them way back then.

"Then we had the public lands. We had all this government-owned land and, at the same time, we had many people on leasehold property and others who just couldn't get lands for small farms or residences. The only way we could make government-owned land available was by public auction and that was bad—the big guys would come in and buy up all the land.

"So the whole theme of my program, which in 1959 I mistakenly named Second *Mahele*, was to give the government the right to put a value on the land and then find the class of people, be they farmers, under-lass urban workers, etc. and make the land available only to those people, at a fair price without auction. Those persons would have to qualify to participate and then their names would be drawn by lot. The few times we did it, it just worked beautifully. But unfortunately, all of it continued to be cursed by the Mahele."

From an editorial in *The Advertiser* January 27, 1961, "Pockets of Prejudice":

> Governor Quinn's land proposals are broadly stated and embrace many aspects of the problem. They need much study. But certainly it's hard to quarrel with one of the suggestions that the state outlaw "onerous discriminatory terms and conditions in leases."
>
> In reply to questions, the governor said his proposal is aimed, among other things, at neighborhood racial restrictions.
>
> ...Hawaii prides itself on racial harmony, but there are a few pockets of prejudice. You can't pass laws that change the way people feel about other people, but you can pass laws to prevent discrimination of this sort. The governor's proposal would be such a law and we're for it.

"The heart of this thing was to avoid public auction, putting aside the land for specific purposes and then doing it by drawing by lot. That was the broader new program," said Quinn.

"Another phase of it was to amend the tax laws so that large landowners like Campbell and Bishop Estate, after selling to lower- and middle-income groups, would pay the capital gain tax, which is less than the ordinary income tax."

On the morning before the opening of the legislative session of February 15, 1961, several hundred Republicans and Democrats, Catholics and non-Catholics, spent a solemn hour together attending the traditional Red Mass in Our Lady of Peace Cathedral on Fort Street. The mass was celebrated by the Most Reverend James J. Sweeney, Catholic bishop of Honolulu. After the service, the group walked to Richards Street and the grounds of Iolani Palace—elected officials, their families and visitors crowded the columned lanai.

Honolulu Star-Bulletin February 16, 1961:

> Preceded by traditional hula dancing and music-making, Hawaii's Legislature convened today in a splash of color to begin its fifth session in the last year and a half. House Speaker Elmer Cravalho banged down his gavel at 10 a.m. in the Koko Head wing of Iolani Palace to call his 50 colleagues to order.
>
> A half-hour later, Senate President William Hill pounded his gavel in the Ewa wing of the palace to call the 25-man Senate to order.

At 11 a.m. the governor addressed the joint session with an hour-long message. *The Advertiser* called it one of Quinn's finest statements since taking office:

> His remarks on land law add up to a philosophy which he and his lawmakers of both parties should reflect in their

actions this session. Here is a philosophy of moderation and flexibility, taking the long view, a philosophy that recognizes there are many differences of opinion and no pat solutions.

...Although the governor emphasized the land problem, he did not neglect other pressing matters such as education, traffic safety and the future of the University of Hawaii.

...All in all it was a good message, thoughtful and realistic. The lawmakers should respond in like spirit.

The *Honolulu Star-Bulletin* reported on February 17, 1961, that the Republican leaders liked Quinn's message. The paper said it was the "most forceful and dynamic ever given by the governor," "one of his best statements since taking office...a strong pacesetter for accomplishments to come in the session."

Others, such as Democratic Speaker of the House Elmer Cravalho, had a different view: "There was no doubt that the governor displayed an uncanny ability to pick up the Democratic Party platform and attempt to give it the appearance of a Quinn original."

It was likewise with Thomas Gill, Democrat, House majority leader: "In the protection of lessees the governor has adopted our music, but we are still waiting for the words. What does he specifically propose?"

Senate President William B. Hill, the crusty Republican, who could be found every morning at 7 a.m. at his desk, drinking his breakfast Coca-Cola and puffing on his Salem cigarette, had this reaction: "It was a good, thorough speech, nothing wishy-washy about it."

And, if the plan Quinn outlined in his talk coincided with that of the Democrats, Hill added, "That's fine. There shouldn't be any trouble getting the bills through."

Under the Reorganization Act of 1959 passed by the Legislature, the governor had until the 10th day of the legislative session to name a new Board of Regents for the University of Hawaii.

Quinn says, "There was a formula required that made it very difficult to make a good selection; five regents out of the nine had to be University of Hawaii graduates."

To the press he said, "There are many fine graduates of the university who could do a splendid job in the governance of the institution. However, a restrictive limitation such as this drastically narrows the field of community leadership from which a blue-ribbon board can be chosen.

"I asked legislators to rescind the UH clause, but the leaders rejected the idea. So I abided by it. There were other requirements, too: representation of both Republican and Democratic parties, both districts, fifth and sixth, and the outer islands. I ended up with a blue-ribbon board but it took many weeks of searching."

No sooner had the governor turned in his appointees' names to the Legislature, he was taken to Queen's Hospital with viral pneumonia. "The move to the hospital was to provide him with complete rest," reported Roger Coryell, his press secretary.

Those who worked closely with the governor admitted that he had been suffering with a cold ever since his quick, frigid trip to Washington, D.C., to attend President Kennedy's inaugural.

"The governor, Mrs. Quinn and I were at the inauguration together," said John Henry Felix. "We'll never forget that it was one of the coldest days on record. The 50th state was the last in the parade and by the time they got to the grandstand, it was dark and the cameras had gone. That evening we went from ball to ball in knee-deep snow. It was pretty strenuous."

Meanwhile, the governor's list of UH regents' nominees became the best-kept secret in legislative history. Said one GOP senator on rejecting a reporter's request for the names, "I tell you, we had to sign our names in blood on a pledge to keep quiet." A mention of the policy was noted in the morning sheet, which reported, "The secrecy clamped on the list as discussed by the Senate majority was regarded as a test of the Republican senators because previous nominations had leaked out before formal submission."

It is interesting that the article made no mention of the Democratic senators. It appears that the slate was known only to the 14 GOP senators and Quinn's office.

The governor was back in the office by March 1st and raring to go. UH regent confirmation by the Senate was imminent, but the heat from the legislative session was like jumping into an open fire. While all that was going on, a blazing headline told of another battle:

Star-Bulletin February 18:
WEINBERG-QUINN BUS TALKS STORMY

> Evidence that the meeting between the governor, Harry Weinberg, Ed deHarne and other officials was stormy at times, came when loud talking could be heard through the closed door of Quinn's executive office.

"The mayor called me one morning and told me how he was trying to settle the HRT (Honolulu Rapid Transit) bus strike. He asked me to step in to try to get it settled....It was a Sunday afternoon that we met and Mayor Blaisdell, Art Rutledge and the new owner of HRT, Harry Weinberg, were there. It was the first time I met him (Weinberg).

"...The first thing he said to me was, 'Oh, I know you. We'll never get a fair shake here...because when I took over I took the HRT account away from Robertson, Castle & Anthony."

"I reached over and with one hand, grabbed his shirt front. I didn't shout but I was angry. 'Listen, Mr. Weinberg, you can talk like that all you want to Bill Quinn but don't you dare talk to the governor of Hawaii that way.'

"From then on we got along well and the next time I was running for office, Harry came up with a big campaign contribution."

The strike was averted and the buses kept rolling. A union official who had been in the conference room reported, "The governor handled it beautifully. They would go off on tangents and he'd bring them back...he finally ground it down."

Quinn had other labor dispute successes. He was given credit for ending a statewide sugar strike of 15 sugar plantations less than 12 hours after it began. The ILWU and Hawaii's sugar industry agreed on a new two-year contract. Jack Hall, the big union boss, complimented Quinn for his role in mediating the dispute. He said, "The fact is that if he is ever out of a job as governor, he can always pick up a few bucks as a mediator."

But Quinn was not that fortunate with the Legislature.

"There was so much going on and I realized, when the session's time was coming to a close, that the legislators were intending to do the same thing they had always done; they were going to stop the clock. Stop the clock, no deadlines, they would pay each other every day. Charles Kauhane had stopped it in the 1957 Legislature for 30 days. For 30 days it was April 1st and they got paid for 30 days.

"I announced that I was not going to stop the clock, that it was unconstitutional and I wouldn't allow it. Instead, I granted a five-day extension and put the pressure on them." In the end there were four extensions—making 30 days of extended time in all.

The governor's press release said, "Despite the repeated extensions, a great deal of work has still not been properly completed. The time is short. The need is great. The people are impatiently waiting."

The governor's statement brought quick replies from several House leaders, including one from Majority Floor Leader Thomas P. Gill:

> "It is also the will of the people that the governor spend a little more time doing his job. If he had spent more time in town last fall getting his budget, reorganization and manpower requests in proper order, we could probably have saved several weeks during the session.
>
> "It is interesting to note that this last series of remarks by the governor was issued while he was out of town attending a rodeo and making a speech."

The Advertiser editorial, June 7, 1961:

> On May 23, the governor complimented the house for being "more interested in stopping the clock than getting their jobs done." This brought such dignified retorts as these:
>
> From Speaker Cravalho: "His intemperate remarks indicate that he still lacks the political morality he lacked when he dashed to Washington to steal the governorship..."
>
> From Floor Leader Howard Miyake:
>
> "Crass...irresponsible...an egotistical rhetorician inebriated by his own verbosity, engaged in penny-ante politics."
>
> As much as it may seem like it, these were not children thrusting out their tongues at one another. These were grown, experienced men, engaged in conducting the business of this sovereign state. What they said about one another—and they kept it up throughout the session—reflects a deep-seated mistrust, even contempt. This could not help but have adversely affected the work of the Legislature.
>
> As far as the House is concerned, the governor is licked

before he starts. Almost every proposal he makes is given only the most perfunctory attention. Because he is the governor and a Republican, he is automatically discredited.

Meantime, the fine speeches go on about a unique Hawaii and its potential in the service to mankind. They are inspiring speeches until the hearer looks closely at the behavior of the speech-makers. Then it becomes depressingly clear that Hawaii will never achieve these high-sounding goals until our lawmakers make up their minds to act in a mature, responsible fashion.

The first step is to grow up.

On June 3 legislators adjourned their 1961 session at midnight, running right up to the maximum time allotted them without stopping the clock. In the dying minutes, they passed the $35 million capital improvements bill but they killed a lands bill that would have enacted a whole new code of land laws for the state.

Quinn severely rapped the House Democratic leaders, saying that they must take full responsibility for the failure of the Legislature to pass an omnibus land bill.

"A comprehensive land bill, the result of long, bipartisan efforts by the Senate committee and adopted unanimously by the Senate, was brusquely shunted aside by the House. The House Policy Committee treated the bipartisan Senate effort with utter contempt and instead produced a puny, politically motivated measure.

"The abbreviated House bill given to the Senate on a take-it-or-leave-it basis made no provisions for transferring functions between departments, the main reason why a law was needed in the first place."

House Speaker Cravalho rebutted by saying that he would refuse to have any more conferences with the governor.

"If he has anything more to say to me, he'll have to put it in writing." Whereupon the speaker called the governor "a squeal-ing pig."

Later Quinn remarked, "I can't tell you all that didn't pass, but much of it didn't, including the land law. The antitrust law passed and it was a good one. It had an impressive impact on this community. We had certain occupations, like the barbers and cosmetologists and a few others, and the way they were working was in violation of the old law, as a matter of internal commerce within the state of Hawaii.

"It meant a big change. Many of the business people used to serve on the board of Bank of Hawaii, on the board of Hawaiian Trust Company, maybe even on the board of First Hawaiian Bank, lots of them on the board of Castle & Cooke and the board of Theo Davies. That was all gone. We gave them a little time to get their affairs in order because the notice was that that was no longer tolerable."

In an interview at the conclusion of the session, Senate President "Doc" Hill called it "a run-of-the-mill one." He said, "On the minus side, the most regrettable thing was that no land bill passed. The land committee of the Senate, composed of five Republicans and three Democrats, worked hard for over nine months to get a land bill ready.

"Every Democrat and every Republican voted for it. It went to the House, but the leadership there had its own ideas about land bills. There was no conscientious consideration given the Senate bill and there is no question that the House group were determined to embarrass the governor and the administration as much as they could."

The omnibus bill was a bust and the lawmakers never ceased their name-calling. A Harry Lyons' cartoon, aptly entitled Thank Heaven, School's Out, captured the sentiments of the poor tax-payers. They had never dreamed that the Legislature was actual-ly the Iolani Palace Kindergarten.

≈ Chapter Thirty ≈

The Governors Arrive
(But None by Ship)

*..Many governors will be seeing the newest state for the
first time while others haven't been here since World War
II days....*

THE HONOLULU ADVERTISER
June 21, 1961

The plans for the 53rd annual National Governors
Conference, June 24 to 30 at Waikiki, were as detailed
and precise as a military operation. John Henry Felix,
administrative assistant to the governor, presented a 90-
minute briefing to police, hoteliers and military officers,
covering every arrangement: arrival times, motorcade routes,
even where to stand and what to say.

Half of the governors would stay at the Royal Hawaiian Hotel
and the other half at the Hilton Hawaiian Village. "The official
party," Felix said, "including governors, families, staff and newsmen, will number 550."

Hotelman Dick Holtzman, head honcho of the Royal, said,
"I've seen a lot of similar functions, but I've never encountered
anything more beautifully planned."

In planning the conference the Quinn administration had
detailed help from a 22-page brochure entitled "Governors
Conference Annual Meeting," a preliminary memorandum on
suggested arrangements, facilities and procedures. The docu-

ment outlined everything from baggage handling to music, flowers and state dinner. It even covered documents, typewriters,
desks, message centers and main conference tables. It asked for
"four short boys for handling roving microphones."

As expected, there were last-minute changes: Vice President
Lyndon B. Johnson was coming in place of President John F.
Kennedy. Johnson, accompanied by Mrs. Johnson and a party of
13, had reserved the entire 17th floor of the Diamond Head
Tower of the Hilton Hawaiian Village.

The vice president had been here before. In May, LBJ came
to initiate the groundbreaking of the East-West Center and to
receive an honorary degree at the University of Hawaii. He and
Lady Bird were welcomed with a marching band, a gun salute,
flowers, dancers, music and crowds. There were several invita-
tional affairs planned in his honor, including a private dinner
party co-hosted by Congressman Dan Inouye and Jack Burns,
the ex-delegate to Congress.

"It's just a horrible mess," said one of Burns' volunteer aides.
"There are sure to be hurt feelings." Political observers
remarked that Burns was making everybody forget Governor
Quinn's past invitation problems.

"As far as we were concerned," said Nancy, "the entire
Johnson visit was terrible, from start to finish."

Nancy Quinn, a gracious woman, was generally the last to be
critical. Yet the Johnson visit for the East-West Center groundbreaking remained an unpleasant memory for her.

"Bill and I were at Hickam Air Field to welcome the
Johnsons. I carried a big red carnation lei for LBJ and a double
white for Lady Bird. After the official military greeting, we rode
through downtown to the ceremonies at the palace. She and I
were in the back seat of an open convertible and Burns was seated up in front with the driver. Whatever I said to her was
ignored. She refused to speak to me. She spoke only to Jack

Burns during the entire ride.

"When the vice president halted the motorcade and stepped out on King Street to greet the crowd, the only conversation was between the two, Jack and Lady Bird. There was a ceremony at the palace where the Legislature was in session and we were seated on the stage at the foot of the entrance steps. Bill stepped up to the mike and introduced the vice president. Johnson, in turn, addressed the seated officials and the few thousand gathered, but did his best to ignore the governor. He purposely avoided any recognition of Bill until he had acknowledged everyone else."

Quinn recalled Johnson's visit for the governors' meeting. "When we arrived at the Hawaiian Village for dinner," Quinn said, "the vice president's reception was just concluding so we went to the dining room. We found our way to the head table. It was full! Two seats remained for the Johnsons. Admiral Don Felt was embarrassed for us. He stood and offered us their seats. Of course we declined. We left the head table and started looking around for a place to sit. We found a table for two near the back of the room and took our seats there."

If that was not enough, when Johnson addressed his guests in his dinner speech, he acknowledged Quinn's presence after recognizing everyone else—Jack Burns, Dan Inouye, the mayor, the police, the military, etc. Then, finally, he mumbled "the governor," without even calling him by name.

Another last-minute change came when six of the governors, who were scheduled to sail to Hawaii on Matson's SS Lurline, had to rearrange transportation hastily and take to the air; a sudden maritime strike spread across the nation and into the Pacific zone.

Evidence that the shipping strike had hit Hawaii was everywhere. At the piers, containers of general cargo sat loaded on idle, strike-bound freighters. In the markets, panicked buyers depleted some staples; fresh produce from the Mainland was practically gone from the bins.

"The shipping strike was a major thing and it went on for a long time," said Quinn. "I quickly got in touch with the Kennedy administration. I said that the strike was disastrous to Hawaii and that we depended on transoceanic shipments for our food and medical supplies (and we did in those days). I reiterated that we could quickly be in an emergency situation if essential shipments didn't get to us. There was all that and the Governors Conference, too."

On the opening day of the conference, just before Quinn was to officially welcome them in the Monarch Room of the Royal Hawaiian Hotel, he received word from Washington that the bosses of all five striking maritime unions rejected an administration plea for an immediate 60-day truce.

Quinn replied immediately.

Honolulu Star-Bulletin June 24, 1961

> In a radiogram to President Kennedy on Friday, Quinn said: "Surface shipping to and from Hawaii has stopped almost entirely due to strike. Situation has drastic impact on health and welfare of our people. I implore you to invoke your powers under the Taft-Hartley Act to require resumption of ship movements during cooling-off period while complex issues of this dispute can be settled."

"In subsequent calls, I was able to persuade Arthur Goldberg, secretary of labor, that our situation was critical. As a result, the Kennedy administration applied for a Taft-Hartley injunction, an unusual procedure," explained Quinn. "They asked for an affidavit from me stating the consequence of the lack of shipping to support the injunction application. With the help of the staff, I put together a long affidavit.

"...Something amusing happened. A day or so before they were going to apply for the Taft-Hartley injunction in the District Court of San Francisco, I got a call from a fellow who was an assistant attorney general. He said, 'Governor, I have your affidavit here. It's just what we wanted, but do you mind if I make a couple of changes?'

"I asked him what he was talking about and he explained: 'One of the things, Governor, that you say will be in scarce supply is sanitary napkins. Now I think that's a serious problem and can be a great difficulty, but I have to take this into court and face Richard Gladstein, attorney for the ILWU and a brilliant trial attorney. I can just see him before a judge saying, "Your Honor, just think. They've got to go without sanitary napkins and isn't that a national emergency." Take my advice, Governor, you've got enough in the affidavit without it.'

"I agreed. They edited the affidavit, filed it and got the injunction."

The Governors Conference continued. Each morning the governors attended business sessions from 9 until noon and then the fun began. There were air tours of the Islands, catamaran rides, golf, tennis and yachting, a Hawaiian feast, a luncheon fashion show, a formal banquet and the opening night reception at Washington Place. The organizers prepared the social calendar with great thought and plenty of aloha.

Nancy and Bill Quinn lived at the Royal Hawaiian Hotel during the festive week while the kids held the fort at Washington Place and got invited over in relays to share host duties. The day that Nancy honored the governors' wives at Canlis, for instance, Stevie co-hosted a buffet lunch at the Hilton Hawaiian Village Beach Club for the governors' children.

The evening paper reported on the Quinn's reception-buffet:

Honolulu Star-Bulletin June 26, 1961:

> The gods grinned at the governors last night, when rain
> fell during the opening event of the 53rd National Governors
> Conference.
>
> The 675 guests were seated under the stars on the man-
> sion's lawn listening to "How About You?" sung by
> Honolulu Police Choral Group when the first drops fell.
> Governor Quinn explained that rain in Hawaii means the
> gods are smiling and nobody minded a bit.
>
> As Arthur Lyman's group launched into "Legend of the
> Rain," it began to pour and guests scuttled for cover under
> the trees and the lanai roof, looking like a flock of Dutch
> cleanser ads with linen napkins covering their heads.

The next day, after the morning's meeting, Quinn and New
York's Governor Nelson Rockefeller took a few hours from the
conference and flew to the Big Island. They went to see what
would be the Mauna Kea Beach Hotel, a project of the New York
governor's brother, Laurance. A press item described the resort
as being developed on property belonging to the Parker Ranch.
"It's billed as a luxury resort comparable to the Rockefellers'
resort in Puerto Rico, and as Rockefeller says, he's committed to
preserving the beauty of the land and the culture of the Hawaiian
people." At the time, it was nothing but an unimproved land-
scape with trees growing down to the water. Nelson Rockefeller,
however, could visualize Laurance's dream.

The final event of the Governors Conference was a formal
banquet in the grand ballroom of the Royal Hawaiian Hotel.
"Steve" Wilcox in her column the next morning described the
affair:

> It was a show of first ladies at their most gracious and
> gowned in their best...and distinguished governors constitut-

ing half a hundred of the nation's most successful and politically talked about men...More than that there were our own
U.S. Vice President Johnson and Japan's Prime Minister
Hayato Ikeda with their wives...and hundreds of leading citizens from Hawaii.

After cocktailing on the terrace, the first ladies filed in to
sit at a long table on a double-tiered horseshoe dais facing
the Monarch Room. Howard Donnelly, manager of the
Royal, seated each first lady personally...a fast-paced gesture
to chivalry....Then came the governors to sit along the top
tier beneath a row of flags of the states and territories flanking the U.S. flag, the Japanese flag, and the personal flag of
Vice President Johnson...

Wilcox's column described how the party revved up: Each
state song played and the audience applauded as each governor
and his wife stood. She reported how Governor Quinn in well-
timed, rapid introductions brought each governor and his wife
back to their feet with a few appropriate words, including the
state's nickname, flower or principal product. Maple syrup for
Vermont. Camellias for Alabama. Treasure state for Montana.
Flickertail state for North Dakota. Gem state of Idaho.

Prime Minister Ikeda's speech called for an increase in trade
between the United States and Japan. Vice President Johnson,
hitting on a great national concern of the time, vowed that
Soviet saber-rattling would not drive the United States out of
Berlin.

The business of the conference came to a successful conclusion with the passage of 18 resolutions. Among the topics of primary concern were mental illness, finance in education, juvenile
crime, student-teacher ratio and the perpetual problem of the
relationship between the federal and state governments.

The governors addressed their last resolution to the local

people and organizations for their help in the conference:

"We are deeply grateful to the lovely Land of Aloha and to its people for their unfailing courtesy and kindness." The governors' "mahalo" was extensive; the resolution stated that "it was a privilege to have our annual meeting in these beautiful Islands."

Two days after the governors' meeting ended, the *New York Herald Tribune* printed a caustic observation. An excerpt appeared in *The Advertiser:* "The governors of several states, assembled in Honolulu, have just ended their annual conference with a series of resolutions which would do credit to a minor patriotic society, but which are not likely to carry any greater weight."

Far more sarcastic was the *New York Mirror's* Lee Mortimer's "Confidential" column:

> Pacific: But It Is Paradise...The conference which was staged by Hawaii's tenor-singing Governor Quinn in an effort to get national political support for himself was a waste of time and the taxpayers' money.

Criticism aside, for one week during June 1961, Honolulu was the most important city, outside of Washington, D.C., in the entire nation.

Chapter Thirty-One

To Realize a Dream

The new regents of the university meet for the first time tomorrow to commence service of unparalleled opportunity to the youth of the state, to the nation, and to the peoples of the Pacific and Asia....

THE HONOLULU ADVERTISER
March 12, 1961

Governor William Quinn was an eloquent proponent of higher education. In Forest Grove, Oregon, in March 1960, he gave a stirring address at the inauguration of Dr. Miller A.F. Ritchie as president of Pacific University. Quinn spoke of the "spirit of the university...this spirit that enlivens the wisdom of ages and, God willing, infuses it, changes it and advances it as the university moves from generation to generation."

In that address, Quinn showed his respect for educational institutions and the importance of the jobs of those who led them.

The inauguration of a university president is like the planting of a giant redwood. His actions and policies will influence the stream of history just as the great tree will give shelter to unborn generations. No one knows how the tree will grow, but there are great expectations at the planting.

A university president can change and affect the minds of men far beyond his age. A university is the most lasting of human institutions, surviving governments and civilizations. To be at the helm of such an institution is to give force and direc-

291

*tion to the stream of history. Through his leadership, the univer-
sity president will mold and form the characters of young people
who will lead the world of tomorrow. He will for a time control,
and forever influence, the most potent and sensitive weapon
known to man, his mind. Whatever influence he has will be
indelibly imprinted on mankind as students continue the
divine plan of peopling the earth.*

A year later, March 12, 1961, Quinn addressed a new group
of university leaders, the Board of Regents of the University of
Hawaii. The new state Constitution, called for different criteria
for the Board of Regents. There had to be a balance in representation from the different Island counties. So it was an entirely
new board.

At the swearing-in ceremony in Bachman Hall on the Manoa
campus, Quinn warned the nine members of the board that their
"job will be anything but easy." One of the board's toughest jobs
would be to select a president for the university.

There had been a ruling that the president of the University
of Hawaii, like all other department heads, had to be a three-year
resident of the Islands. Quinn felt that "would very seriously
limit our choice of president of the university."

"I therefore did some independent research of my own,
because I felt that just wasn't right. I read the Constitution and
its recognition of the university. Then I called Shiro Kashiwa and
asked for a another opinion on the matter. That was the only
time I ever did that, but he did come in with a different opinion."

In August 1961 Attorney General Shiro Kashiwa opined that
the University of Hawaii Board of Regents was not bound to the
three-year residency law in selecting a new president.

"The opinion is a far-reaching one," said Kashiwa. "This
takes the UH out of the realm of the law that requires executive
department heads to have lived in Hawaii three years immedi-

ately prior to their appointment. The university under this new opinion will have much independence. I can envision the University of Hawaii becoming an independent institution."

Quinn's new regents represented specific areas of the state: East Hawaii, West Hawaii, Maui, Kauai and five from Honolulu.

"Among them were Herbert Cornuelle, president of Dole Corporation; Art Lewis, president of Hawaiian Airlines, and Bob Hughes from Maui," Quinn said. "All nine regents were fine people and highly regarded in the community.

"The first thing that the regents did was to arrange for the retirement of the president, Laurence Snyder, and begin their search for a new president. Their action set tongues wagging and soon after that a few senators demanded that some of the regents be fired because they weren't doing a competent job.

"So began all this pulling and hauling...it was just terrible. But I met with the board and encouraged them to go nationwide and find a really top man to be president of the university, and that is what they did."

At their first meeting the regents chose Cornuelle to act as chairman. Tall, with a quiet, thoughtful manner, Cornuelle, 40 years old and chief executive officer of Dole Corporation, represented the new managerial spirit in Hawaii.

"We fired Snyder in a very gentle way," Cornuelle said. "I went to see Mr. Philip Spalding, who was chairman of the regents prior to my arrival, and asked him why they hired Snyder."

Cornuelle said he wanted to be sure letting Snyder go was the right thing and to find out what Snyder's strengths were. Spalding told him it had been a mistake to hire Snyder, Cornuelle recalled.

"That made it easier to go ahead. The idea was to try to make the university a center of the Pacific. When we were recruiting, we had a projection with a map of the world with Hawaii right in the center of it," said Cornuelle.

As chairman, Cornuelle appointed a search committee of four regents. He was not on the committee; he stayed neutral. Cornuelle designated Robert Hughes, superintendent of Alexander & Baldwin's two sugar mills on Maui, to conduct the initial search.

"The map was our focus for putting the university's opportunity at the forefront," Hughes said, "I think of the entire board, Herb was the key person. I attribute what transpired to his skill and his perceptions."

By November, the search committee had compiled a list of 100.

"By February '62, we were ready to meet the final list of 14 nominees. Three of us traveled from the West to the East Coast interviewing. Art Lewis, regent and member of the search committee, was a very aggressive and forceful chief executive officer of Hawaiian Airlines and a thoughtful, personable kind of guy. He set up all of our airline transportation when we traveled from San Francisco, to Portland, to Los Angeles...to Iowa, from there to Chicago and Chicago to New York. We went to Albany and it was there that we interviewed Thomas Hamilton."

Quinn said, "I'll never forget how elated we were when Tom Hamilton, head of the university system of the state of New York arrived here. Tom came down, accepted the job, and the university started to move forward."

"We were lucky and very happy to get Thomas H. Hamilton," says Cornuelle. "Tom accepted and hit the ground running, as the saying goes. He did a good job. I left soon after...that was in the mid-1960s and that was a good thing. It was good for Tom to have me out of the way because I had been so active in the process, process meaning the governance of the university."

With a slight smile, Cornuelle added, "Everybody knows how

to run a university. It's like building a fire, making a martini or managing a hotel. But in this state, I used to say, people revere education because there are so many of us from Asia where education is the fundamental yearning....That's a good thing in a way, but in another way you find many who want to latch on to the control of it...that meant that the Legislature and other people in the state government wanted to run the university..."

During the period when Hamilton was being hired, Hawaii was able to keep the university relatively free of controlling interests. Cornuelle said state universities need to remain quasi-independent to interest the best people.

"At that time we were able to attract good people such as Tom Hamilton or Fred Harrington, president of the University of Wisconsin. They were persuaded that Bill Quinn and the rest of government were in favor of having the university run in a traditional way," Cornuelle said.

"There is one more thing that I'd like to mention," he said. "The Atherton family deserves all the credit for giving College Hill (the UH president's residence) to the university. But the fellow who really had the idea and made it happen was Alex H. Castro. It seems to me to be important. The home still has an enormously positive effect on the university. It's a wonderful 'town and gown' kind of relationship that's reinforced by having a place at the university. The whole idea that the president's home be not right on the campus, which would be deadly, but almost on the campus and have the history that it has, was Alex's idea."

Castro, after meeting Hamilton, gave the distinguished mansion a nickname: Uncle Tom's Cabin, an affectionate term for the stately Victorian residence sitting high on its Kamehameha Avenue hill one block ewa of University Avenue.

As the university was making progress during 1961, so was the East-West Center.

The Advertiser August 10, 1961:

> Governor William F. Quinn praised the "almost unbelievable amount of progress" made to date by the East-West Center ground-breaking for the first of six center buildings on the campus of the University of Hawaii.
>
> Quinn, who termed the center a "crucible for cultural blending," said that "a remarkably fine beginning has been made under the guidance of acting chancellor Murray Turnbull, his staff and other university officers.
>
> "The selection of Dr. Alexander Sphoer as chancellor-elect is an exceedingly enlightened one," the governor said.

"It was in 1959 after the Statehood Act that Congress passed the mutual aid bill," said Quinn. "Tacked to it was a single phrase: There shall be at the University of Hawaii a center for technical and cultural interchange between East and West. I think (Lyndon) Johnson wrote that, although Jack Burns probably had suggested it. There had been no prior study on the concept."

Quinn called some university people together, including Murray Turnbull, an art teacher, and John "Jake" Stalker, an outgoing, politically minded professor. From that single sentence in the congressional bill, Quinn's committee fleshed out a two-inch-thick document on what the East-West Center could become.

"We sent the book back to Washington and then we brought the State Department representatives out here to review it with them. Next we got President Eisenhower and the secretary of state to accept it. We laid out how the center could function. We outlined how it could deal with students from Asia and students from the United States and how they would mix together. We laid out the technical and cultural considerations. We obtained a $10 million appropriation to get it started."

George Chaplin, editor of *The Honolulu Advertiser* at the time, noted, "David Benz and I started raising money in support of the East-West Center movement. We tried to get people like Walter Cronkite and James Michener out here to speak and we collected some money."

Before Chaplin's group could put the plan into action, though, the East-West Center bill moved rapidly through Congress and federal money was appropriated. Chaplin's group stopped collecting and returned what they'd gotten. Chaplin, one of the founders of the Friends of the East-West Center, was instrumental in those pennies Hawaii's schoolchildren gave President Eisenhower when he came to Hawaii in 1960.

"Art Lewis, president of Hawaiian Airlines, Hal Lewis (J. Akuhead Pupule), radio disk jockey, and I, with permission of the DOE (Department of Education) asked each public school student to donate a penny to the center."

They ended up with a chest of thousands of pennies.

"We gave him a check, of course, and sent the equivalent money to Washington...it was called "Pennies for Peace," Chaplin said.

At first, the plan was that the East-West Center would function as part of the University of Hawaii, with major decisions about the center's operations being made by the secretary of state.

"However, it didn't work out that way," Quinn said. Through more study "it was decided that the center ought to have an independent status and its own chancellor."

Eventually, the center achieved even greater autonomy, with its own president, considerable independence and power over its budget.

"That was what it needed before it could take off," Quinn said.

Chaplin served on the East-West Center board for some time.

At his retirement dinner several years ago, he spoke of others who'd been instrumental in the center's development.

"That evening I paid tribute to Governor Quinn, to Jack Burns and to Vice President (Lyndon) Johnson. But Johnson had a totally wrong idea about what the center should be. He thought it would be a place where people would learn foreign language so they could talk with each other."

Quinn remained proud of the East-West Center and his role in its creation.

"Somehow or other the whole East-West Center organization has been a crowning feather in the Jack Burns/Johnson political cap," said Quinn. "That's fine with me because no matter who was responsible, the East-West Center is a great institution. The notion that Johnson and I didn't get along is certainly true. I have absolutely no respect for him or his memory."

≋Chapter Thirty-Two≋
An Impossible Triangle

*"...History teaches us that the fruits of victory are not
always entirely sweet. With accomplishment comes responsibility, sometimes burdensome..."*
GOVERNOR WILLIAM F. QUINN
Republican State Convention, 1962

What became known as the "great prison controversy" simmered for months behind Social Services Department doors despite Governor Quinn's efforts to have Social Services Director Mary Noonan and Oahu Prison Warden Joe Harper bury the hatchet. Now, in the last quarter of 1961, the feud was getting out of hand.

Unfortunately, as happened 15 months before, Quinn was on the Mainland when the battle roared through the iron gates, and Lieutenant Governor James Kealoha, as acting governor in Quinn's absence, called for an investigation.

The press reported that Corrections Chief Ray V. Belnap ordered Harper to stop writing his opinions and observations on prison problems. Harper answered that such an order not only violated the principles of free speech, it would also curb a subordinate while leaving the superior "free to build an uncontested record as his purposes may dictate." Harper then said that Belnap and Noonan had systematically and unfairly built a record of bad performances against him to force him out of office. Harper made his memos public, including the gag order sent by Belnap.

299

Pundits compared the feud to a volcano eruption. Noonan fired Harper. Harper had no sooner cleaned out his desk when some Oahu Prison inmates staged a sympathy sit-down strike. It was questionable that Social Services Director Noonan had the authority to fire the prison warden and that set up a series of legal complications. Charles C. Smith, head of the Kulani Honor Camp on the Big Island, was named to succeed Harper. The same day Smith arrived at his new position, he was put "on leave." Later that afternoon, it was disclosed that Smith had been dishonorably discharged from the Army 28 years before; Noonan gave Belnap the prison warden's job pending further investigation of Smith.

The acting governor, busy with his own investigation, summoned a parade of witnesses to his office. State Representative Thomas Gill said Kealoha should suspend Noonan as state social services director during his investigation. On the third day, a third person was named to be the warden of the prison. Belnap went back to his position as state corrections chief and Alfred 0. Souza, superintendent of Olinda Prison Camp on Maui, took his place.

The morning of Quinn's return home, *The Advertiser* published a long editorial, a severe warning to the governor about the "hot potato" steaming atop his desk.

October 12, 1961:

> Governor Quinn today returns to his desk to find thereon the hottest potato of his career—which he blithely dismissed months ago as completely cooled off.
>
> But it wasn't. Instead it is now:
>
> 1. A potentially serious threat to his own personal political future; and,
>
> 2. Far more important, the basis for serious questioning whether a major department of the state government is being run right.

How the governor handles this matter can greatly affect public confidence in his administration and employee morale in the storm-swept Department of Social Services.

The governor can treat this as a simple case of a department head disciplining an unruly and uncooperative employee as he has done up until now with lamentable results. Or this time he can dig to the bottom of what is obviously a tangled and unhealthy situation.

...It is up to Governor Quinn to find out whether justice has in fact been done Warden Harper, but beyond that to find the real source of trouble and, if necessary, perform drastic surgery—instead of merely applying more publicity Band-Aids.

Quinn responded to reporters that swarmed into the terminal at his arrival, saying, "On the information so far, there was no alternative for the department head. It would be a terrible thing for the state's future if a subordinate could continue to disagree, conduct a public fight and disrupt the department."

He made it clear, based on his present knowledge of the dispute, that he felt Noonan was justified in dismissing Harper, but he promised a new probe. He ended his press meeting with a blast at the Democrats for their full-scale legislative hearings during the last session concerning Noonan's department. Quinn charged that the House investigation of the department earlier this year was the "most aggravated" case of "McCarthy-type approach" and "character assassination" the state has ever witnessed. "You don't have to be a lawyer to be shocked by it."

That was just what the Democrats wanted to hear. As *Star-Bulletin* columnist Forrest Black wrote, "It has become crystal clear now that the Democrats are banking on the fuss in the Social Services Department to help them unseat Republican Quinn in next year's election."

The Advertiser, October 15, 1961:
Dan Tuttle, Columnist

> Did Governor Quinn unwittingly deliver his own political funeral oration when upon arrival from the Mainland he instantly supported Social Services Director Mary Noonan's firing of Warden Harper?
>
> ...The governor has returned, backed Miss Noonan's solution, and blasted his political opponents in the process. It is a position in which it will be extremely difficult for the governor to retreat. And, however unusual it would be, the governor has, on occasion, shown signs of being an unusual politician...evidence of an ethic and fair play above and beyond the normal pattern of politics.

Letters from irate citizens flooded the editor's desk. Some were bored with the press coverage, others claimed the editorials were biased, while the Democrats lambasted Quinn for not cleaning up "the mess."

George Chaplin, now-retired editor-in-chief of *The Honolulu Advertiser,* said about Governor Quinn, "I'd say the only real handicap Bill had was that as a Harvard lawyer, he thought like a lawyer. For instance, a controversy would come up; let's say, a guy like Frank Fasi will respond instantly...a gut reaction. Bill would do what a good lawyer does. He would separate the elements, he'll think about it and sometimes a couple of days would pass before he'd arrive at a conclusion, by which time the opportunity for our point of view had passed.

"You can hardly fault a guy for thinking things through and coming to a rational conclusion and making his statement. Because of his training, he always wanted to know what he was talking about and getting it right," Chaplin said.

To deal with the Department of Social Services flap, Quinn found a good man to conduct a fair and impartial probe into the matter. The governor retained Edward P. Shaw, a visiting professor of industrial relations and personnel management from San Jose State College.

"By employing Shaw, the governor has moved to minimize the partisan political aspects of the situation," *The Advertiser* said in November 1961, "and has made it much more possible to get a factual and unbiased picture of Miss Noonan's department."

"Ed Shaw was a student of government and of organizational relationships," said Quinn. "He had been hired by many corporations to see how they could make things better...he studied it at great length, then told me that there was really only one solution. He recommended the replacement of Mary Noonan. He really shook me up, as did the 48 hours with Mary trying to get her to resign."

Chaplin remembered that this diabolical triangle continued on and on:

"It's getting towards the end of 1961, and the creatures of war against Quinn are gathering. Bill Quinn was away at the time that Mary Noonan fired Joe Harper. Whenever the governor was away, something would go awry....It turned out that Noonan was to blame, so Quinn asked for her resignation. Now both Noonan and Harper were out. Considering the fact that Mary had a long career with the Republican Party and as such had her following, it was a bad situation for the Republican governor. She was a handsome woman with silver hair drawn up high in a chignon. She was a forceful speaker and a leader."

Dan Tuttle, political observer for *The Advertiser*, saw the situation differently:

"Quinn took a long time to issue any political action....I feel that Mary Noonan double-crossed Bill Quinn. Even when the governor announced that she would be resigning, Noonan denied that she would be doing so and acted as though the whole fuss never happened. Joe Harper was quite an unusual personality and the last person in the world you'd pick to run a prison. He was quiet, religious to the point where he would take prisoners home with him. The feud went on much too long and as a result, helped to split the Republican Party badly."

Roger Coryell, Quinn's press secretary at the time, said, "Mary Noonan was a good person. It was too bad. I suppose you could say that she was the cause but hard-headed manipulation was the cause in that time. The politician's political opponents tend to side with everybody who has a complaint against him, the politician. In other words, everybody opposed to Quinn, for whatever reason, sided against Mary Noonan...."

But the press didn't quit. The stories were a daily calendar of who did what to whom.

"People who get elected to public office frequently tend to develop a proprietary air," Chaplin said. "The office belongs to them after awhile and since it belongs to them, they do what they want. You need a couple of reporters out there who dig around.

"Even with a fine governor like Bill, there will be times when he and the press are bumping into each other. It's inevitable. The press tends to be, if not adversarial to the governor, at least suspicious—as they should be. Otherwise the reporter will be snowed and through him the public will be snowed...," Chaplin added.

Quinn had liked facing the media—and the public—by way of the weekly telecasts. By the time of the prison administration controversy, however, these had been discontinued, Quinn alleged for political reasons. During those telecasts, "the press was there and able to ask any question that they wanted. Then in the last five or 10 minutes of the 30-minute show, we opened it to a phone-in by the public. I'd try to get the answer as best I could....Then at least a year, perhaps a year and a half before the '62 election, somebody got to the media on the basis that I was probably going to be a candidate and I was getting all this press coverage. So the show was cut off. That's exactly what happened and yet there was nothing political about that telecast—not a thing."

Years later, Quinn still did not know who brought the influence to bear to stop such a public service. "I could see cutting it off three months before election," he said, "but this was over a year before and it was so valuable. I got so many good reactions from the people who were finding out some answers."

During the course of those weeks of prison controversy, the governor went ahead with the plan to take government to the different islands. John Henry Felix said Quinn was the first governor to take his cabinet to the Neighbor Islands. "It was very challenging, as some of those first meetings were away out in the hinterlands."

"We held our cabinet meetings at various spots on the outer islands," said Quinn. We'd conduct our regular meeting and then invite people in an orderly way to get up and ask any member, the head of any agency, whatever question they had.

"I can't estimate how many questions were resolved right on the spot. In some cases, people said that they had been writing for five years and were still waiting for answers. In those meetings they got their answers right there with the concurrence of the leading department heads who would go back and implement it."

Roger Coryell remembered once such session on Maui: "One group were the scientists from Haleakala....Some equipment was already in place and they had others they wanted to put in place for their studies in the upper atmosphere. They pleaded to get the radar off of Haleakala because it interfered with their work."

The scientists reported the radar blotted out reception of signals from space, and they explained the work they were doing was terribly important, pure science. The scientists said Haleakala was "one of the most remarkably perfect places in the whole world for this kind of research," Coryell recalled.

Without hesitation, Coryell said, Quinn called Fred Makinney, commander of the National Guard, which operated the radar. "'Fred, do we have to have the radar up there?' Bill asked. After a strong objection, the commander said that they probably could re-install it on Mount Kaala on Oahu. Quinn said, 'OK, so do it.' And Haleakala was saved for science," Coryell said.

Finally, in early February 1962, the impasse in the Noonan-Harper controversy broke. The *Star-Bulletin* reported:

MARY NOONAN TO LEAVE POST ON FEB. 15
She Blasts Shaw, Harper and Politics

The report of Noonan leaving office was bumped to page two, however; bigger political news took the front page that day:

POLITICAL TRIANGLE
The triangle, the tried and true device of the dramatist, seems destined to provide the basic pattern for Hawaii's gubernatorial contest this fall.

It will, that is, if the three apparent candidates for the Republican nomination—Governor William F. Quinn, Lt. Governor James K. Kealoha and Mayor Neal S. Blaisdell—are all on stage when the curtain goes up for the campaign.

≈ Chapter Thirty-Three ≈
The Bandwagon

"...Is our brilliance like the sudden flash of a mirror in the bright sunlight on a distant hill? Will we drop our booster and sustainer engines but fail to get into orbit? In other words, have we reached our zenith?"
GOVERNOR WILLIAM F. QUINN
to the First State Legislature
February 23, 1962

Nineteen sixty-two was shaping up to be a tough year for the budding state of Hawaii. The governor's "State of the State" message to the Legislature reported a slippage in Hawaii's economic growth that forced a downward revision in his budget requests. Later in the year, another shipping strike would further stymie the economy. But it was also the year Quinn got his land bill through the Legislature.

ECONOMY BANDWAGON ROLLS IN THE LEGISLATURE
The Honolulu Advertiser, Feb. 23, 1962:

"Economy will be the pet phrase of both Republicans and Democrats at this state legislative session. The tone was set in a somber report by a committee of fiscal experts a few days ago and now everybody seems to be getting into the act."

Quinn chopped the budget by $4.4 million and planned to trim $1.6 million more.

"This was a budget session, which means that under the laws that then existed, only the budget can be considered," Quinn said. "Other urgent items could be submitted but must be approved by two-thirds of each house. It was to be a 30-day rather than a 60-day session.

"I sent my land bill down marked 'urgent.' It had run into a huge hassle in the last legislative session of 1961 and it wasn't passed by August 21, our second year of statehood."

Quinn had said the year before that the new state couldn't operate without this and other measures being passed before August 21, 1961. Yet, "here we were still operating. That made me out a liar," Quinn said.

There had been an earlier legal opinion that these laws were necessary to supplant the federal law that had governed Hawaii under its territory status. Another opinion by the attorney general "said that what we were doing was legal."

Quinn finally saw the success of his land bill. It was passed by more than two-thirds in each house.

"After it became law we were able to do the farmer development at Laiamilo and the farms and house lots in Waimanalo. It really began to work the way we thought it should. In each instance, we could select a qualified class of buyers, set a price— by appraisal not auction—and choose the buyers by lot.

"The bill, however, had many restrictive things added to it by the House that subsequently had to be amended out. For example, if you wanted to get lease land, you had to have legislative approval. So when you obtained a lease, subject to legislative approval, you had to go to the next Legislature to gain that approval.

"That was just terrible," said Quinn, "but I think they did that for a particular reason. I was accused of representing special interest groups. At one point they thought I was Dillingham's boy; there was a ranch over on the Big Island that had come up for lease and there were negotiations between the Land Department and Dillingham and others who wanted to operate this land as a ranch.

"It was pretty much wasteland, so I figured that if we gave them a term lease and required in the lease certain plantings and foresting, it would be a good thing. So we negotiated and leased it. As a result I was charged with handing things to the Dillinghams on a silver platter.

"They just pilloried me on that until the problem of the Oahu Railway and Land (OR&L) station and the railroad tracks running all the way to Haleiwa came along."

The state needed the land under the tracks, Quinn said, "So we started moving against OR&L and Dillingham.

"We finally filed suit in court, got the property appraisals and nailed down a settlement. The state got the OR&L station and all that track land and got it on a very favorable basis. Then, of course, they couldn't say I was Dillingham's man. I had to be somebody else's man."

When Quinn heard that Matson Navigation Co. and OR&L had been talking about bringing containers to a pier near the OR&L station, then transporting the containers by limited rail to a special yard for reloading, he called Fred Simpich, the man in charge of the Castle & Cooke terminals.

Quinn recalled telling Simpich, "We've got Pier 2 available. It's an ideal location for container ships to dock. The state will assist in putting up the unloading lifts and other facilities. It's not being used and that's where we need a transportation center."

Simpich was negative to the offer, Quinn said. His recollection of Simpich's response was, "Governor, we've already checked that out. The currents and tides are much too great there. We can't possibly do it."

That didn't stop Quinn. He called in a couple of experts and proved that it could be done.

"They abandoned the deal with OR&L, came to us and the state put some money in to help," said Quinn. "Matson paid rent for Pier 2 and that was a good deal for the state. So I became Matson's boy until I went into court to try to prevent Matson from getting a rate increase.

"Then I became...who knows? I couldn't be my own man. Didn't have anybody. I didn't have the (Republican-controlled) Senate, I didn't have the House. When I look back, I don't know how we made it. I had a few people working with me and fortunately there was so much to be done, and we got an awful lot done. I don't know how. But we did."

Quinn had to extend the legislative session, first for 10 days, to deal with the latest shipping strike "that was once again crippling Hawaii's waterfront and the economy. "There is only one man in the nation—the president—who has the power to order the maritime strike to end," said Quinn.

Honolulu Star-Bulletin, March 28, 1962

The governor's statement followed the breakdown of strike negotiations in San Francisco indicating that only federal intervention can get supplies rolling here again from the West Coast.

Quinn says that he has been asked why doesn't he invoke the dock seizure law and reopen the waterfront.

But he pointed out, "The waterfront itself is open; there is no trouble on the docks. It is the ships that are strikebound by their own crews, and the state has no authority over them."

Star-Bulletin, April 4, 1962

Governor William F. Quinn last night proclaimed a state of emergency existed in Hawaii due to the West Coast shipping strike and sent a radiogram to President Kennedy asking for immediate shipping relief.

The governor explained that his proclamation is a step taken in order to give him legal powers which he would not otherwise have. By declaring a state of emergency, he is able to charter ships or make any other transportation arrangements to prevent the state from running out of needed commodities.

The next day all major radio and television stations broadcast the governor. Quinn promised that "no one would starve because of the shipping strike but that Hawaii's economy will suffer, hurting each of us sooner or later, until normal shipping is restored."

As usual, Quinn carried himself with his distinctly executive look, but his voice was somber.

"I still believe the Taft-Hartley injunction (forcing the ships back to sea) should be obtained by the president. For Hawaii's health and safety are obviously imperiled and this affects national interests," he said.

The following day, Quinn extended the legislative session another six days to help ease the Legislature through some 11th hour financial struggles.

Not to negate the seriousness of the situation but Quinn recalls a certain phone call from Washington. "In my efforts to persuade Washington of our perilous predicament, I was able to persuade Arthur Goldberg, secretary of labor, that that was so. The administration was going to apply for a Taft-Hartley injunction, which was quite unusual. I had to take my hat off to the Kennedy Administration because that was not exactly their cup of tea. But they were going to do it.

"They asked for an affidavit from me to support the application of all of the things that would happen here with this stoppage. I put together with the help of staff, a long affidavit of everything. So they filed and got the injunction. And that strike settled within the forty-five day period before they were free to strike again."

As if there weren't enough problems facing the governor, more trouble percolated within his own party. A power play between two Republican state senators caught Quinn in the middle. Senators William H. Hill and Randolph Crossley fought over whether nominees to the state Transportation Commission should be screened initially by a standing committee headed by Crossley. As a result, two bigger issues arose:

Would the Hill-Crossley hassle cause defeat of any of Quinn's nominees?

Would Hill, the Senate president, be able to beat back Crossley's challenge to his leadership?

Considerable unhappiness was reported among the Senate Republicans about some Transportation Commission nominees. They conferred with Quinn several times but failed to agree on a slate.

On April 11, *The Advertiser* reported that the "State Senate dumped two more of Governor William F. Quinn's nominees, including Quinn's former campaign manager, Howard Hubbard, and Mary K. Robinson, Hawaiian Homes commissioner."

Quinn took these defeats hard and speaks sadly of the episode:

"Howard Hubbard, one of my dearest friends, who had been my campaign manager and who was such a sweet, dedicated, unselfish person, had served, at one point, on the Territorial Board and he was one of those on the state Land Board they refused to confirm. It was just a real kick in the face to the governor by the Republicans in the Senate. It was terrible because it was the Senate that did all the confirming. The House had nothing to do with it. It wasn't the Democrats," Quinn said. Members of his own party were responsible.

"As soon as that 1962 budget session was over, I think you can say that everything turned strictly to politics," Quinn said.

Jack Burns, however, had started long before that, Quinn said.

"...Burns was back in the picture making comments about this and that, starting at about the latter half of '61 and from then on.

"They started coming out with polls," Quinn said. "The first poll was a university-sponsored poll that had Burns ahead. Then there were two or three other polls where I was leading the pack by a big margin. Art Woolaway was the party chairman, Ben Dillingham, the county chairman. They tried hard to pull Kealoha and Quinn back together but Jimmy said that was out of the question. It just got worse and worse."

Woolaway, who had shepherded the Republican Party from the territorial days, told the Central Committee in April 1962 that the party faced the prospect of obliteration by a Democratic juggernaut in the November election. He presented everyone with a warning list:

• Lack of party unity.
• Failure to realize and analyze the opposition's power.
• Lack of support by precinct and district leaders.
• Lack of party discipline.

"Art was right. The Democratic Party was very strong," Quinn said.

"They owned the House and they virtually owned the Senate because Randy Crossley would vote against anything the governor wanted," said Coryell later.

On August 13, former Delegate to Congress Jack Burns formally entered the contest for governor on the Democratic ticket. It was his second bid; Quinn defeated him to become the first governor of the state of Hawaii in the 1959 election. In his campaign address, the Democratic political chief, "the wheelhorse of his party," lashed out at the Quinn administration for "failing to keep us abreast of new times and new opportunities."

The day before, an editorial in the *Star-Bulletin* razzed U.S. Representative Dan Inouye on a political speech in which he stated: "I am certain a change is needed at Iolani Palace." Inouye prefaced his conclusion with the observation that while the Quinn administration has talked a lot and busied itself with surveys, the voters will be asking this fall what it has done.

HOW'S THAT AGAIN?

Mr. Inouye can be excused for saying this. He has spent most of the last three years in Washington, which was where he belonged. He has had to depend on his Democratic colleagues for news of the Quinn administration and some of the colleagues are probably partisan. Since evidently he has not been reading the Honolulu newspapers very closely, we offer him this rundown of the Quinn administration's accomplishments.

The editorial was lengthy and detailed. A few of the major subjects included:

Education—state department's budget increase by 50%, its staff by 2,000, teacher pay increases, special classes for gifted, retarded and physically handicapped, etc....

University of Hawaii—enrollment up 6,000 to 10,000, faculty up from 500 to 1,000, 37 new buildings in Manoa campus, 13 others on Neighbor Islands, three new colleges, 27 new academic departments, 10 new institutes, East-West Center acquired, Hilo campus built.

Land Department—expanded under reorganization; backlog of land leases cleared up; continuing drive for equitable distribution of land to homeowners and small farmers;

water projects completed in Kona, Kula, Waimanalo, Waianae; forestry and parks program developed, etc....

Economy—pushed through 20-year general plan; contributed to settlement of major labor disputes in shipping, sugar, pineapple, buses; 15 major new industries; highway, harbor and airport construction and championed Neighbor Island development.

Government administration—completely reorganized state government (109 different agencies incorporated into 18 departments); undated classification of 7,000 state jobs; tighter and more centralized auditing of state's books; improved public health and social services (mental health program recognized as one of the best in the nation) etc.

"Dan Inouye and I had been good friends. We had worked together from time to time, but you know, politics is politics," said Quinn. "He had a lot of time to work against me. He, Masato Doi and Matsuo Takabuki went into all those Japanese precincts which had supported me in the 1959 election. It wasn't long before I began to feel those voters going the other way."

Many believed Dan Inouye secretly supported Bill Quinn in the early stages of the 1962 election.

"For some time there was beneath the surface talk that Dan Inouye was supporting the election of Governor Quinn very much under the table," says Coryell. "Inouye was immensely popular and was also running for the U.S. Senate. Some well-meaning idiot who was mailing out Inouye fliers stuck in Quinn fliers. Of course, this found its way to the press and was broadcast and, as a result, Inouye had no choice but to come out and say, 'Any rumors that you might have heard that I am supporting William Quinn for governor are absolutely wrong. I am for Jack Burns 100 percent.'

"So what happened was that we engineered an endorsement

for Jack Burns from one of the most popular politicians in the state—or somebody engineered it. I think it was just some envelope-stuffer who thought they were doing something smart. It hurt hard."

The hottest political race of the primary was that between incumbent Governor Quinn and Lieutenant Governor James Kealoha for the Republican gubernatorial nomination.

"If you want to see your local boy, your native son of the land be governor, this is your chance," said Jimmy.

Coryell, who from his post as press secretary with day-to-day contact with the lieutenant governor, said, "Kealoha had a very substantial appeal to the Hawaiian people and to the gentle, easy-going people of the Islands because he was of an old-time family. Jim saw this race as his last hurrah. He wanted very much to be governor."

Coryell said Kealoha saw his position as lieutenant governor as a stepping-stone.

"He began rooting for himself and trying to shape the operation of the administration of the state as much as possible through his political needs. Quinn saw him, of course, as a political opponent. They were both of the same party. There was absolutely no love lost and very little communication in the upper hall of Iolani Palace. Jimmy was on the Waikiki corner. I was in an office next to Bill," Coryell said.

On the eve of the primary, Governor Quinn paid a surprise visit to the Republican wind-up rally in Hilo, Kealoha's hometown. After Kealoha spoke to about 600 seated in the armory, Quinn appeared from the wings, took the platform and spoke extemporaneously:

My friend Jimmy has even repudiated me, his (former) running mate, because I do not have what his friends believe is the right color of skin.

My skin has not changed color since 1959....I would like to
plead with all of you: Do not let this type of argument ever be
made in this new and great state of Hawaii.

The audience seemed astonished at Quinn's sudden appearance and gave him an applause at least as heavy as the applause given the Big Island's own Jimmy Kealoha earlier in the evening.

The primary election held the next day brought out a record vote and the defeat of Kealoha for the Republican nomination for governor.

⪜Chapter Thirty-Four⪜
What Went Wrong?

"Will Hawaii's second state governor be William F. Quinn or John A. Burns?"

DAN TUTTLE, COLUMNIST
The Honolulu Advertiser
October 14, 1962

"With just three weeks to go until the general election in November, the best analysis of the recent primary results points up the formidable task facing both contenders," wrote Dan Tuttle. "There are some 80,000 or more votes suspended in the air until November 6. The 80,000 is calculated on the number of votes Kealoha received in the primary, the number of persons who did not vote or who spoiled ballots and the remaining are those who did not get to the polls or haven't registered.

"But how to motivate the voter to place an X by one name or the other? That's the tough task facing Quinn and Burns."

Those last frenzied weeks were a haze of coffee hours, mid-morning rallies, luncheon and afternoon meetings, on into the evening with cocktail or dinner gatherings and two- or three-day swings around the Neighbor Islands. Still, the best opportunity for the voter to see and hear the candidates became the television debates. Burns stalled. For 10 days he refused to agree to face-to-face debates or to appear in a series of debates with no restriction on subject matter.

The Honolulu Advertiser, October 23, 1962:

...Mr. Burns says he's still willing to debate Governor Quinn on television. But he imposes so many restrictions that the "full discussion" he says he wants would be impossible to achieve.

The conclusion has to be that Mr. Burns just doesn't want to be pinned down, that he prefers the controlled situation, that in his view, any genuine test or challenge is to be meticulously avoided.

ALL THE GOVERNOR'S MEN

Finally, plans for a face-to-face hour-long debate between Quinn and Burns was set. On Friday, November 2 at 7:30 p.m., KGMB radio and TV would broadcast it. Professor Daniel W. Tuttle of the University of Hawaii and political analyst for *The Advertiser,* would moderate. They agreed to eliminate reporters; Burns and Quinn would ask questions of each other on issues involving the administration of the government. The sides agreed Tuttle would eliminate any question that strayed from issues directly related to the governor's office.

Meeting to discuss the debate format were Robert Alderman and Ed Sheehan, representing Burns. Representing Quinn were Roger Coryell, press secretary, Howard Hubbard, campaign manager, and campaign aides Wayne Collins and Jack Fox.

"Before the TV debate...we woodshedded," said Coryell. Quinn and several staff members spent a couple days holed up at the Royal Hawaiian Hotel. Coryell remembered Leo Pritchard, Tad Kanda, George Miyasaka and Jess Walters being there, and probably some others who came in and out.

"At the Royal we trained Bill. We asked biased questions, loaded questions like, how come you haven't done anything to help us get land in Hawaii? Of course, he had done all kinds of things to get land and all of them were bad-mouthed by the Democrats who were appalled to find a Republican suggesting land reform," Coryell recalled.

"Quinn had an incredibly fine mind. He'd put the information into his computer mind. When we asked him something that he didn't have an answer to, staff was right there to get it for him. That convinced us, I think, that we were really going to whip Jack Burns in the debate on the basis of the obvious grasp of the government and facts of the state administration that Quinn had and Burns didn't have."

By the time the debate evening arrived, Quinn's staff believed he would easily outdistance Burns.

"The debate went on and in terms of grasp of administrative skills and techniques, Quinn clobbered him. He knew all about the state administration. Quinn had a dominating appearance. He had the look of eagles. He was glib and articulate," Coryell said. "But in the radio-television audience there were thousands and thousands of viewers who thought that this Mainland haole was cruelly picking on the people's boy. So, if they were wishy-washy to begin with, they were then convinced that Quinn had beaten Burns over the head. Bill lost them with his own brilliance, his own grasp. Furthermore, they thought, he's not the kind of guy they could ever talk to and Jack Burns won that debate on that basis," Coryell concluded.

After the debate, the last days of campaigning intensified.

"We kept working to get Bill elected. The day before the general a whole bunch of us from the office got together at the Prince Kuhio restaurant and we talked about the campaign. All of a sudden somebody said, 'Hey, let's everybody put up 20 bucks or so and state by how many votes and in favor of whom the election is going to go.' Everybody started in...'I'll take Quinn by 10,000 votes'; 'I'll take Bill by 7,500'; or somebody said 'by 15,000.' Leo Pritchard, his (Quinn's) administrative director, was the only one who said, 'I think Bill's going to lose by about 10,000.'

"Leo came away with about a hundred and fifty (dollars) or so and there was nothing bad about Leo. He was the only cool, calculating, sensible person in that whole gang....Of course, Quinn did lose and badly, by about 30,000 votes," Coryell said.

In bold, black, capital letters, the morning-after headlines read:

DEMOCRATS SWEEP NATION AND HAWAII;
BURNS IN STUNNING VICTORY OVER QUINN

In a smaller article on the same front page was a picture of Nancy and Bill Quinn:

DEFEATED QUINN SINGS
"IRISH EYES ARE SMILING"

Governor William F. Quinn sang "When Irish Eyes Are Smiling" as his swan song last night after conceding defeat at his party headquarters on Kapiolani Boulevard.

"I hate to tell you we've lost it, but the only thing to do is to recognize we've lost it," he said. "But we've got a great state and we've got to keep trying to build it."

It was hard for everyone in that room to keep a dry eye, including the Quinns.

Honolulu Star-Bulletin:
A GOOD GOVERNOR BUT NO POLITICIAN
By A. A. Smyser, Managing Editor

...Given the rule of thumb that four incumbents out of five are reelected in Hawaii, why was the governor defeated on November 6? There seems to be a consensus around these reasons:

1. The split with his Lieutenant Governor and their primary fight.

2. The disunity of the Republican Party.

3. The general weakness of the GOP ticket.

4. The Second Mahele and other 1959 issues that were used against Quinn.

5. The unity of the Democrats.

The purpose of this piece is to suggest that there is a deeper reason, one that Quinn himself expressed when he quoted others as saying "Quinn is not a politician." Had a politician been given all the patronage that was within his grasp in 1959, he probably would have been reelected in 1962.

But the governor somehow failed to turn it into political advantage.

For whatever reasons, the governor turned for advice from public relations people and radio personalities (and then didn't get the ones most experienced at politics).

One observer I respect highly agrees that the governor is not a politician but does not consider that too serious. What is really too bad, he says, is that there was no tested, trusted politician in the innermost circle giving advice.

For Art Woolaway, state Republican Party chairman, the aftermath of the Republican-Quinn defeat was bitter. Woolaway, sugar executive and noted sports figure, endured considerable grumbling.

"When I'd go into a restaurant, I got accused of losing the election for Bill Quinn. Once he was in office, he was surrounded and his people didn't want anything to do with me or the Republican Party. I've always respected Bill, but I was kept from him. When I went to see him, he was busy. They isolated him and Bill Quinn was not a politician. He lost the local-boy touch when they isolated him. They even shut me out.

"One day Hubbard, his campaign chairman, said to me, 'Why don't you guys (the party) just follow us?' What are you talking about, I asked. No way we're going to follow you...we're trying to help you. We're trying to tell you the mistakes you're making. They were running their own game and they lost it," Woolaway said.

George Mason, part of the Samuel King administration's economic planning authority, and later the first director of the new state Department of Economic Development, agreed that Quinn wasn't a politician.

"Our programs were initiated in an effort to bring new industries and new manufacturing into Hawaii," Mason said of his time in the Quinn administration, "Bill and I got on well even when we disagreed. I'd have as many as 30 or 40 projects going at one time, including the agricultural loan program, small-business disaster program and, of course, the tourist business. We encouraged small enterprises.

"Bill was a good governor but a poor politician. In 1962 all the department heads, including myself, held secret meetings. We were trying to find a way to help Bill's disastrous campaign.

"The whole time he refused to play the political game and milk every situation for what it was worth. All of us tried our best to create news and spread the good word about him," Mason said.

George Chaplin said Bill Quinn could just as easily have been a Democrat as a Republican.

"I think of him as being a Republican in terms of fiscal conservatism and being a Democrat in terms of social welfare and programs. Hawaii needed a lot of changing. The oligarchy had run this place for centuries and there was need for reform. Bill saw things that needed changing, that lay dormant for all those years.

"But you need good politicians. You need people who know how to get things done, through your legislators, offices, through the governor's offices and through the mayor's offices. It's a question of how you get things done. Bill would not fit the image of a traditional politician. In an office like the governorship, compromise is the name of the game. If you just say this is it and don't budge from it, you're not going to get things done and you ain't going to be there another time."

John Henry Felix spoke of his former boss not as a politician but as a statesman:

"That is not a criticism but an observation of what was fact. One of the things that impressed me most about Bill was his attention to detail. His total commitment was doing the very best job for the people of Hawaii. At times he even put in jeopardy and sacrificed his political career. He did not take into account his personal political agenda and that sort of thing contributed to his loss of the election. If only he had paid more attention to the politics of politics."

Tuttle, whose political observations included prophecies of doom for the Republican Party, said years later, "Bill Quinn, a talented guy, a natural leader, 6-foot and more, never quite arrived in Hawaii. That was his biggest fault. No one ever gave him a quick-study lesson in what makes Hawaii tick. Therefore, he was susceptible to certain things. Somehow the St. Louis in him never mixed with the Hawaiian, Filipino, grass roots, etc. of Hawaii.

"Then there was Jimmy Kealoha, who really did him in. As a matter of principle Bill Quinn would not give Jimmy what he wanted. And as a matter of principle whatever Kealoha wanted as lieutenant governor—either he gets or he's going to take it out on whoever won't give it to him—which was Bill Quinn."

Republican Party Chairman Woolaway spoke of another crucial campaign happening: "One day I got a call from Judge (Albert N.) Felix in Hilo to come on over for a meeting. There in the back yard was Kealoha and ILWU veeps George Martin and Eddie DeMello. We had a drink, then they said, 'Come on, Woolaway, why don't you come out and support Jimmy in the primary for governor.' I said, 'Wait a minute, you guys, you think I'm just born yesterday? You answer this question first. We have a closed primary and when you get your ballot you say whether you want a Republican ballot or a Democratic ballot. Are you telling your voters to take a Republican ballot in the primary? Hell, no. You're not going to do that, no way.' They used Jimmy to split the vote with Bill Quinn and that was a big reason he lost the election. The ILWU was rough.

"Bill Quinn shouldn't have lost. He was a good governor. Labor took over and labor has never looked back. Labor runs this place and we have no business leadership in government at all. This is a labor state and it all started when Quinn lost that election. The power of labor is person-to-person contact and that machine works in each precinct.

"Unfortunately," said Woolaway, "the Republican Party lost its contact with the masses. We don't represent the masses. We represent the *haole*, the rich, and business. We not only lost Bill Quinn but we lost the future as a party. But they'll never take one thing away from Bill...he was the first state governor."

"Besides the above," says Ward Russell, one of the most loyal Republicans of long standing, "the election was poorly run. Not one incumbent was reelected to office. Hebden Porteus was a holdover so he didn't have to run for the Senate. But everyone of us in the House and the Senate was defeated. The whole state was out. Never had there been such a debacle and it was all due to the backbiting, double-crossing and weakness of the party. That was the death of the Republican Party, and Bill Quinn was part and parcel of it."

Post-election analysis came from all points of the Islands. Newspaper reporters and columnists were swamped. Accusations of who should bear the blame became the order of the day; some were helpful and some petulant. One of the angriest reports printed was that made by Frank R. Hicks, Republican Party chairman, Oahu County Committee. He coupled his announcement with a three-page attack on President Kennedy, Governor-elect John Burns, local and national Democrats generally and *Advertiser* Editor George Chaplin.

Bob Midkiff, Quinn's campaign co-chairman, who raised a couple of million dollars on the governor's behalf, was back at Harvard Business School when he heard of Bill's defeat. "That's when I quit the Republican Party. Hell, Bill could have won that election, but you know, I found out that a lot of Republicans didn't even vote and that made me mad." Midkiff had also worked hard and long as co-chairman with Representative Scotty Koga on the governor's Architect Selection Committee for the new Capitol building.

Ed Johnston, last territorial secretary under Quinn, held Kealoha responsible.

"Lieutenant Governor James K. Kealoha's outstanding work in wrecking the Republican Party" aided the Democratic sweep in the state's elections. "He was more interested in politics than in good government," said Johnston.

Frank Fasi, speaking to 400 people at the Hawaiian Sugar Technologists Conference held in the Princess Kaiulani Hotel, blamed Kealoha for the Republicans' crushing defeat.

"The Republican Party decided to keep hands off in order to be fair in the Quinn-Kealoha battle," Fasi said. "By the time the primary was over, it was already too late for the Republicans to put on an organized campaign."

The day after the general election, upstairs at Iolani Palace in the governor's chambers, Bill Quinn sat and talked with *Advertiser* interviewer Gardiner Jones:

> Governor Quinn, weary and hurt, sat amid the wreckage of his defeat, groping for the answer to the big question - Why?
>
> "I know I lost. The heavy attack laid on the same basic theme by the Democrats, fraud, deceit, fraud, deceit, fraud, deceit. Broken promises. Secret land deals with the Dillinghams. Lack of integrity. I didn't answer because everyone said don't. But it had an impact beyond what anybody thought.
>
> "Well, I can't be cynical about it. There's a saying. Someone once said that if you win an election, everybody did it for you. If you lose an election, you did by yourself. I accept that.
>
> "But again, we got a warm reception everywhere. In 1959 we could tell we were doing well. Not this time. I think there's a backlog of goodwill, even among those who voted against us.
>
> "Many people respect me. But more love Nancy."

Washington Place

"There was very little time left for us in the old mansion," Nancy recalled. "We had to move out by December 3, the inaugural date set for Jack Burns."

Star-Bulletin, November 29, 1962

Governor Quinn and his family have been offered the 14-room home built by Frank C. Atherton in

Manoa. Quinn owns a home in Portlock but it's too small for the family, which has grown since he became the state's chief executive. The arrangement is on an interim basis, for a period of weeks or months until he finds a permanent home.

"There was so much to do," added Nancy. "Every day I'd load up the station wagon and in between dropping the children off at school and meeting our official commitments, I'd dash up to the Manoa house. In the midst of all the confusion, I received a call from a dear friend, Mary Ann West. She said that a few mutual friends wanted to have a luncheon for me. I was honored but explained that I really didn't think that it was possible. She was determined and convincing, and on November 30 I was swept into the time of my life. What a beautiful, wonderful luncheon it was and so many friends were there. I'll never forget it."

The Advertiser, December 1, 1962:

WELL DONE, NANCY QUINN
by Steve Wilcox

Admirers and friends crowded into the Hilton Hawaiian Village Long House...overflowing it just as their hearts overflowed with affection and respect for the guest of honor.

A standing ovation from the more than 500 women guests was made three times during the luncheon...multiracial leaders...from the grand dames of Hawaii to the young stenographers and housewives who've rejoiced in the way Nancy has conducted public life and her own private life as Mr. Quinn's wife and the mother of his rollicking brood of seven children.

Mrs. Rodney West, unofficial head of the group that organized the luncheon, explained that Nancy's friends...in a burst of aloha had wanted to encircle all of Washington Place with a lei for her in appreciation of her service as first lady...decided instead on the luncheon and so..."we're all here in lieu of a lei." Then she presented Nancy with a string of jade beads for which each woman present...and many who could not come...had donated...saying, "Never did so little say so much."

Nancy thanked everyone and said..."I loved serving with you and for you. It was a great privilege to serve as Bill's first lady and your first lady. Thank you, I love you all."

On Monday, December 3, the *Star-Bulletin* printed an editorial salute to public servant William F. Quinn:

"TO THE DEPARTING CAPTAIN"

The people of Hawaii say aloha today to one of the more distinguished of its public servants, William Francis Quinn.

No man in any capacity in the state or territorial governments has faced a more difficult task than did Governor Quinn upon the passage of the Statehood Act of 1959. No one could have faced it more courageously or with greater drive and decision.

Today we have Governor Quinn to thank for a smoothly operating governmental organization that has been designed for the needs of the present and the future, that provides a solid foundation for future executives to build on.

At the inaugural Bill stood alongside the newly elected governor and his first lady while Jack Burns raised his right hand and was sworn in. Quinn stood tall, dressed in a dark business suit with a double white carnation lei draped on his shoulders. The ceremony was held in the Bandstand and the 3,000 guests sat in chairs across the wide lawn fronting the palace steps. A reception was held immediately after the inauguration. Nancy and Bill Quinn followed after the new governor's family.

After properly congratulating the Burnses, the Quinns ducked out the back entrance of the palace and walked to their white station wagon. There was no driver awaiting and it did seem odd after five and a half years of having car doors opened for them. Just then a crowd of onlookers spotted the couple...they waved and shouted their aloha.

It wasn't until Bill drove out of the palace grounds and along King Street that it hit him—he, William Francis Quinn, private citizen, father of seven children, was unemployed.

In the afternoon's *Star-Bulletin* salute "To The Departing Captain," it couldn't have been said better:

> So we say aloha to the governor and wish him well in all his endeavors. Bill Quinn is not the sort of man whose light can be hid under a bushel, or who can be easily discouraged. We and all of us are much in his debt. Whatever he does, we know he will continue to be a credit to the state and the people he has served so well.

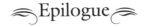

Epilogue

By

William Francis Quinn

It is an exhilarating and exhausting experience to try to relive the late '50s and early '60s—certainly the most exciting years of my life. It was an enormous surprise to everyone in Hawaii when I was appointed governor in 1957. I was the most surprised of all. I had been in the Islands only a decade. I had been an active Republican for five years, and had run for office (to fill a candidacy) in 1954. I had supported Governor King's reappointment and had never dreamed of being appointed to succeed him.

The battle for statehood was bloody. Thanks to the heroism of the 100th Infantry Battalion, we were able to overcome the opposition because of our large Japanese population. Then came the charge of communism because of Harry Bridges' control over the ILWU.

Eventually, the statehood battle was won. We were distressed when Congress set Hawaii aside and made Alaska a state in 1958. Then we realized that they could no longer withhold equal status from our Islands.

Our campaign for statehood, the realization of our dream, and the building of our new state was a most exciting and demanding time. I can't believe that my election as first state governor was more than thirty-five years ago. The recollections are so vivid it seems like yesterday.

The demands were tremendous. To create a state organization, I had to make about 550 appointments, starting with all the

justices and judges and including all appointed executive officials.

That was just the beginning. Many Hawaiian governmental
functions had been handled by the federal government when we
were a territory. The transfer of these duties required long and
difficult negotiations.

I must confess that in those days I was an unrelenting ideal-
ist. I had such great power, creating the whole organization of
our new state. My appointments could have been based on the
appointees' loyalty to Quinn and the Republican Party and will-
ingness to do whatever was necessary to advance the cause. But
no—I sought the best people I could find, with wide racial, sex-
ual and, yes, political backgrounds. I thought I could set a course
for our new state to follow. And as I look back over all those
years, despite the political developments, I do not regret what I
did, and if faced with the same situation, I would do it again.

Mary Richards's book lays out the many problems I faced,
the many criticisms I received, and the many public and legislative rebuffs that were heaped on me. Nevertheless, I look back
on those days, a third of a century ago, as the most exciting,
interesting and productive time of my life.

I gave my life then to the wonderful people of Hawaii. I am
so thankful for the opportunity.

"What one wish do you have for the future of our state?"

Glancing back has been exciting and I find it equally exciting
to try to foresee what is in store for our beautiful islands after
Nancy and I are gone.

Hawaii is and will remain one of the most beautiful and comfortable places in the world; beautiful because of its location, its
geology and its tropical vegetation; comfortable because despite
its placement in heat latitude, the blessed trades provide a cool-

ing atmosphere not often found in the tropics. Therefore, tourism, properly promoted, can and probably will remain Hawaii's chief economic activity.

Even when tourism was just getting started, long before my day, sugar and pineapple were our main economic activities. By the time I left the governor's office and became president of Dole Pineapple Co., pineapple was suffering from competing crops imported from Asian countries whose labor was paid daily the rate Hawaii pineapple workers earned in an hour. Canned pineapple is no longer a major industry here. The plantation lands are seeking other usage.

A later and more serious development is the demise of the sugar industry, again because of cheaper production elsewhere in the world. What can be done with the hundreds of thousands of acres that once were sugar plantations? There is no apparent agricultural answer. Golf courses, clubs, resorts and housing developments can rise upon much of the area. If those spacious areas are covered with such activities, our future will suffer. So far other export crops demand only a small amount of the former plantation lands. Continuous agricultural study of other alternatives is imperative.

I once called Hawaii "the crossroads of the Pacific." The term became rather commonly used. As we enter the new Pacific century, our location, our culture, and our understanding can still make our Islands a melting ground for the various cultures of East and West. Our East-West Center, our university, and most of all, our people can make Hawaii a gathering place for cultural, business, and social meetings serving all Pacific lands. This remains my dream for the future of our great state.

Index

≈About the Author≈

Mary C. Kahulumana Richards, journalist and lecturer, is the *kama'aina* author of *Sweet Voices of Lahaina*, which was published by Island Heritage in 1990.

Mrs. Richards has been a contributing editor and columnist for *RSVP* magazine, *Vintage News*, and *Aloha* magazine. Her interviews about celebrities in the Islands, people and places, have appeared in national and international publications.

She is the past-president (1994-96) of the National League of American Pen Women, Honolulu Chapter, and a life member of the Daughters of Hawaii. A graduate of Punahou School, she attended Dominican College in San Rafael, California and has also served as a volunteer for a variety of Hawaii historic and non-profit organizations including Honolulu Community Theatre, Junior League of Honolulu, and as a docent for the Honolulu Academy of Arts.